ABOUT THE AUTHOR

ROBERT B. REICH, a member of the faculty of Harvard's John F. Kennedy School of Government, is one of America's foremost political economists. A graduate of Dartmouth College, Yale Law School, and Oxford University, he served as Assistant to the Solicitor General in the Ford administration and Director of Policy Planning for the Federal Trade Commission in the Carter administration. He is now serving as President Clinton's Secretary for Labor. He is a contributing editor of *The New Republic*, chairman of the editorial board of *The American Prospect*, a frequent contributor to the *Harvard Business Review* and *The Atlantic*, and a regular commentator for both National Public Radio and public television. He is the author of *The Resurgent Liberal, Tales of a New America, New Deals: The Chrysler Revival and the American System, The Next American Frontier, Minding America's Business,* and other books. Reich lives in Cambridge, Massachusetts, with his wife and two sons.

To the memory of Frances Freshman

THE WORK OF NATIONS

Preparing Ourselves for 21st-Century Capitalism

ROBERT B. REICH

SIMON & SCHUSTER

LONDON·SYDNEY·NEW YORK·TOKYO·SINGAPORE·TORONTO

Patriotism is easy to understand. . . . It means looking out for yourself by looking out for your country.

CALVIN COOLIDGE

First published in Great Britain by
Simon & Schuster Ltd in 1991
A Paramount Communications Company
This paperback edition first published 1993

Simon & Schuster Ltd
West Garden Place
Kendal Street
London W2 2AQ

Simon & Schuster of Australia Pty Ltd
Sydney

A CIP catalogue record for this book is
available from the British Library
ISBN 0-671-71275-6

Typeset in Baskerville
Printed and bound in Great Britain by
HarperCollins Manufacturing, Glasgow

Contents

Part Three: The Rise of the Symbolic Analyst

Part Four: The Meaning of Nation

Acknowledgments

THIS book is the product of several years of research, interviews, and discussions, undertaken with many people whose insights appear on almost every page. To thank them adequately would take up much of the space in this volume. Some of them occupy responsible positions in business and government, here and abroad. I list their organizational affiliations at the end of the book, but I have usually refrained from identifying them by name in the text. Others are scholars and academicians, less squeamish about receiving credit where it is due. Jack Donahue, David Ellwood, Bill Hogan, Lawrence Katz, Frank Levy, John Meyer, David Riesman, Dani Rodrik, Robert Solow, Laura D'Andrea Tyson, Raymond Vernon, and Shirley Williams provided helpful comments on earlier drafts. I am also grateful to several diligent students. Paul Ameer, Karen Kornbluh, Tom Pendry, and Kim Walesh persisted against all odds in tracking down obscure data and sources. John Heilemann sharpened both my prose and my ideas so gracefully that he spared me the realization of how dull they were to begin with. Several friends subjected earlier drafts to the sort of withering criticism that only friends can be trusted to provide. Here, James Dillon, Doug Dworkin, John Isaacson, Marc Lackritz, Bennett Marks, Dorothy Robyn, and Erik Tarloff played their customary role. Robert Wright and Martin Peretz of *The New Republic*, Alan Webber of the *Harvard Business Review*, and Jack Beatty and Bill Whitworth of *The Atlantic* all encouraged me to develop earlier versions of several of the ideas contained herein. Katie McDermott, Margaret Brooke, Scott Samenfeld, and Alison Thompson provided much-needed technical support; Jeff Faux and the Economic Policy Institute, much-needed financial support; Rafe Sagalyn and Bill Leigh, much-needed advice. Through it all, Clare Dalton tolerated my obsessive musings, and assured me that the fever would pass. Not the least, I am indebted, as before, to Jonathan Segal, my editor and friend, for his encouragement, thoughtfulness, and kindness.

ROBERT B. REICH
Cambridge, Massachusetts
November 1990

Introduction
The National Idea

WE ARE living through a transformation that will rearrange the politics and economics of the coming century. There will be no *national* products or technologies, no national corporations, no national industries. There will no longer be national economies, at least as we have come to understand that concept. All that will remain rooted within national borders are the people who comprise a nation. Each nation's primary assets will be its citizens' skills and insights. Each nation's primary political task will be to cope with the centrifugal forces of the global economy which tear at the ties binding citizens together—bestowing ever greater wealth on the most skilled and insightful, while consigning the less skilled to a declining standard of living. As borders become ever more meaningless in economic terms, those citizens best positioned to thrive in the world market are tempted to slip the bonds of national allegiance, and by so doing disengage themselves from their less favored fellows. This book describes this economic transformation, and the stark political challenge it presents.

2

WITH numbing regularity we hear of the gross national product, the nation's trade balance, the nation's rate of economic growth, the nation's savings rate, the nation's unemployment rate, national productivity, the value of the nation's assets, the profitability of the nation's corporations. Incumbent politicians point to some figures with pride; their challengers point to others (and sometimes even the same ones) with dismay. It has become a national sport. Each new set of figures brings a frenzy of speculation: Are we doing better or worse? Is another nation beating us? Are we pulling ahead? What does this mean for our economic future? Numerous talking heads (mine included) appear on television and solemnly deliver the indispensable answers.

The optimists point ever upward: Look at the number of new jobs! Marvel at all the small entrepreneurial firms! Wonder at the number of new patents in exotica like monoclonal antibodies and digital optics! Take pride in all the foreign capital pouring into the nation as a result! The economy is booming as never before! The pessimists point downward: Bemoan the loss of manufacturing. Bewail the trade deficit, and our huge debt to the rest of the world. Abhor the loss of assets to foreigners. The economy is collapsing around us.

Who is correct? Are we becoming better off or worse off? Where are we heading?

It depends on whom you mean by "we."

Underlying all such discussion is the assumption that our citizens are in the same large boat, called the national economy. There are different levels of income within the boat, of course (some citizens enjoy spacious staterooms while others crowd into steerage). Yet all of us are lifted and propelled along together. The poorest and the wealthiest and everyone in between enjoy the benefits of a national economy that is buoyant, and we all suffer the consequences of an economy in the doldrums.

The national economic boat is thought to be piloted by a number of citizens: the President or Prime Minister, the Director of the central bank, several thousand chief executives of major national corporations, the leaders of organized labor; and, arrayed around this core group, the executives of smaller companies, investors and venture capitalists, and a wide-ranging collection of scientists, inventors, and entrepreneurs. A nation's citizens depend on these "pilots." Their collective wisdom, foresight, and ambition spell the difference between national prosperity and stagnation. Other citizens must faithfully do their parts as well, of course. All must work hard, save as much as possible, and inculcate in their children similar habits of diligence and frugality.

The metaphor is readily extended to other boats, one of them called the Japanese Economy, another the German Economy, a third the South Korean Economy, and so on, including every nation on earth—all comprising a grand flotilla of national economies sailing on the same wide sea. One boat's speed and safety depend somewhat on the speed and safety of the others (there is need for some coordination lest we collide with one another or run aground on the same shoals, and there are substantial advantages in selling them some of our goods in exchange for some of theirs), but everyone knows that each boat is also competing with every other in a worldwide regatta whose prize is economic preeminence. Boats that are in the lead at one point in history may fall behind at another time. Thus we must maintain our vigilance.

This picture, or something like it, has characterized the way most people around the world have come to view their economic life together. The public interest is defined as national economic growth; the common good, as a buoyant national economy. We are bound together, if not by the threat of a foreign predator, then at least by a common economic rate. Each of us relies on our nation's economic prowess, which, in turn, depends on how effectively the nation's resources are developed and mobilized.

This vision's clarity and soothing comprehensibility are its only virtues. The problem with this picture is that it is wrong.

3

ABSENT memory, we are, with Santayana, condemned to repeat the mistakes of the past. But excessive reliance on memory can be equally debilitating. A fixation on what was can blind us to what is, blocking the recognition of change. In matters of economic and social organization we are especially susceptible to vestigial thought. Because few of us have occasion to see the whole of society, we learn to rely on pictures taken in the past. Some of these pictures can be remarkably durable—especially those that are the most pleasing to look at. But an outmoded image can be dangerously misleading.

So it is with our picture of the national economic boat, in which all of us sail together. The picture once represented reality, but it no longer does. Its perseverance has led to a fraudulent diagnosis of economic and social problems, and of the challenges ahead. It has distorted discussions about national purpose. The economic pessimists are as misled as the optimists. Both begin from the wrong premises.

There has been no lack of warning that reality has changed. Some of the manifestations of the change are easily observed, in the United States as elsewhere. It is now a commonplace, for example, that large corporations are no longer as profitable as they were twenty-five years ago. From a peak of nearly 10 percent in 1965, the average net after-tax profit rate of America's largest nonfinancial corporations declined in the 1970s, bounced back somewhat between 1982 and 1985, and then resumed its downward slide. When adjusted for inflation, the highest Dow Jones Industrial Average of the bullish 1980s, reached in August 1987, was actually below its peak of January 1966. Further, America's 500 largest industrial companies failed to add any American jobs between 1975 and 1990, and their share of the civilian labor force dropped from 17 percent to less than 10 percent during the same interval.

Organized labor has shrunk to a small fraction of the work force. In 1960, 35 percent of all nonagricultural workers in America belonged to a union. By 1990, the figure was 17 percent. Excluding government employees, the unionized portion of the work force was only a bit over 13 percent—less than it was in the early 1930s, before the Wagner Act created a legally protected right to union representation.

There is a growing awareness, too, that foreigners are coming to own an ever greater proportion of America's productive assets. As recently as 1977, no more than 3.5 percent of the manufacturing capacity of the United States, by value, was owned by non-Americans. By 1990, foreigners exercised effective control over almost 11 percent of American manufacturing and employed more than 10 percent of American manufacturing workers. Meanwhile, American corporations are investing abroad at a furious pace. Between 1980 and 1990, American companies increased their overseas spending on new factories, equipment, and research and development at a higher rate than their investments in the United States.

Money, technology, information, and goods are flowing across national borders with unprecedented rapidity and ease. The cost of transporting things and communicating ideas is plummeting. Capital controls in most industrialized countries are being removed; trade barriers, reduced. Even items that governments wish to prevent from getting in (drugs, illegal immigrants) or out (secret weapons) do so anyway.

At the same time, there has been an increasing divergence in compensation between corporate executives and the workers laboring under them. In 1960, the chief executive of one of America's 100 largest nonfinancial corporations earned, on average, $190,000, or about 40 times the wage of his average factory worker. After taxes, the chief executive earned only 12 times the factory worker's wages. By the end of the 1980s, however, the chief executive earned, on average, more than $2 million—93 times the wage of his (rarely her) average factory worker. After taxes, the chief executive's compensation was about 70 times that of the average factory worker.

This divergence has been matched by an increasing inequality in the incomes of Americans overall. Between 1977 and 1990, the average pretax earnings of the poorest fifth of Americans declined by about 5 percent; during the same interval, the richest fifth became about 9 percent wealthier, before paying taxes. The income disparity has widened fastest between people who graduated from college and those who graduated only from high school or dropped out. This trend is not unique to the United States; many other advanced industrial nations are witnessing a similar divergence.

The divergence in earnings is related to where people have chosen to reside. Until the late 1970s, the average incomes of the inhabitants of different towns or states were slowly converging, as industry spread outward to embrace less developed areas of the nation. Since then, however, the trend has been in the opposite direction. Relatively wealthy towns and states have become even more wealthy; the poorer have grown steadily poorer by comparison. Such regional disparities are growing in many other nations as well—between Tokyo and outlying prefectures, between southern England and the Midlands, between Italy's affluent north and more primitive south.

All of these manifestations of change have the same root cause, which I will explore in the following pages. Americans are no longer in the same economic boat (nor, for that matter, are the citizens of other nations in the same boat). Yet the prevailing image remains fixed in our heads. The old picture gives comfort, suggesting national solidarity and purpose. If we are all in it together, then we can rely on one another in a pinch.

4

THE AIM of this book is to paint a new picture, one more reflective of the realities of the emerging global economy and of the societies that are being shaped as a consequence. As almost every factor of production—money, technology, factories, and equipment—moves effortlessly across borders, the very idea of a national economy is becoming meaningless, as are the notions of a national corporation, national capital, national products, and national technology. The same transformation is affecting every nation, some faster and more profoundly than others; witness Europe, hurtling toward economic union.

So who is "us"? The answer lies in the only aspect of a national economy that is relatively immobile internationally: the American work force, the American people. The real economic challenge facing the United States in the years ahead—the same as that facing every other nation—is to increase the potential value of what its citizens can add to the global economy, by enhancing their skills and capacities and by improving their means of linking those skills and capacities to the world market.

This is not the challenge of "national competitiveness," as typically conceived. There is no longer any reason for any nation to protect, subsidize, or otherwise support its corporations above all others, as some have argued. Nor are there grounds for reducing public expenditures and cutting taxes in order to give the nation's citizens more money to invest—an argument in vogue among those with an often quasi-religious faith in free markets. Neither the profitability of a nation's corporations nor the successes of its investors necessarily improve the standard of living of most of the nation's citizens. Corporations and investors now scour the world for profitable opportunities. They are becoming disconnected from their home nations.

Conventional discussions of the economy—the gross national

product, national economic growth, the nation's competitiveness—are beside the point, as are the predictable range of prognostications concerning the economy's future. The optimist's view is accurate—but only for a small portion of a nation's workers who are becoming ever more valuable in the world economy. Because these citizens are every bit as insightful as their counterparts in other nations, and are successfully selling their insights around the world, talk of a "Japanese challenge" or the "resurgence of Europe" misses the mark. The pessimist's prognosis, on the other hand, is accurate for most citizens, but it neglects this thriving minority, who represent one of the great successes of modern economic history.

The underlying question concerns the future of national *societies* as distinct from national economies, and the fate of the majority of citizens who are losing out in global competition. The answer will depend on whether there is still enough concern about society to elicit sacrifices from all of us—especially from the most advantaged and successful of us—to help the majority regain the ground it has lost and fully participate in the new global economy. The same question of responsibility confronts every other nation whose economic borders are vanishing.

It is not simply a matter of national security. Modern technologies have diffused global power. Even relatively poor nations can now finance weapons of fierce destruction. It is, rather, a matter of national purpose. Are we still a society, even if we are no longer an economy? Are we bound together by something more than the gross national product? Or has the idea of the nation-state as a collection of people sharing some responsibility for their mutual well-being become passé?

Part One
The Economic Nation

1

The Origins of
Economic Nationalism

In a civilized society we all depend upon each other.

SAMUEL JOHNSON,
from *Boswell's Life of Samuel Johnson* (1791)

THE FAMILIAR picture of a national economy whose members succeed or fail together would have appeared novel to someone living as recently as the seventeenth century—even in Europe, where the idea of the nation-state had developed furthest. Before the eighteenth century few kings, statesmen, or political philosophers regarded the nation as in any way responsible for, or necessarily connected to, the economic well-being of its population. National wealth pertained only to the wealth of the sovereign—to the kings and queens and retainers who contrived, financed, and directed various schemes to accumulate foreign riches in order to wage wars and enhance their power and prestige—rather than to the well-being of ordinary individuals within the nation. Patriotism meant devotion to the monarch rather than to fellow citizens.

In the seventeenth century, Louis XIV's minister Colbert employed techniques for stimulating the French economy practically identical to those tried by the modern Japanese, Koreans, Taiwanese, West Germans, French, and any self-respecting governor of an American state. He financed road and canal construction; he provided subsidies and tax exemptions to France's most valued manufacturers (makers of silks, tapestries, glasswares, and woolens); he established a trading company (the French East India Company) which would carry France's products to the ends of the earth; he instituted measures to assure quality, in order to stimulate foreign purchases of French goods; and, in general, he encouraged exports while discouraging imports. But in contrast to his modern descendants, Colbert's motive was not to improve the standard of living of the average French subject. He devised these schemes in order to accumulate silver, with which Louis XIV could finance wars and maintain a large standing army. For Colbert, the logic was obvious: "[E]veryone agrees that the might and greatness of a State is measured entirely by the quantity of silver it possesses."[1] In this mercantilist game, one sovereign's advance was necessarily at the expense of another, because the whole point of the exercise was to gain more power than a potential opponent. "It is clear that one country can only gain if another country loses," noted Voltaire.[2]

Mercantilism already had been the guiding principle of national economic policy for three hundred years. As early as 1462, Louis XI of France had limited the export to Rome "of gold and silver, in coin or otherwise, which might be extracted, carried and transported from this our kingdom."[3] And for centuries, the development of manufacturing had been viewed (in the language of an edict issued by Henry IV before 1603) "as being the only way to stop transporting out of our Kingdom gold and silver to enrich our neighbors."[4] By producing what you needed at home, you could retain precious metals within the nation; by exporting manufactured items, you could accumulate even more precious metals.

According to this same mercantilist logic, England's American colonies, like the colonies of all great powers, existed to enrich the sovereign. They were to provide cheap raw materials, and then purchase the finished products from the mother country. Under no circumstances were the colonies to manufacture prod-

---

[1] Quoted from Ch. W. Cole, *Colbert and a Century of French Mercantilism* (New York: World, 1939), Vol. 1, p. 337.

[2] Quoted in F. Braudel, *Civilization and Capitalism, 15th–18th Centuries*, Vol. 2: *The Wheels of Commerce* (New York: Harper & Row, 1984), p. 205.

[3] Quotation from René Gandilhon, *Politique Economique de Louis XI* (Paris, 1941), pp. 416–17, cited in Braudel, op. cit.

[4] From Isambert, *Recueil Générale des Anciennes Lois Françaises* (Paris, 1829), p. 283, cited in Braudel, op. cit. The classic study of mercantilism is Eli F. Heckscher, *Mercantilism* (rev. ed., 2 vols.; New York: Macmillan, 1955).

ucts of their own or acquire them from a third country. (In "disallowing" a Pennsylvania law to subsidize shoemaking in the colony, a New York law to encourage the manufacturing of sailcloth, and a Massachusetts law to support the production of linen, the colonies' English overseers noted, without inordinate explanation, that "[t]he passing of laws in the plantations for encouraging manufactures, which in any way interferes with the manufacture in this Kingdom, has always been thought improper, and has ever been discouraged."[5]) England also decreed, under the Navigation Acts, that only English vessels could carry cargo back and forth across the Atlantic.

There were, of course, other reasons why the American colonies sought independence from England, but had they been able to develop their own economies uninhibited by England's mercantilist demands, the separation would have occurred much later, and probably more peacefully.

2

THE SHIFT from mercantilism to popular economic nationalism paralleled a political shift from absolutism to democracy—a shift which proceeded, in fits and starts, from the eighteenth century to the twentieth, and which, a contemporary observer of Latin America, Eastern Europe, and the Soviet Union might surmise, continues still. With the spread of democratic ideas and institutions, the overriding economic and political goal changed from increasing the power of the sovereign to improving the well-being of the nation's population. In much of Western Europe and the American colonies, the impetus for change first came from a rising commercial class of merchants and bankers who sought to secure their property, trade freely, and put an end to aristocratic privilege. In much of Central and Eastern Europe, economic nationalism emerged from efforts to beat back or overthrow foreign oppressors.

The evolution occurred earliest in England, where modern democratic institutions first took root. By the eighteenth century,

---

[5]Cited in L. Hacker, *American Capitalism: Its Promise and Accomplishment* (New York: Van Nostrand, 1957), p. 23.

the House of Commons was developing into what the political philosopher Edmund Burke would call a "deliberative assembly," guided by "the general reason of the whole."[6] To Burke and an increasing number of his compatriots, a nation constituted a contract—a form of "partnership not only between those who are living but between those who are living and those who are to be born."[7] The partnership was a moral one; citizens had obligations to one another. Democratic institutions provided a means of both instilling and fulfilling such obligations simultaneously. John Stuart Mill, the English philosopher, argued that democracy cultivated moral attachments "by the utmost possible publicity and discussion, whereby not merely a few individuals in succession, but the whole public, are made, to a certain extent, participants in the government."[8] Democratic institutions, in short, created good citizens.

Throughout the eighteenth century, in England and on the Continent, the word "patriot" appeared with increasing frequency. Now the patriot was "he who in a free government, cherishes his fatherland . . . or more accurately the public welfare."[9] The English philosopher (and failed statesman) Bolingbroke signaled the change in his 1730 essay "The Spirit of Patriotism," in which he observed that every citizen who was a real patriot would "direct all his thoughts and actions to the good of his country"— that is, "to the good of the people," which he deemed "the ultimate and true end of government."[10]

---

[6] Edmund Burke, *Reflections on the Revolution in France* (1790; New York: Penguin, 1968), Vol. 2, p. 221.

[7] Ibid., p. 321.

[8] J. S. Mill, "Representative Government," in *Utilitarianism, On Liberty, and Representative Government* (London: Everyman's Library, 1910), p. 243.

[9] F. Brunot, *Histoire de la Langue Française dès Origines à 1900* (Paris: Renard, 1935), Vol. 6, Pt. 1, p. 135, cited in B. Shafer, *Nationalism: Myth and Reality* (New York: Harcourt, Brace, & World, 1955).

[10] *Bolingbroke's Works* (London: T. Davies, ed., 1775), Vol. 1. Nationalist stirrings did not inspire all eighteenth-century intellectuals, however. Precisely as the idea of nation grew, so did the idea that people owed a greater allegiance to all humanity. Thomas Jefferson and Benjamin Franklin regarded themselves as citizens of the world; so did Goethe, Schiller, and Kant in Germany; Voltaire, Diderot, and Helvetius in France; and Goldsmith and Hume in Britain. Their focus was on the universal rights and duties of man.

Democratic patriotism proved a far more potent force than was loyalty to a sovereign. Sacrificing one's life and property to a monarch living luxuriously in a distant castle seemed far less inspiring (and less sensible) than sacrificing for one's *nation*. The new sentiments found expression in national anthems, flags, pageants, and holidays. "Rule Britannia" appeared in 1740, with this rousing verse:

> *The nations not so blest as thee*
> *Must in their turn to tyrants fall*
> *Whilst thou shalt flourish great and free*
> *The dread and envy of them all.*

Monarchs became the symbol of a nation, rather than the other way around. "God Save the King," first sung at London's Drury Lane Theater in 1745, had less to do with love of king than with love of country. The composer Joseph Haydn was so impressed with the emotional effect the song had upon Englishmen (upon whom emotional effects were somewhat rare to begin with) that he returned to Germany to write the music for what would become "Deutschland, Deutschland, über Alles." Such anthems, and their composers, took on mythic qualities. French children learned how Rouget de Lisle had come to write the "Marseillaise" in 1792; American children, how Francis Scott Key penned "The Star-Spangled Banner" in 1814. National flags developed mythologies of their own—the Union Jack, the Tricolor, Betsy Ross and the first American flag. National law codes and constitutions became sacred documents, like Moses' tablets.

The French Revolution and the subsequent Napoleonic Wars provided an added stimulant. The populations of Central and Eastern Europe had already become interested in their native cultures, partly in reaction to the political domination of the Austrians and Turks and the cultural domination of the French.[11] But France's bloody revolution, followed by the advancing armies

---

[11] In 1784, J. G. von Herder, a Protestant theologian, had called upon Germans to stop emulating the French and develop their own national character—their common German spirit, or *Volksgeist*. He explained that other national groups had their own *Volksgeist* as well, which they should seek to uncover. *Ideas on the Philosophy of the History of Mankind* (1784).

of Napoleon Bonaparte, made many groups acutely aware of their
national identities. Joseph Mazzini, moral philosopher and poli-
tician, told Italians that their duty to nation was intermediate
between their duty to family and to God. The philosopher J. G.
Fichte instructed Germans that the German spirit was nobler
than that of any other nation. The Brothers Grimm, founders
of the modern science of comparative linguistics, traveled over
Germany in search of German folk tales—the *Volksgeist* of Germany. National consciousness spread throughout Europe during
subsequent decades: Poles, Magyars, Russians, Czechs, Slovaks,
Ruthenians, Romanians, Serbs, Croatians, Greeks, all became self-
consciously national, even if they lacked their own nation-state.

Citizen patriots proved better soldiers than paid mercenaries,
especially when defending the fatherland. Democratic governments also depended on committed and educated populations.
For these and other reasons, the creation of "good citizens" became a legitimate national goal. By the last decades of the nineteenth century, in Europe and America, children were expected
to attend free public schools, where they studied their nation's
history and heroes, learned to write and speak the national language correctly, and pledged their allegiance to the nation's flag.
By the end of the century, free, universal education in language
and citizenship had spread eastward through the Balkans and into
Russia.

3

THE IDEA that the citizens of a nation shared responsibility for
their economic well-being was a natural outgrowth of this budding
patriotism. The most influential book of the eighteenth century,
written by the Scottish political philosopher Adam Smith, was
entitled, not coincidentally, *An Inquiry into the Nature and Causes of
the Wealth of Nations*. In it, Smith set forth all the major ideas that
conservative Whigs, Tories, free-traders, and twentieth-century
Republicans and economists would regurgitate periodically thereafter. But Smith was no cosmopolitan. He wrote about universal
economic principles, yet his frame of reference was resolutely
national. He condemned English mercantilism not because it re-

duced the wealth of other nations but because it caused England's citizens to be poorer than they would be otherwise.

Nor did Smith object in principle to government intervention when the nation's interests required it. He opined that the Navigation Acts were "perhaps the wisest of all the commercial regulations of England" because "defense is much more important than opulence," and that Britain should expand its empire by seizing islands from "the Falklands to the Philippines"[12] (views with which Margaret Thatcher would comfortably agree). As to the nation's output, on which its wealth fundamentally depended, he identified two inherent determinants: first, the fraction of the population gainfully employed; second, "the skill, dexterity, and judgment by which labour is generally applied"[13]—factors which are as determinative today as they were more than two centuries ago.

Most nations whose economies lagged behind England's adopted more activist notions of how to enhance the wealth of their populations, but they embraced the same basic objective. One of the most influential plans was offered by Alexander Hamilton, America's first Secretary of the Treasury under George Washington, in December 1791. Hamilton's "Report on the Subject of Manufactures" was one of four reports he presented to the young American Congress, and the only one whose proposals Congress rejected as requiring too powerful a central government. (Anti-Federalists finally agreed to the plea, in Hamilton's "Report on the Public Credit," that the federal government assume the Revolutionary War debts of the states, but only on condition that the nation's capital be moved from New York to a swampy area beside the Potomac River, between Maryland and Virginia; they opposed his second proposal, in his "Report on the Bank," to establish a central bank with responsibility for controlling the nation's money supply, but President Washington followed Hamilton rather than Jefferson and signed the bank bill; while his third, "Report on the Coinage," which called for an independent mint and currency for the United States using both gold and silver, met with little opposition.)

---

[12] *The Wealth of Nations* (1776; New York: Modern Library, 1937), p. 408.
[13] Ibid., p. lvii.

Hamilton's arguments for why the nation as a whole should support the development of industry nevertheless reverberated in America, and in many other nations, for two centuries: A strong manufacturing base would increase the nation's overall "revenue and wealth," would provide more opportunities for employment and thus stimulate immigration, would attract foreign capital, and would render the nation more independent and secure. An economy based on agricultural staples alone would result in "a state of impoverishment, compared with the opulence to which [our] political and natural advantages authorize [us] to aspire."[14]

Yet a strong industrial base would not evolve automatically. Hamilton warned that small manufacturers in the United States could never catch up with the larger and more advanced manufacturers of Europe unless they were protected and subsidized, at least temporarily. There is "no purpose to which public money can be more beneficially applied, than to the acquisition of a new and useful branch of industry; no consideration more valuable, than a permanent addition to the general stock of productive labor." Thus "it is in the interest of the society . . . to submit to the temporary expense—which is more than compensated by an increase of industry and wealth; by an augmentation of resources and independence; and by the circumstances of eventual cheapness."[15]

Hamilton urged tariffs on foreign products as well as subsidies to American manufacturers, but he preferred the latter. He reasoned that subsidies could be withdrawn when no longer necessary, whereas tariffs tended to remain in place long after their justification had disappeared. Industry, it seemed, came to depend on tariffs, and the public was unaware of their true costs. Tariffs

---

[14] "Report on the Subject of Manufactures," from J. C. Hamilton (ed.), *The Works of Alexander Hamilton* (New York, 1850–51), Vol. 7.

[15] Ibid. Albert Gallatin, one of Hamilton's successors as Secretary of the Treasury, commented in 1810 on the problems faced by Americans in export markets when confronted by the English. His arguments echo today, when discussion turns to Americans trying to compete with the Japanese: "The only powerful obstacle against which American manufacturers have to struggle, arises from the vastly superior capital of Great Britain which enables her merchants to give very long term credits, to sell on small profits, and to make occasional sacrifices." Quoted in Jacob Viner, *Dumping: A Problem in International Trade* (Chicago: University of Chicago Press, 1923), p. 38.

enabled domestic businesses to fix their prices without worry that a foreign competitor might undercut them. Ironically, the aspect of Hamilton's plan that received most attention during the nineteenth century was his qualified, wary call for a protective tariff.

4

APART from slavery, the tariff became the most heated economic issue in nineteenth-century America, dividing the nation along regional lines. (It also evoked a spirited debate among academics, with some universities, like the University of Pennsylvania, prohibiting their economists from supporting free trade, and others requiring such support. Cornell apparently could not make up its collegial mind, and appointed two lecturers, one advocating free trade and the other, protection.) Small manufacturers in New England, New York, and Pennsylvania, who wanted to be shielded from European exporters of manufactured goods, argued that the nation's future economic greatness depended on the tariff. On the other hand, Southern farmers, who wanted to be able to purchase machinery as cheaply as possible from whatever source, viewed the tariff, in the righteous words of South Carolina's John C. Calhoun, as "an immense tax on one portion of the community to put money into the pockets of another."[16]

Many Westerners, like Henry Clay of Kentucky, saw tariff duties as a potential source of funds for internal improvements, such as canals and turnpikes, which would link the West to the rest of the nation. "Still cherishing the foreign market," argued Clay, "let us create also a home market, to give further scope to the consumption of the produce of American industry. Let us counteract the policy of foreigners, and withdraw the support which we now give their industry, and stimulate that of our own country."[17] Clay was passionate, if not persuasive. "There are few, if any, governments which do not regard the establishment of domestic manufacturers as a chief object of public policy," he bellowed during

---

[16]Cited in H. W. Furber (ed.), *Which? Protection or Free Trade* (Boston: Boston Publishing Company, 1888), p. 551.
[17]Quoted in F. W. Taussig (ed.), *State Papers and Speeches on the Tariff* (Cambridge: Harvard University Press, 1892), p. 275.

the Senate debate over the tariff of 1832. "When gentlemen have succeeded in their design of an immediate or gradual destruction of the American system, what is their substitute? Free trade! Free trade! The call for free trade is as unavailing as the cry of a spoiled child, in its nurse's arms, for the moon, or the stars that glitter in the firmament of heaven. It never existed, it never will exist."[18] Passions became so inflamed after Congress had passed the 1832 tariff that an angry South Carolina legislature barred federal customs agents from collecting duties within the state, thus forcing President Andrew Jackson to dispatch reinforcements to the federal garrisons at Forts Sumter and Moultrie, which in turn prompted the South Carolina legislature to summon volunteers to protect the state from "invasion"; the crisis was averted only when Clay and his fellow Whigs backed down and agreed to reduce tariff rates.

After the Civil War, when the protestations of Southern Democrats were drowned out by the victory celebrations of Northern Republicans, tariff rates were hiked again. ("I do not much know about the tariff," said Abraham Lincoln, in his characteristically folksy manner, "but I know this much, when we buy manufactured goods abroad we get the goods and the foreigner gets the money. When we buy the manufactured goods at home we get both the goods and the money."[19]) Until 1913 the average duty on imports was often close to 50 percent, even higher on iron, steel, cotton textiles, and woolens. In fact, so much money flowed into the federal coffers during the latter decades of the nineteenth century from high tariff duties that Republican administrations found themselves in the embarrassing position of running large budget surpluses. In order to reduce the surpluses and help justify a continuing need for tariff income, the Republicans dramatically increased federal spending on just the sorts of internal improvements that Henry Clay had advocated many years before: canals,

---

[18] Ibid. The German economist Friedrich List brought Hamilton's and Clay's ideas back to Germany. In List's *National System of Political Economy* (1840), he argued that any nation wishing to be wealthy and civilized must develop its own industries and financial capital. High tariffs would be necessary, at least temporarily, in order to protect infant industries from the more advanced British manufacturers.

[19] Ibid., p. 213.

...oads, harbor construction, bridges, and roads. The Union Pacific and Central Pacific railroads, for example, were granted $65 million in one swoop to build a single railway connecting the East Coast to the West.

5

PERHAPS the most interesting feature of the tariff debate in America was the form of argument used by all sides: Whatever sacrifices might be entailed would nonetheless be good for the national economy as a whole and would redound to the benefit of those who paid the tariff. This was no appeal to honor or duty; each section of the country appealed to the others on the basis of what was in the others' economic interest. "[T]he aggregate benefit to the whole society from a public improvement, may be such as to amply justify the investment . . . of capital in its execution," argued Clay, for example, in support of his system of internal improvements to be financed by the tariff.[20]

Europeans of the nineteenth century had also begun to view their national economies as tied to the well-being of their populations, but in justifying tariffs or other devices that imposed economic burdens unequally they employed a different kind of argument. A young French magistrate named Alexis de Tocqueville, on a tour of the United States in 1831, noted the distinction. He observed that in France, as elsewhere in Europe, sacrifices were legitimated in terms of patriotism and honor. The usual European argument was that "men should sacrifice for their fellow creatures *because* it is noble to make such sacrifices" (emphasis in the original). Such claims, in Tocqueville's view, were often hypocritical. "[A]mong us, men still constantly feign abnegation which they no longer feel." In America, by contrast, sacrifices were justified as being in the enlightened self-interest of those who incurred them. "The Americans," Tocqueville noted, "are fond of explaining almost all the actions of their lives by the principle of self-interest rightly understood; they show with complacency how

---

[20]This is from one of Clay's speeches to the House of Representatives in 1818. It can be found in Calvin Colton (ed.), *Works of Henry Clay* (New York, 1857), Vol. 5.

an enlightened regard for themselves constantly prompts them to assist one another and inclines them willingly to sacrifice a portion of their time and property to the welfare of the state."[21]

It is an important insight. Americans have willingly sacrificed for the nation's well-being because—Americans have repeatedly claimed—such sacrifices are ultimately in their own best interests. This is not to suggest a lack of patriotism in the United States, of course. The young Tocqueville witnessed a strong social solidarity and commitment among Americans. But these sentiments emerged from their interdependence, rather than the other way around. "It would be unjust to suppose that the patriotism and the zeal that every American employs for the welfare of his fellow citizens are wholly insincere," Tocqueville observed. "The free institutions which the inhabitants of the United States possess, and the political rights of which they make so much use, remind every citizen, and in a thousand ways, that he lives in society. They every instant impress upon his mind the notion that it is the duty as well as the interest of men to make themselves useful to their fellow creatures."[22]

But what if such claims no longer seem convincing? What if Americans have grown far less dependent on one another, so that sacrifices no longer benefit them personally? Will civic virtue survive? I will return to these questions, and to Tocqueville's observation, in subsequent chapters.

---

[21] Alexis de Tocqueville, *Democracy in America* (F. Bowen, trans.; New York, 1862), Bk. II, Ch. 8.
[22] Ibid., Bk. II, Ch. 4.

2
Economic Nationalism and High-Volume Production

> But in spite of all temptations
> To belong to other nations,
> He remains an Englishman!
> He re-mains an Eng-lish-man!
>
> W.S. GILBERT *and* A. SULLIVAN,
> *H.M.S. Pinafore (1878)*

THE IDEA that a nation's citizens shared a common economic fate became more widely accepted during the last decades of the nineteenth century. A revolution in the methods of manufacturing and moving goods transformed what had been loosely knit networks of local economies into national ones, thus creating a worldwide competitive arena in which the primary battles were waged nation against nation.

Between 1870 and 1900, a stream of inventions, many of which had been pioneered in Britain, spread throughout Europe and America: steam engines, railway locomotives, the telegraph, electric turbines, and iron and steel machinery with interchangeable parts. Each played a crucial role in the transformation of production. These inventions made it possible to manufacture all sorts of things in large volume, by gathering raw materials and components from hundreds or thousands of miles away, fabricating, assembling, or mixing them in large batches within huge factories, and then sending the finished products off again to all quarters. Mechanical industries that processed tobacco, grain, soap, and canned foodstuffs dramatically increased their output through the use of continuous-process machinery. A cigarette-making machine developed in 1881 was so productive that just fifteen of them satisfied America's entire annual demand for cigarettes. Procter & Gamble developed a new machine for mass-producing Ivory soap. Diamond Match began using a machine that produced and boxed matches by the billions. Industries that distilled and refined petroleum, sugar, animal or vegetable fats, alcohol, and chemicals reaped enormous savings from new heat and chemical technologies, giant furnaces, whirling centrifuges, converters, and rolling and finishing equipment. Standard Oil, American Sugar Refining, and Carnegie Steel, among others, gained unprecedented efficiencies. Metalworking industries benefited from larger and more efficient machine tools and a wider variety of semifinished materials. International Harvester and Singer Sewing Machine expanded their production far beyond the imaginings of past generations.

The average worker in the earlier decades of the nineteenth century—seeding and harvesting crops, logging, fishing, or applying his craft with hand tools—had produced each year a minuscule 0.3 percent more than the previous year. By the end of the century, productivity surged to nearly six times that rate.[1] The result was similar in America, Britain, Germany, and France: Production of cotton and woolen fabrics expanded furiously, as did farm implements, nails, pots, guns, utensils, washboards, and hundreds of other items. Iron output doubled between 1870 and 1890; steel production multiplied twentyfold during these years. As manufacturing equipment continued to improve and factories expanded, the volume of production grew. In the United States alone, manufacturing investment ballooned from $2.7 billion in 1879 to $8.2 billion in 1899; the annual value of the nation's manufactured products escalated over the same years from $3.8 billion to $11 billion, in constant dollars.[2]

America's railroad and telegraph networks perfectly comple-

[1] Figures from Simon Kuznets, *Economic Growth and Structure* (New York: W. W. Norton, 1965), pp. 305–27.

[2] Figures from U.S. Bureau of the Census, *Historical Statistics of the United States: Colonial Times to 1970* (Washington, D.C.: U.S. Government Printing Office, 1975), Vol. 1, pp. 201–2, 224.

mented its industrialization by lubricating the flow of goods into and out of the new enterprises. The nation had 23 miles of railroad track in 1830. By 1890 it had 208,152 miles. The telegraph developed in tandem. Invented in 1844, it was being used commercially by 1847.[3] Railroad and telegraph systems extended over Europe as well, tying together local economies. Fast, regular, and reliable transportation and communication were essential to high-volume production. In order to cover the high fixed costs of plant and machinery, the nation's new industries depended on a constant flow of production into and out of the factory. Such a flow depended in turn on a predictable stream of materials and products throughout the economy. Manufacturers could afford neither the cost of maintaining huge inventories at each end of their production process nor the risk of suddenly running out of materials or merchandise. The railroad and telegraph reduced these risks and costs by allowing manufacturers to schedule the shipments they needed and to sell their wares directly to wholesalers nationwide.

It is a rudimentary principle of economics, indeed perhaps the only principle whose truth has been demonstrated with persuasive regularity: When the supply of a particular item increases faster than the demand for it, its price will tend to decline. This principle applied itself with a particular vengeance in the late nineteenth century. Production expanded, but there were too few consumers ready to buy all the new goods suddenly available. Mass consumption is an acquired taste of modern society. Although the average worker was moving from farm to factory, the average consumer possessed the self-sufficient thriftiness learned on the farm. Mass distribution and retailing networks were not yet in place to cajole and conscript reluctant buyers into the great army of consumers that the new productive capacity required.

The result, predictably, was a general decline in prices. The wholesale price index, which had stood at 193 at the end of the Civil War in 1864, dropped to 68 by 1890. So too in Europe, where prices fell about 40 percent in the 1870s and 1880s. A severe depression jolted much of Europe and America in 1873.

---

[3] Figures from U.S. Bureau of the Census, *Historical Statistics of the United States: Colonial Times to 1970* (Washington, D.C.: U.S. Government Printing Office, 1975), Vol. 2, p. 731.

Another, in the summer of 1893, impoverished several agricultural areas, closed thousands of banks, and threw more than one-quarter of America's unskilled urban work force out of jobs.[4] There were political consequences. In many European and American cities, a growing number of socialists proclaimed the imminent collapse of capitalism. On the Western farmlands of America, a swelling cadre of populists (mindful of the abundance of silver in Rocky Mountain mines) demanded that currencies be inflated through the simple expedient of converting from the gold standard to silver, an approach which would have reduced their debts to Eastern banks and likely brought prosperity to the West.

2

ONE OF the most important consequences of industrial over-capacity was its effect on national sentiments. At least since Alexander Hamilton had urged subsidy and protection of America's infant manufacturers, the nation had been aware of the threat posed by European manufacturers to its nascent industries. Now, in the face of high-volume production and the overcapacity of industry, the threat was more immediate. Manufacturers on both sides of the Atlantic aggressively sought out new markets for their overabundance of goods and willingly cut prices to gain market share. Germany, Italy, France, and Russia all increased their tariffs in order to protect their manufacturers from predatory foreigners. Not surprisingly, America's tariff rates surged to even higher levels.

Only Britain, whose manufacturers were the most advanced, and thus had been among the primary beneficiaries of free trade, declined to join in this escalating protectionism. As a result, other manufacturing nations (especially the United States and Germany) subjected Britain to a strategy that, it has been argued, Japan adopted a half century later: By protecting themselves from foreign competition within their home markets, they could sell their goods domestically at prices sufficiently high to cover expenses and allow a healthy profit. Then, having established scale

---

[4] Ibid.

efficiencies, they could sell the remaining lot in Britain at cut-rate prices—thus boosting earnings while grabbing market share away from British manufacturers on their home turf. The unsurprising result was that even as world industrial production expanded between 1870 and 1913, Britain's share plummeted, from 31.8 percent to about 14 percent; Germany's share, meanwhile, expanded somewhat, and America's ballooned from 23.3 percent to 35.8 percent.[5] Britain's free trade policy, as the British press was not reluctant to observe, was fine so long as most others were playing by the same rules. Now, however, it was inviting German and American "economic invasions."[6]

3

IF THE home market could not fully absorb the new goods, and if foreign markets that produced manufactured goods were closing, there remained one further outlet: poorer nations and territories. The term "imperialism," with its rather unpleasant ring in late-twentieth-century ears, never appeared in the writings of Karl Marx. Though first used in the 1870s, the term did not enter common speech until the last decade of the century, by which time every major manufacturing nation was looking to more backward regions of the globe as potential markets for the overabundance of goods. Competition for such "spheres of influence" further intensified the popular feeling that, in the new manufacturing age, one nation's economic success was sure to come at the expense of another's.

Politicians of the age were proud to call themselves imperialists. National expansion, influence, and economic growth were wrapped in the same cloak. "Territorial expansion," explained an

---

[5] Figures from F. Crouzet, *The Victorian Economy* (London: Methuen, 1982).
[6] Beginning in the 1890s, the average British citizen was treated to a series of lurid exposés about the German and American economic onslaught and its baleful consequences for Britain. Among them were E. E. Williams, *Made in Germany* (London, 1896), and Frederick A. MacKenzie, *American Invaders* (London, 1902). In form and substance, these jeremiads bore remarkable resemblance to accounts of Japanese "invasions" offered American readers a century later.

official of the U.S. Department of State in 1900, "is but the by-product of the expansion of commerce."[7] Teddy Roosevelt, teeth clenched in a ferocious grin, proclaimed America's imperial destiny in Latin America; Britain and Germany equated their economic prowess with their nations' global reach. The size and influence of a national economy came to signify the nation's strength and determination. "Great power" became synonymous with "great economy."

The spread of economic nationalism among manufacturing nations provoked similar sentiments elsewhere around the world. The subjugation of China by the great powers convinced the leaders of Japan's Meiji restoration that Japan's survival depended on its rapid economic development. Only a modern economy could create and maintain a modern military; only an economy that was powerful relative to others could ensure the nation's security.[8] Education, industrial development, and national security were seen as tightly interrelated. Fifty years later, Sun Yat-sen, who sought to overthrow China's Manchu dynasty, based his revolutionary program of economic development on a similar logic. The West had been able to dominate China not simply because of its superior military strength but also because of the economic might on which that military power was based. In *The International Development of China*, Sun Yat-sen rejected Marxist demands for a more equal distribution of wealth in favor of a strategy of national economic development financed by the West, emphasizing education and industrialization. "Our economic rights are leaking away. . . . If we want to recover these rights . . . we must quickly employ state power to promote industry, use machinery in production, and give employment to the workers of the nation. . . . So we shall certainly have to borrow foreign capital to develop our communication and transportation facilities, and foreign brains and experience to manage them."[9] This view—linking

---

[7] Cited in W. A. Williams, *The Tragedy of American Diplomacy* (New York: World, 1959), p. 44.

[8] D. S. Landes, "Japan and Europe: Contrasts in Industrialization," in W. W. Lockwood (ed.), *The State and Economic Enterprise in Japan: Essays in the Political Economy of Growth* (Princeton: Princeton University Press, 1965).

[9] Sun Yat-sen, *The International Development of China* (New York: Putnam, 1922), p. 8.

national security and independence to the nation's economic development—was to become increasingly dominant in Asia, Africa, and Latin America, but it was by no means universally accepted among colonial nations. Mahatma Gandhi, rejecting the pleasures of material well-being, denounced manufacturing machinery as "the chief symbol of modern civilizations," representing "a great sin."[10]

In his 1902 *Imperialism*, the British economist J. A. Hobson, after examining the events leading up to the Boer War, predicted that the logical end point of competition for markets would be warfare. Businessmen, he warned, opt for war when they have exhausted their home markets and have nowhere else to sell their wares. Like John Maynard Keynes three decades later, Hobson urged instead that advanced nations increase their domestic demand by enlarging the number of people capable of buying domestically produced goods: "The most convincing condemnation of the current economy is conveyed in the difficulty which producers everywhere experience in finding consumers for their product. . . . If apportionment of incomes were such as to evoke no excessive saving, full constant employment for capital and labor would be furnished at home."[11] Hobson had no way of knowing, of course, that the less desirable alternative he posited would, within fifteen years, contribute to the death or injury of some 20 million people.

4

HIGH-VOLUME manufacturing also stimulated economic nationalism by drawing large numbers of people away from villages, farms, and extended families and into cities—where they were exposed to political movements, news of foreign plots and maneuvers, national spectacles, and waves of immigrants that further reminded them of their national identities. In 1870, fewer than 8 percent of America's workers were engaged in manufacturing, while only one out of five Americans lived in a city with 8,000 or

---

[10] "Hind Swaraj," in *The Collected Works of Mahatma Gandhi* (Allahabad: Government of India, 1963), Vol. 10, p. 26.

[11] J. A. Hobson, *Imperialism* (London, 1902), p. 112.

more inhabitants. By 1910, almost a third were involved with manufacturing, and almost half of the population lived in cities. New York City's population increased fourfold between 1860 and 1910. In 1860, Chicago had 109,260 inhabitants; by 1910, it was the nation's second-largest city, with 2.2 million people.[12] Here, in the burgeoning industrial cities of the world, the idea of nation found concrete meaning. The word "nationalism" itself, like "imperialism," was a product of these times. First used to describe right-wing groups in France and Italy, by the late nineteenth century "nationalism" came to signify expansion and competition, in which loyalties toward homeland became linked to national ambitions.

Not only did vast numbers of laborers move from village to city, they moved to the world's major industrial regions from other nations. In these years 15 percent of the population of the territory of Poland traveled to Germany in search of gainful employment. Almost half of the population of Ireland abandoned the Emerald Isle between 1841 and 1911, many of them landing in Boston or New York. By the 1870s, 280,000 immigrants were arriving in the United States annually; at the end of the century, the yearly average was over 1 million. Immigrants comprised the majority of workers in many of America's new manufacturing industries. A 1908 government study found that almost three-fifths of the wage earners in twenty-one principal branches of American industry were foreign-born.[13]

The new immigrants further ignited national feelings. Some of the Americans already here wanted to close the door to the newcomers. Conveniently forgetting that their own forefathers had shared the corn with and taken the land of New England's real native Americans, the founders of Boston's Immigration Restriction League pledged, in 1893, to "prevent the destruction of American ways by unimpeded Immigration." Other Americans devised a more constructive approach. The goal was to cultivate in the immigrants a love and respect for their newly adopted country, along with an ability to speak its language and function as productive citizens. Thus in America, as in other nations where

---

[12] Figures from *Historical Statistics of the United States*.
[13] Figures from Jeremiah Jenks and Jeff Lavek, *The Immigration Problem* (New York: Funk & Wagnalls, 1926), p. 148.

they disembarked, the new immigrants were required to write and speak the national language and to know the basic principles of the nation's government before being granted citizenship.[14]

5

BY THE start of the twentieth century, economic nationalism had taken firm root in many places around the world. Citizens of the United States, Britain, Germany, France, Italy, Japan, and elsewhere understood that their personal well-being was bound up with their nation's economic prowess. Patriotism and economic nationalism were inextricably linked. Nation competed with nation. And despite Karl Marx's call for the workers of the world to unite, national allegiances remained strong even among the new urban working class. On the battlefields of national economic ambition, the production worker was the new foot soldier.

---

[14]There remained the question, in the minds of many Americans, whether the new immigrants had the appropriate capacity for patriotism. Henry Cabot Lodge argued that the very idea of devotion to one's country was Roman in origin, while the idea of devotion to the head of state was Byzantine. Thus, according to Lodge, immigrants from Southeastern Europe were importing into America the wrong form of patriotism. See his "Immigration—A Review," in Philip David (ed.), *Immigration and Americanization* (Boston: Boston Publishing Company, 1920), p. 55.

3

The Corporation
and the National Interest

We must wage a crusade against the powers that have governed us ... that have determined our lives [and] set us in a straightjacket to do with as they please.

WOODROW WILSON (1912)

NEITHER high tariffs that blocked foreign imports nor exclusive "spheres of influence" in the less developed regions of the world solved the problem of overproduction. So long as manufacturers competed vigorously against one another at home, adding capacity and cutting prices, profit margins would remain too slim to keep the businesses going. Thus a third solution emerged in the closing decades of the nineteenth century which, like the other two, shaped how people of the twentieth century came to understand the purpose and organization of the national economy. The solution was to reduce domestic competition by consolidating production within large, nationally based corporations. Here was the final plank of economic nationalism: The well-being of citizens was linked to the success of the national economy, which depended in turn on the success of its giant corporations.

2

THIS solution came somewhat more naturally to Europeans, and subsequently to the Japanese, than it did to Americans. Cartels, guilds, and other restraints on trade had been common in Europe and in Japan since the Middle Ages. Royal monopolies, like the East India Company, had enriched the sovereign. Perhaps most importantly, government bureaucracies charged with mobilizing resources and directing trade were firmly established within Germany, France, and Italy by the 1870s, and in Japan by the 1890s. When markets became unruly, bureaucrats organized manufacturers into groups that coordinated their investments, shared financial capital, jointly purchased raw materials and jointly marketed their goods, and fixed prices. Since price-cutting was apt to be enormously profitable for any member who quietly broke ranks, the bureaucrats also performed the invaluable service of policing against such disloyalty. Thus, by the end of the nineteenth century, the newly industrializing sectors of Europe and Japan were dominated by the likes of large consolidations, syndicates, cartels, giant joint-stock banks, *zaibatsu, Grossbanken, grande industrie, Grossindustrie*.[1]

The shift from competition to national consolidation was far less assured in America. From colonial times, Americans had learned to distrust monopolies, special charters, and other royal prerogatives. Abuse of economic power was feared almost as much as the abuse of political power. Just as government authority needed to be held in check—balanced among three branches and dispersed among localities, states, and the nation—so too was economic power to be fragmented, or so most Americans believed. Unlike Europe or Japan, nineteenth-century America possessed no large administrative bureaucracy experienced in regulating markets and encouraging industry. The only government department of any size was the Post Office, whose employees were sufficiently challenged by rain, snow, hail, and the dark of night without taking on the added burden of economic planning.

Nor were American judges prepared to sanction monopolies and cartels. The common law of the colonies, and then of the states, looked unfavorably upon agreements among businesses

---

[1] For a thoughtful history of the European shift to large, integrated corporations, see Leslie Hannah, "Mergers, Cartels, and Concentration: Legal Factors in the U.S. and European Experience," in N. Horn and J. Kocka (eds.), *Law and the Formation of the Big Enterprises in the 19th and Early 20th Centuries* (Göttingen, West Germany: Vandenhoeck und Ruprecht, 1979), pp. 306–14.

that caused, in the typically vague but Olympian words of the law, "restraints of trade." Almost as soon as America's emerging enterprises began discovering ways to maintain their prices and tame domestic competition, public concern prompted the passage of the Sherman Antitrust Act of 1890, which prohibited price-fixing and barred market-dividing "agreements." The official language of the act barred "monopolization" as well, but Congress did not define what it meant by "monopolization" and, in any event, the explicit agreements—usually in the form of written contracts—were far easier to root out.

It was not to be the last time that well-intentioned legislation would have a practical effect precisely the opposite of that intended. If American firms were prohibited from agreeing with one another on prices and markets, the easiest path for them was simply to merge into huge corporations whose component parts could coordinate prices and markets with impunity inside the giant firm. The result was America's first great merger boom, which gathered momentum during the last decade of the nineteenth century and culminated in a vast implosion between 1898 and 1904. Approximately one-third of the nation's manufacturing assets were consolidated into 318 giant companies with a combined capitalization of $7.3 billion. The high tariffs that America imposed on raw materials and supplies from abroad encouraged further consolidation: The new giants preferred to buy up domestic suppliers rather than pay them high, protected prices. Thus, when tariffs prevented U.S. Steel from obtaining cheap pig iron and coking coal from Canada, the firm simply purchased Pennsylvania iron and coal producers outright rather than let them enjoy the extra profits of the protected market.

Thus was the core corporation born in America. Some of the mammoths that emerged bore names that would become synonymous with American industry—names that reflected the unambiguously national identities to which they aspired: U.S. Steel, American Sugar Refining, American Telephone & Telegraph, American Rubber, United States Rubber, American Woolen, National Biscuit, American Can, American Tobacco, Aluminum Company of America, General Electric, General Motors, Standard Oil, and, even more grandiosely, International Harvester.

Large size and centralized management permitted even easier

control over markets and sources of supply, and greater scale efficiencies, than before. Production could now be concentrated in one or two huge facilities, operations could be streamlined, materials could be purchased in bulk at great savings. The entire production process, from raw materials onward, could now be planned. Bottlenecks could be eliminated or at least reduced, smoothing the flow of materials to the place where they were refined, assembled, or processed in ever-greater quantities and then shipped to wholesalers and retailers on a predetermined schedule. (Notably, where giantism failed to produce such efficiencies, the consolidated firm collapsed under its own weight. Few people today remember the ambitious beginnings of U.S. Leather, National Wallpaper, Standard Rope and Twine, or National Starch.)

3

THE GREAT *fin de siècle* consolidation of American industry hardly stilled the political debate. Just as the tariff question had dominated much of the nineteenth century, debates over the role and legitimacy of the giant American corporation dominated the first half of the twentieth. And the defenders of the giant corporation wielded many of the same arguments that had been used to justify the tariff: It was necessary in light of foreign competition (just look at the cartels and syndicates of Europe!); it was a natural and inevitable step in the evolution of industrial economies (Charles Darwin's celebrated theories provided convenient justification for any economic trend of the time by which the rich grew richer and more powerful); it generated enormous efficiencies; it ensured jobs. In short, the giant American corporation was the vehicle by which the resources of the American economy were to be mobilized and directed. It would bring prosperity and greatness to the nation, or so the argument went.

Many Americans found these arguments unpersuasive. Giant corporations might be efficient, but they also seemed dangerously powerful. They might be the vehicle for mobilizing national resources, but they were unaccountable to the nation. They were sheltered from competition, and thus from any specific demands that the marketplace might place upon them; they also were free from democratic oversight, and thus immune from any political demands that the public might make on them.

During the first half of the twentieth century public passions were periodically ignited by the specter of malicious corporate giants plotting against the body politic. "The masters of the government of the United States are the combined capitalists and manufacturers of the United States," stormed Woodrow Wilson in the 1912 presidential campaign. "The government of the United States at present is a foster-child of the special interests."[2] Twenty-five years later, Franklin Delano Roosevelt sounded a similar theme when he blamed the nation's economic woes on "economic royalists" sitting atop giant corporations, who fixed prices and thwarted competition.[3] By contrast, European politicians who presided over the great national economic consolidations of European industry—David Lloyd George, Otto von Bismarck, Georges Clemenceau—were conspicuously quiet about the evils of concentrated economic power, their silence presumably reflecting the European public's relative indifference to it. The giant corporation remained a uniquely American obsession.

How to control these giants? They could not be dismembered without America's sacrificing the efficiencies of large-scale production. In any event, as the nation soon discovered, antitrust prosecutions rarely had the desired effect. After years of litigation, the Supreme Court finally insisted in 1911 that both Standard Oil and American Tobacco be dismembered; sixty-five years later a similar fate would befall AT&T. But for every such antitrust victory there were scores of prosecutorial failures, resting on technicalities that only an antitrust lawyer could truly appreciate: insufficient evidence of intent to monopolize, improper definition of relevant market, inadequate data on market share, no proof of an agreement. The passionate concerns that had first caused Congress to enact antitrust legislation, and which flared in campaign rhetoric for decades thereafter, were gradually extin-

---

[2] Chicago, October 10, 1912. *Papers and Speeches of Woodrow Wilson* (Princeton: Princeton University Press, 1926).

[3] Acceptance address, Philadelphia, June 27, 1936. *Speeches of Franklin D. Roosevelt* (New York: Dutton, 1949).

guished by the steady, boring, interminable drips of protracted litigation. Antitrust, once a political movement, became a legal specialty.[4]

4

IF LARGE corporations should not—and in any event could not —be disassembled and subjected to the discipline of the market, could they nevertheless be rendered more accountable? In 1909, Herbert Croly, a young political philosopher and journalist, argued in his best-selling *The Promise of American Life* that the large American corporation should be regulated by the nation and directed toward national goals. "The constructive idea behind a policy of the recognition of the semi-monopolistic corporations is, of course, the idea that they can be converted into economic agents . . . unequivocally for the national economic interest," he wrote. National regulation would preserve the efficiencies of large scale and "convert [the corporation] to the service of a national democratic economic system."[5] Theodore Roosevelt's New Nationalism embraced Croly's idea, and World War I put it into effect.

World War I provided Americans with their first experience in national corporate planning. Government functions that would be taken for granted a half century later had their origins here. A War Finance Corporation, which underwrote bank loans to war industries, was the direct precedent for Herbert Hoover's Recon-

---

[4]On the transformation of antitrust from political movement to legal specialty, see Richard Hofstadter, "What Happened to the Antitrust Movement?" in his *The Paranoid Style in American Politics and Other Essays* (Chicago: University of Chicago Press, 1952).

This is not to suggest that antitrust ceased to have any significant effect on the structure of American industry, of course. But as the public gradually lost interest in antitrust, government enforcers and the courts came to rely ever more on the test of whether the large enterprise or proposed merger promoted *efficiency*. The original fears about unaccountable aggregates of political power played a dwindling role in such analyses, until they virtually disappeared by the 1980s.

[5]Herbert Croly, *The Promise of American Life* (New York: World, 1909), pp. 362, 379.

struction Finance Corporation in 1929, and for the various schemes of government-backed loans and loan guarantees which continued through the New Deal and culminated with the Chrysler bailout of 1979 and the Savings and Loan bailout of 1989. A U.S. Housing Corporation condemned land and built housing for defense personnel—thus inaugurating federal responsibility for the nation's housing stock. A War Labor Board to settle industrial disputes became a model for a national system of labor-management relations two decades later. A Fuel Administration enforced "gasless Sundays"; a Food Administration (under Hoover) fixed commodity prices; a Shipping Board oversaw the production of vessels.

All this was overseen by the War Industries Board, which promptly scrapped the Sherman Antitrust Act in favor of national industrial cooperation. The board functioned as what one participant called a "town meeting of American industry." Its institutional progeny could be traced years later to Hoover's elaborate programs to "rationalize" American industry through trade associations; then to Franklin Delano Roosevelt's ill-fated National Recovery Administration (which succumbed to internal squabbles, cartelized prices, and public distrust); followed by, on an even larger scale, the War Production Board of World War II, and through the 1950s and 1960s by subsidies and production cartels governing military contractors, oil companies, banks, airlines, and much of the telecommunications and aerospace industries.

National planning on an even more ambitious scale was being attempted in several other nations during the first four decades of the twentieth century, with apparent success. So long as government oversight was confined to heavy industries producing large volumes of identical things, it was a relatively simple matter to establish and enforce production quotas of this or that. Some Americans of the 1920s looked wistfully at the comparative efficiency of Benito Mussolini's centrally directed system of national production. *The Wall Street Journal* put its admiration for him into rhyme:

> *On formal etiquette*
> *He seems a trifle shy;*
> *But when it comes to "go and get,"*
> *He's some two-fisted guy.*

The national commander of the American Legion proudly noted that his organization resembled Mussolini's in all but name: "Do not forget that the Fascisti are to Italy what the American Legion is to the United States."[6] The Soviets, meanwhile, were implementing their own form of national planning, with similar resolve and success. Russian industrial production rose precipitously; steel output alone increased by about 9 percent a year all the way through the 1950s. (Indeed, by 1959 Nikita Khrushchev could credibly boast that at the rate his economy was growing, it would overtake America's within twenty years.)

5

BUT WITHIN America's more ad hoc system of national planning, the question remained: How, exactly, were the managers of America's largest corporations to be held accountable to national goals? Wartime planning was one thing, but how would political oversight work the rest of the time? In 1932, Adolf A. Berle and Gardiner C. Means, lawyer and economics professor, respectively, published *The Modern Corporation and Private Property*, which documented what most people already knew but had not seen revealed so starkly: The top executives of America's giant companies, who controlled the nation's most important economic resources and received most of the government's largesse, were not even accountable to their own shareholders. Executives operated corporations "in their own interests, and . . . divert[ed] a portion of the asset fund to their own uses."[7] The only solution, suggested Berle and Means, was to enhance the power of all groups within the nation who were affected by the large corporation, including employees and consumers. "Neither the claims of ownership nor those of control can stand against the paramount interests of the community," they warned. "It remains only for the claims of the

---

[6]Quoted in Norman Hapgood (ed.), *Professional Patriots* (New York: World, 1928), p. 62; for additional encomiums to Mussolini, see John Booth Carter, "American Reactions to Italian Fascism, 1919–1933" (Ph.D. thesis, University of California, 1953).

[7]A. A. Berle and G. C. Means, *The Modern Corporation and Private Property* (New York: Macmillan, 1932), p. 300.

community to be put forward with clarity and voice."[8] Berle and Means envisioned that the corporate executive of the future would become a professional administrator, dispassionately weighing such claims and allocating benefits accordingly. "It is conceivable—indeed it seems almost essential if the corporate system is to survive—that the 'control' of the great corporations should develop into a purely neutral technocracy, balancing a variety of claims by various groups in the community and assigning each a portion of the income stream on the basis of public policy rather than private cupidity."[9]

This ideal of the large corporation as a national resource managed by professionals accountable to various national constituencies seemed within reach as New Deal legislation bolstered the bargaining positions of various groups affected by corporate decisions. Under the Wagner Act of 1935, employees were given the right to form labor unions and bargain collectively. Small investors gained protection under the Securities and Exchange acts of 1933 and 1934. Small retailers gained bargaining leverage against the big chain stores under the Robinson-Patman Act and state "fair trade" acts. And so on. Such "countervailing powers"[10] would, in fact, render legitimate the role and purpose of the large corporation in America. Gradually, the top executives of America's largest corporations would come to view themselves as "corporate statesmen," responsible for balancing the claims of stockholders, employees, and the American public. Surprisingly, the public would come to share this view.

---

[8] Ibid., p. 312.

[9] Ibid.

[10] John Kenneth Galbraith, *American Capitalism: The Theory of Countervailing Power* (Boston: Houghton Mifflin, 1952).

4

The National Champion

BY THE 1950s, the well-being of individual citizens, the prosperity of the nation, and the success of the nation's core corporations seemed inextricably connected. Most of the larger questions about the role of the giant corporation in American society had been resolved. Nothing stills political debate like success. This was, not incidentally, the decade in which most of today's business and government leaders encountered American industry for the first time. Their initial impressions have proven remarkably durable; vestigial thought is most convincing to those whose obsolete views are shared by associates and friends.

To ensure against any return to wartime controls or the seductions of statism and communism, the American business community at midcentury launched a spirited public relations campaign promoting the wonders of the profit system. General Motors produced a full-length Hollywood movie illustrating the advantages of American capitalism. Outdoor billboards erected by the Advertising Council proclaimed the benefits of free enterprise and the evils of government planning. The National Association of Manufacturers distributed free to hundreds of thousands of workers a comic book which explained that the American Revolution was caused by "government planners" in London. The president of the organization summed up the prevailing concern: "Today's challenge, today's dire necessity, is to sell—to resell, if you will—to free Americans the philosophy that has kept us and our economy free."[1]

---

[1] Cited in *Fortune*, September 1950, p. 77.

Such efforts were hardly necessary. If any Americans during the Depression decade of the 1930s or the war decade thereafter harbored lingering doubts about the legitimacy of the large American corporation or about the viability of American capitalism itself, such doubts were erased by the explosive prosperity of the 1950s. Even the staunchest critics were by now convinced. David Lilienthal, a New Deal planner, rhapsodized over the giant American corporation in his 1953 book *Big Business: A New Era*: "Our productive and distributive superiority, our economic fruitfulness, rest upon Bigness."[2] Richard Hofstadter, whose historical writings had sometimes dwelled on the less admirable qualities of American capitalism, now embraced big business: "An occasional big-business leader may stand out for his enlightenment and urbanity, as compared with the small-businessman, who more often than not proves to be a refractory anti-union employer, a parochial and archaic opponent of liberal ideas, a supporter of vigilante groups and of right-wing cranks."[3] *Fortune* magazine, reporting on a 1953 public opinion survey which showed that the vast majority of Americans approved of big business, concluded, with its customary enthusiasm, that "the huge publicly owned corporation . . . has become the most important phenomenon of mid-century capitalism. Corporate bigness is coming to be accepted as an integral part of a big economy. Whatever attacks may be made against them in theory, the large corporations have met the test of delivering the goods."[4]

While the world's other major economies had been shattered by World War II, America's had surged forward. Government spending on an unprecedented scale had pulled the nation out of the Depression; American industries had accomplished un-

---

[2] D. Lilienthal, *Big Business: A New Era* (New York: World, 1953), pp. 47, 190.

[3] Richard Hofstadter, "What Happened to the Antitrust Movement?" in his *The Paranoid Style in American Politics and Other Essays* (Chicago: University of Chicago Press, 1952).

[4] *Fortune*, October 1955, p. 81. The same trend appeared in a 1951 survey undertaken by the Institute of Social Research at the University of Michigan. When asked to give a general characterization of the social effects of big business, more than 75 percent of the respondents agreed that "the good things outweigh the bad things." See B. Fisher and S. Withey, *Big Business as the People See It* (Ann Arbor: University of Michigan Press, 1951).

imagined feats of production; American corporate leaders had distinguished themselves in service to the nation. Now, at war's end, the widely anticipated high levels of unemployment failed to materialize, and production escalated to ever-greater heights. GIs swarmed back to set up families, buy homes with government-subsidized loans (in 1950, young families were moving into new houses at the unprecedented rate of 4,000 a day), and fill the houses with dishwashers, clothes dryers, electric skillets, air conditioners, washing machines, baby carriages, refrigerators, and television sets. And to top it all off: at least one car in every driveway. Automobile ownership surged from 10 million in 1949 to 24 million by 1957. In computing 1951's Consumer Price Index, including all articles that entered into the cost of living for "moderate income" families, the Bureau of Labor Statistics for the first time added TV sets, electric toasters, frozen foods, canned baby foods, home permanent wave lotions, and group hospitalization —a collection of newly minted necessities that prompted the New York *Herald Tribune* to ask, wryly, "What, no caviar?"[5]

Large-scale mass production went hand in glove with mass consumption, of course. Here, finally, was the society that J. A. Hobson had wished for a half century before—one which could find its market at home. Americans took it as their patriotic duty to consume, and understood the purpose of the American economy as enabling them to do so. "Economic salvation, both national and personal, has nothing to do with pinching pennies," declared a 1953 advertisement for Gimbels, the New York department store. "Economic survival depends upon consumption. If you want to have more cake tomorrow, you have to eat more cake today. The more you consume, the more you'll have, quicker."[6] The chairman of Eisenhower's Council of Economic Advisers made it official: The "ultimate purpose" of the American economy, he solemnly intoned, was "to produce more consumer goods."[7]

---

[5] January 17, 1951, p. 18. See also *Fortune*, February 1954, p. 64.
[6] *Fortune*, December 1953, p. 99.
[7] *Fortune*, September 1953, p. 94. A noted investment banker of the era put the matter even less ambiguously: "Not purchasing power but purchases, not production but consumption, are the ruling factors in the economy." Paul Mazur, *The Standards We Raise: The Dynamics of Consumption* (New York: World, 1953), p. 29.

2

THE AMERICAN economy of the 1950s was the engine of mass production. Its defining characteristics are still solidly fixed in America's collective memory, and although the image bears almost no relation to how the economy is organized today, it continues to condition the thinking of many Americans at century's end.

At its core stood about five hundred major corporations which, by midcentury, produced about half of the nation's industrial output (about a quarter of the industrial output of the free world), owned roughly three-quarters of the nation's industrial assets, accounted for about 40 percent of the nation's corporate profits, and employed more than one out of eight of the nation's nonfarm workers. The largest of these corporations were very large indeed: The top twenty-eight accounted for about 10 percent of all manufacturing employment.[8] General Motors, the biggest manufacturing company on earth, was single-handedly responsible for 3 percent of America's gross national product in 1955, equivalent to almost the entire GNP of Italy (Wall Street's prior encomiums to Mussolini notwithstanding). GM's well-publicized expansion program that year was even credited with forestalling a national business slump.[9] Standard Oil of New Jersey and AT&T each had revenues greater than Denmark's.

This set of core corporations was in turn divided, by twos or threes, into twenty to thirty major American industries, for which the core corporations set industry norms on prices, wages, and methods of high-volume production. The steel industry was dominated by three behemoths: U.S. Steel, Republic, and Bethlehem; the electrical equipment and appliance industry, by two—General Electric and Westinghouse; in basic chemicals it was Du Pont, Union Carbide, and Allied Chemical; in food processing, General Foods, Quaker Oats, and General Mills; tobacco, R. J. Reynolds, Liggett & Myers, and American Tobacco; jet engines, General Electric and Pratt & Whitney; automobiles, General Motors, Ford,

---

[8]Figures from M. A. Adelman, "The Measurement of Industrial Concentration," *Review of Economics and Statistics*, Vol. 32 (November 1951).
[9]*Time*, January 2, 1956, pp. 40–51.

and Chrysler; and so forth, across the great expanse of American industry.

Around these core corporations were arrayed several thousand large but not immense industrial corporations and a few substantial service firms that catered to the needs of the core corporations—banks, insurance companies, railroads, and mass retailers like Sears, Montgomery Ward, and J. C. Penney. Encircling them, like the outer rings of Saturn, were hundreds of thousands of smaller firms that filled market niches for specialized goods that could not be efficiently produced in large volume, along with small retailers involved in marketing or selling the mass-produced goods. The rest of the private economy comprised restaurants, law firms, barbers, realtors, and the other occupants of Main Street, and a dwindling number of family farms. Unlike the core corporations, whose output could be planned far in advance with a fair degree of confidence that it could be sold at a predetermined price, these peripheral businesses were subject to the whims of the marketplace. Facing the continuous threat of competition, their owners and employees lived a relatively precarious existence.

Because of their size and central role in the economy, America's core corporations came to identify themselves, and be identified by Americans and others around the world, with the American economy as a whole. They were the champions of the national economy; their successes were its successes. They *were* the American economy.

The great headquarters buildings of the core corporations were the shrines of American capitalism, representing the country's power and confidence: GM Headquarters in Detroit, the RCA Building in New York, Lever House, the Chrysler Building. Their corporate logos and slogans everywhere reminded consumers around the world of the dynamism of American enterprise. U.S. Steel unabashedly chose for its company motto the grandiose claim: "As steel goes, so goes the nation." (Advised by its public relations office that the motto might invite blame for any subsequent economic downturn, the firm quietly reversed the phraseology a few years later, to read: "As the nation goes, so goes steel."[10]) Charles Erwin ("Engine Charlie") Wilson, president of

---

[10]*Fortune*, April 1950, p. 91.

General Motors when Eisenhower tapped him to become Secretary of Defense in 1953, voiced the conventional view at his confirmation hearing when asked whether he would be capable of making a decision in the interest of the United States that was adverse to the interest of GM. He said that he could, but that such a conflict would never arise. "I cannot conceive of one because for years I thought what was good for our country was good for General Motors, and vice versa. The difference did not exist. Our company is too big. It goes with the welfare of the country."[11]

3

THE CORE corporations not only flooded America with goods but also created millions of the jobs that swelled the ranks of America's middle class, and in turn enlarged the mass market for such goods. By the mid-1950s, almost half of all American families fell comfortably within this middle group (defined as family units receiving from $4,000 to $7,500 after taxes, in 1953 dollars). Notably, most of these middle-class families were headed not by professionals or business executives but by skilled and semiskilled factory workers and clerks, who managed the flows of product and paperwork through the great corporations.

The prosperity and growth of America's middle class was one of American capitalism's greatest triumphs, for which the core American corporation could claim significant credit. In 1929, the highest-paid 5 percent of Americans received 34 percent of total individual income, but by 1946 their share was down to 18 percent ("more than halfway to perfect equality," enthused the National Bureau of Economic Research[12]). The top 1 percent of income earners took an even bigger plunge, from 19 percent of total income in 1929 to 7.7 percent in 1946.[13]

In the 1920s it had looked as if American capitalism would

---

[11] U.S. Senate, Armed Services Committee, *Confirmation Hearings on Charles E. Wilson as Secretary of Defense, February 18, 1953.*

[12] Quoted in *Fortune*, June 1951, p. 67.

[13] From U.S. Bureau of the Census, *Historical Statistics of the United States: Colonial Times to 1957* (Washington, D.C.: U.S. Government Printing Office, 1960).

split along class lines, a fate that would not have surprised Karl
Marx. Sociologists Robert S. Lynd and his wife, Helen Merrell
Lynd, after observing life in Muncie, Indiana (a small city of
35,000 which the Lynds took to be representative of America and
which they called "Middletown"), recorded a distinct division: "At
first glance it is difficult to see any semblance of pattern in the
workaday life of a community exhibiting a crazy-quilt array of
nearly four hundred ways of getting its living. . . . On closer scru-
tiny, however, this welter may be resolved into two kinds of activities. The people who engage in them will be referred to
throughout this report as the Working Class and the Business
Class. Members of the first group, by and large, address their
activities in getting their living primarily to things, utilizing material tools in the making of things and the performance of services, while the members of the second group address their
activities predominantly to people in the selling or promotion of
things, services, and ideas. . . . There are two and one-half times
as many in the working class as in the business class. . . . [I]t is
after all this division into working class and business class that
constitutes the outstanding cleavage in Middletown. The mere
fact of being born upon one or the other side of the watershed
roughly formed by these two groups is the most significant single
cultural factor tending to influence what one does all day long
throughout one's life."[14]

A college sociology textbook of 1956 entitled *The American Class
Structure* noted how far America had come from the class divisions
of Middletown in the 1920s, and attributed much of the change
to the newly dominant organization of production. America's core
corporations had blurred the distinction between those who used
tools and those who sold services and ideas by creating a large
middle group of skilled and semiskilled workers, foremen, supervisors, middle managers, and technicians. "All are employees,

---

[14]R. S. Lynd and H. M. Lynd, *Middletown* (New York: Harcourt, Brace, 1929),
pp. 21–24. In 1935, Robert Lynd returned to Middletown to discover a
larger city of 47,000 inhabitants whose major corporations were centralized
into larger units than before and were more subservient to national corporations. The gap between the worker and the manager—between the
working class and the business class—had widened. *Middletown in Transition*
(New York: Harcourt, Brace, 1937).

not owners. Their places in the system depend upon the rules of bureaucratic entry and promotion; business is coming more and more to assume the shape of the government civil service. A man chooses the basic level within which he will work by the amount and type of schooling he gets; the rest depends upon bureaucratic competition." The author of the textbook went on to show how corporate bureaucracies had a leveling effect on incomes, as the bottom rungs were elevated and the top rungs constrained by the civil service–like job categories. "Income is determined by functional role in the bureaucracy. The trend of income distribution has been toward a reduction in inequality. Owners have been receiving a smaller share relative to employees; professionals and clerks have been losing some of their advantages over operatives and laborers."[15]

Corporate bureaucracy had created a new, growing middle class of Americans, whose incomes were based not on ownership of assets but on bureaucratic rank. "Most of us are employees," noted *Life* magazine's chief editorial writer in a 1952 address. "As individuals we may own a lot of property, but typically not the property that gives us our livelihood. But neither is the corporation's ownership of physical property . . . the only reason we work for it. We work for it because the organization itself . . . has become the unit of production."[16]

America of the 1950s still harbored vast inequalities, of course. The very poor remained almost invisible. Blacks were overtly relegated to second-class citizenship. Few women dared aspire to professions other than teaching or nursing. (In 1957 United Airlines proudly announced that its "executive" service between New York and Chicago featured comfortable slippers, a steak dinner, and "no women on board except for two stewardesses."[17]) It would be decades before such barriers would begin to fall, even as more

---

[15] J. Kahl, *The American Class Structure* (New York: Holt, Rinehart, 1956), pp. 109–10.

[16] John Knox Jessup, Harvard Business School, June 7, 1952. See also Hofstadter, op. cit., p. 218: "[T]he modern corporation has proved to be a better medium for social mobility and opportunity than the old system of individual and family entrepreneurship."

[17] *Fortune*, May 1957, p. 106.

and more Americans joined the large, stable, standardized bureaucracies of corporate America.

4

AMERICA'S corporate bureaucracies were organized like military bureaucracies, for the efficient implementation of preconceived plans. It is perhaps no accident that the war veterans who manned the core American corporations of the 1950s accommodated so naturally to the militarylike hierarchies inside them. They were described in much the same terms as military hierarchies—featuring chains of command, spans of control, job classifications, divisions and division heads, and standard operating procedures to guide every decision. When in doubt, go by the book. All jobs were defined in advance by preestablished routines and responsibilities. Organization charts graphically mapped out internal hierarchies, starting with a large box at the top containing the chief executive officer, and proceeding downward through levels of ever smaller and more abundant boxes. As in the military, great emphasis was placed upon the maintenance of control—upon a superior's ability to inspire loyalty, discipline, and unquestioning obedience, and upon a subordinate's capacity to be so inspired.

Absolute control was necessary if plans were to be implemented exactly. And exactitude was necessary in order to achieve efficiencies of scale in mass or commodity production and to assert effective control over prices and markets. Here, too, the similarity with military commands was notable. As in war, strategic planning required a decision about where you wanted to be, followed by a plan for mobilizing your resources and troops to get there. The core corporation wanted to be at full production of a high volume of goods, at a price that would cover costs and provide a respectable profit. Production was guided by preestablished production goals, and sales by preordained quotas.

The system was not without innovation. But new inventions came in dramatic leaps rather than small increments. Small-scale improvements could not be planned or efficiently controlled. Large changes, on the other hand, lent themselves to meticulous preparation. New product designs emerged fully formed from the laboratory. Then, if the financial strategists and marketers thought well of the new product, the entire production process would be altered to accommodate it. New machinery would be installed, assembly lines reconfigured, new suppliers lined up, new advertising and marketing campaigns carefully planned. Highly detailed preparation was essential for high-volume production, since every step had to be perfectly synchronized with every other. And because the large midcentury American corporation reinvested fully half of its earnings in new plant, equipment, and research and development, it could not afford an unreceptive market. RCA spent most of a decade developing the first commercially available television set. Du Pont worked for twelve years to get nylon into production. It took Union Carbide more than seventeen years to achieve coal hydrogenation. The occasional product failure, such as Ford's Edsel, was noteworthy only as an exception to this general rule of meticulous and successful preparation. (A bad omen, symptomatic of intemperate planning: The first newspaper photos of the doomed vehicle, which had been on display at Ford's lavish kickoff party amid the smooth sounds of the late Glenn Miller's famous orchestra, gave less prominence to the car than to the music stands in the background, emblazoned with the orchestra leader's unfortunate—for Ford—initials.)

5

AT THE top of the large bureaucracies and occupying a box too large for any organization chart were the corporate statesmen, who lost no opportunity to tell the nation—in words describing the precise ideal propounded by Adolf Berle and Gardiner Means two decades before—that their job was to balance the needs of everyone affected by the corporation, including the public at large. "The job of management," proclaimed Frank Abrams, chairman of Standard Oil of New Jersey in a 1951 address that was typical of the era, "is to maintain an equitable and working balance among the claims of the various directly interested groups . . . stockholders, employees, customers, and the public at large. Business managers are gaining in professional status partly because they see in their work the basic responsibilities [to the public] that other professional men have long recognized in theirs."[18] *Fortune* solemnly lectured its executive readers on their duty, as corporate statesmen, to maintain a broad national perspective: "To take the professional point of view, the executive must adopt a detached, reserved attitude toward the opportunities and tactics of the moment. He must become an industrial statesman."[19]

This was no pose. The role of industrial statesman came naturally to these men, many of whom had served at high levels of government during World War II and continued to serve on government advisory panels, commissions, special committees, and task forces throughout the 1950s. When "Engine Charlie" Wilson brought with him to the Pentagon a platoon of GM executives, Adlai Stevenson quipped that America had taken government out of the hands of the New Dealers and given it to the car dealers. These self-described corporate statesmen frequently testified before Congress and were generous both with their time and with their opinions about what was good for the nation. Their views attracted attention, if for no other reason than because these men exercised not inconsiderable power over the economy. Their decisions about whether to raise prices and by how much, whether to build or close factories, and whether to hire more workers or lay workers off were often critical to entire regions of the country and to the nation as a whole.

Their personal influence was compounded by their tendency to agree with one another on major issues of the day. This was no conspiracy or cabal, but rather the consequence of having shared many of the same formative experiences and gained many of the same perspectives along the way. They had attended the same preparatory schools, Ivy League colleges, and business schools. They read the same newspapers, belonged to the same clubs, vacationed at the same resorts. They served on the boards of directors of one another's companies. (On leaving his Defense post in 1957, Engine Charlie told the press, with characteristic candor, that he looked forward to joining a few corporate boards "just to keep contacts with some old friends."[20]) In short, the

---

[18] Quoted in *Fortune*, October 1951, p. 98.
[19] Ibid., p. 99.
[20] Quoted in *Fortune*, July 1957, p. 94.

corporate statesmen of America viewed the problems and opportunities facing the nation in much the same way because they
viewed everything in much the same way.

Beneath them were the top executives and strategic planners
who plotted ever-larger volumes of production. And directly beneath them, a layer of senior vice presidents, division heads, and
senior managers who translated the plans into day-to-day operations. Beneath them, in turn, came layers upon layers of middle
managers—assistant vice presidents, assistant directors, unit managers, sales managers, supervisors, and so on—who conveyed the
orders downward, carried information upward, and mediated
conflicts.

The middle manager of the core American corporation at midcentury was not, by most standards, a rugged individualist. Indeed, his tendency toward conformity was the subject of considerable comment at the time. He was, according to sociologist
David Riesman's best-selling book *The Lonely Crowd*, anonymous
and "other-directed,"[21] a faceless "organization man" (according
to another best-seller of the era).[22] But conformity and tractability
were perfectly consistent with the standardized, high-volume system of production he oversaw. The system neither required nor
rewarded much in the way of original thought. In a mid-1950s
survey of corporate personnel managers charged with hiring and
promoting middle-level managers, 70 percent agreed with the
statement: "Because the rough-and-tumble days of corporation
growth are over, what the corporation needs most is the adaptable
administrator, schooled in managerial skills and concerned primarily with human relations and the techniques of making the
corporation a smooth-working team."[23]

The "organization man" joined the corporation fresh out of
college, and often remained there until retirement. Of 800 senior
executives in 300 major corporations surveyed in 1952, three-
quarters had been with the same corporation for more than twenty

---

[21] D. Riesman, *The Lonely Crowd: A Study of the Changing American Character*
(New Haven: Yale University Press, 1950).
[22] W. H. Whyte, Jr., *The Organization Man* (New York: Simon & Schuster,
1956).
[23] Cited in ibid.

years.[24] Like the "salaryman" of Japan in the last decades of the twentieth century, America's core manager at midcentury was a loyal bureaucrat.

6

BENEATH the middle manager came the foot soldier of American capitalism—the production worker, sporting a blue collar and toting a lunch bucket, doing the same task hour after hour, day after day. By midcentury, 15 million of them—fully 70 percent of America's factory workers, miners, and railway workers—belonged to trade unions. Before and just after the war they had been locked in bitter disputes with management, but by the 1950s the tumult was over. This was partly due to the Taft-Hartley Act, passed in 1947 by a Congress wondrously attuned to the new ascendancy of American business. The Act outlawed "closed shops" and secondary boycotts and gave the President power to enjoin strikes endangering national health and safety and to require a ninety-day "cooling-off" period before a strike was declared.

The peace between labor and management was even more a function of the growing bureaucratization of the American economy. Increasingly, confrontations occurred not in lockouts and on picket lines but in conference rooms stuffed with lawyers and clerks. Big Labor had become a bureaucracy all its own, mirroring the structure of Big Business. Walter Reuther and John L. Lewis were as notorious, and almost as powerful, as Engine Charlie. And almost as respectable: "The new labor leader is a member of the new class," opined the editors of *Fortune*. "His salary is high. He is a public figure. He enjoys a powerful place in society."[25] Big Labor had joined the establishment. "Labor leaders [are] eagerly welcomed on civic boards, community chests, and patriotic organizations. . . . A growing number of union leaders have come

---

[24] The Editors of *Fortune, The Executive Life* (Garden City, N.Y.: Doubleday, 1956), p. 30.
[25] *Fortune*, October 1951, p. 114.

to sport, with academic éclat, the gown and scarlet hood of honorary degrees."[26]

Each union had a national headquarters, housing top officials, their staffs, middle-level managers, and assorted specialists. Under them were regional managers and their staffs, and so on, all the way down to shop stewards. At bargaining time, while national union leaders and top corporate executives made menacing noises to the press, the bureaucrats and specialists on each side sat down behind closed doors, compared numbers and financial data, and came to agreement.

Such accommodation was possible because unions were organized by industry—automobile, aircraft, steel, rubber, shipbuilding, glass, paper, electrical equipment, chemicals—thus automatically extending any increase in wages and benefits to workers in every company in the industry. Because the core corporations within each industry were already coordinating prices, it was relatively easy for company negotiators to accede to generous wage and benefit increases and then pass them along to consumers via higher prices. Corporate executives found this benign arrangement superior to strikes and work stoppages, which jeopardized the smooth flow of large-scale production. Labor leaders likewise came to understand how far they could push their demands without causing undue alarm among politicians concerned about inflation. "Where you have a well-established industry and a well-established union, you are going to get to the point where a strike doesn't make sense," observed George Meany, the president of the AFL-CIO.[27]

The unionized segment of the American work force declined slightly in the 1950s and 1960s, but generous labor agreements nonetheless established industry-wide wage levels that continued to move steadily upward. For more than a quarter century, from the end of World War II until 1973, the real wages of America's production workers grew, on average, 2.5 to 3 percent each year. Benefits grew in tandem. In 1950, only 10 percent of union contracts provided for pensions and only 30 percent included social insurance; five years later, 45 percent provided their workers with pensions and 70 percent offered life, accident, and health insur-

---

[26] Daniel Bell, "The Language of Labor," *Fortune*, September 1951, p. 86.
[27] Quoted in ibid.

ance, including hospitalization and maternity care. Paid vacations became the norm, as did supplemental unemployment benefits (beyond those provided by the states) for workers who were laid off. Within the decade, wages were automatically adjusted upward for any increase in the cost of living brought on by inflation.

Symbolic of this transformation was the way organized labor came to be viewed within American culture. No longer a social movement, labor was by now an established political and economic institution, sharing with Big Business the credit and the responsibility for ensuring the nation's ever-rising prosperity. The 1930s had been the era of proletarian drama, like Clifford Odets' biting one-act play *Waiting for Lefty*, about workers exploited by their employers. "We're stormbirds of the working class," proclaims one of them defiantly in the concluding scene, after Lefty, who tried to organize a union, is murdered by the bosses, "and when we die they'll know what we did to make a new world." The curtain then falls to the angry chants of the workingmen: "Strike, strike, strike!"

By the 1950s, the proletarian drama had been superseded by the musical comedy, like the 1954 Broadway hit *Pajama Game*. Here, too, a strike is threatened, this one at the Sleep Tite Pajama Company. But the denouement is somewhat different, and emblematic of the new era. After a series of slapstick confrontations, the company's reactionary young president finally grants his employees' demand for a seven-and-a-half-cent-an-hour raise. In the finale, the president appears at the employee pajama party for a happy romp.

5

The National Bargain

> Just as an individual business seemed to run better if you
> plowed some of its profits into improvements, so the busi-
> ness system as a whole seemed to run better if you plowed
> some of the national income into improvements in the in-
> come and status of the lower income groups, enabling
> them to buy more goods and thus to expand the market
> for everybody.
>
> FREDERICK LEWIS ALLEN,
> *The Big Change* (1952)

IN RETURN for prosperity, American society accepted the legitimacy and permanence of the core American corporation. Government no longer would intrude on management prerogatives.
While harmful side effects upon public health, safety, the environment, and civil rights would eventually be regulated (with varying degrees of ardor), there would be no return to wartime
controls, no Depression-era industrial planning, and no flirtation
with public ownership, as there would be in some European and
Asian nations. Nor would government enforce the antitrust laws
with the rigor and passion that periodically had gripped reformers
in decades past. Tacit collusion among the largest firms in each
industry (or in the more technical and less alarming language of
economics, "oligopolistic coordination") would be an accepted feature of private-sector planning for high-volume production.

Instead, government officials took as one of their primary responsibilities the continued profitability of America's core corporations. Government would provide low-interest loans for the
purchase of new homes, an important stimulus to mass consump-

tion. It would attempt to smooth out the business cycle, so that the core corporation could more easily plan high-volume production without undue concern about suddenly falling or suddenly escalating demand for products. Planners at the Federal Reserve Board and the Bureau of the Budget would alter, respectively, the money supply and government expenditures, in efforts to counterbalance the economy's tendencies toward surges and sags. Presidents might "jawbone" the chief executives of core corporations and labor leaders, in order to persuade them to forgo a price and wage increase that seemed too generous, but only under emergency conditions would government try to control prices directly.

How much inflation was tolerable remained a point of contention, however. Conservative Republicans, whose constituents included many of the leaders of American business, preferred to steer far clear of inflation even at the risk of substantial unemployment. This preference was understandable, given that their constituents tended to be lenders, the value of whose loans was undermined by inflation, and they tended not to be among those most likely to be laid off in the event of an economic dip. Democrats, on the other hand, preferred higher employment even at the risk of some inflation. This preference, too, was understandable, given the proclivity of their constituents toward debt and relatively less secure employment. When this partisan clash played itself out in Congress, the result was a compromise—the Employment Act of 1946—that substituted "maximum" for "full" employment (its original objective), yielding a vague mandate that provided little by way of guidance.

2

PREPARING America's children for gainful employment was another realm of public responsibility. Given America's system of high-volume, standardized production, the responsibility was not terribly burdensome. The only prerequisites for most jobs were an ability to comprehend simple oral and written directives and sufficient self-control to implement them.

Thus did America's grammar schools and high schools at mid-century mirror the system of mass production. Children moved from grade to grade through a preplanned sequence of standard subjects, as if on factory conveyor belts. At each stage, certain facts were poured into their heads. Children with the greatest capacity to absorb the facts, and with the most submissive demeanor, were placed on a rapid track through the sequence; those with the least capacity for fact retention and self-discipline, on the slowest. Most children ended up on a conveyor belt of medium speed. Standardized tests were routinely administered at certain checkpoints in order to measure how many of the facts had stuck in the small heads, and "product defects" were taken off the line and returned for retooling. As in the mass-production system, discipline and order were emphasized above all else.

Here, too, standardization produced scale economies. Like factory workers, teachers had little discretion over what they did at each stage along the line. They were required to follow plans devised by specialists at the highest rungs of the educational hierarchy and transmitted down to them through layers of commissioners, superintendents, assistant superintendents, and principals. And, as in factory production, the larger the better: Smaller school districts were steadily consolidated into ever-larger ones, which gave rise to vast centralized factories called regional schools, through which ever-greater numbers of children could be processed smoothly and continuously.

It was the perfect preparation for the world of high-volume production. In the early 1930s, educational expert Elwood P. Cubberly had anticipated the ideal American school in similar terms: "Our schools are, in a sense, factories in which the raw materials are to be shaped and fashioned into products to meet the various demands of life. The specifications for manufacturing come from the demands of the twentieth century civilization, and it is the business of the school to build its pupils to the specifications laid down. This demands good tools, specialized machinery, continuous measurements of production to see if it is according to specifications, [and] the elimination of waste in manufacture."[1] Not even the Soviets' successful launch of *Sputnik* in 1957, which caused the nation momentarily to question the quality of American education, challenged this vision in a fundamental way. America's

---

[1] E. P. Cubberly, *Public Education in the United States* (Boston: Houghton Mifflin, 1934).

response was not to rethink the organizing principles of American schooling, but to appropriate additional funds for training teachers to be more efficient at mass production—particularly in mathematics and the sciences.

The top 15 percent of high school students, those processed most expeditiously on the fastest track, went on to attend four-year colleges or universities, whence they moved onto an executive track toward the top of the corporate bureaucracies. Slightly more than half of the remainder would not complete high school. Notably, no severe financial penalty attached to this impertinence. Well-paying factory jobs awaited high school graduates and nongraduates alike, as the core American corporation fulfilled its side of the implicit bargain.

3

NATIONAL defense was the third domain of public responsibility. The nation's preoccupation with the Soviet Union gave new meaning to the presumed identity among the national economy, its core corporations, and the welfare of Americans. The contest between capitalism and communism was to be waged not only on the edges of the Soviet empire but also on the battlefield of the world economy. Thus was America's economic prowess at midcentury seen as an aspect of its defense preparedness, and nothing better represented that prowess than the core American corporation.

The Cold War defense mission served as a ready justification for public-sector investment. *Sputnik*'s indirect contribution to American education was called, appropriately enough, the National Defense Education Act. Its avowed purpose was to prepare more scientists and engineers, so that the Russians could not surpass us in space. In similar fashion, the legislation launching a new national highway system—40,000 miles of straight four-lane freeways to replace the old two-lane federal roads that meandered through cities and towns—was called the National Defense Highway Act, and justified in the halls of Congress as a means of speeding munitions across the nation in the event of war. The manifestly real possibility of other consequences, good and bad —that it might also generate sprawling suburbs and shopping malls, harm downtown retailers, fatten the construction industry, boost auto sales, create an entire trucking industry, displace barges and railroads, and radically lower the cost of transporting and distributing goods across America—was not openly discussed.

Nor was it explicitly acknowledged that the billions of dollars dedicated to researching, designing, and constructing intricate and complex weapons systems would also generate technologies with commercial possibilities. Defense contractors invented small transistors, which eventually would find their way into everything from televisions to wristwatches. Also from the military-industrial complex, as Eisenhower so decorously dubbed it, would emerge hard plastics, optical fibers, lasers, computers, jet engines and aircraft frames, precision gauges, sensing devices, and an array of electronic gadgets, many of which also would create commercial advantage for America's core corporations. (From Pentagon-induced technologies have come many of the indispensables of modern life, such as solar-powered hand calculators, graphite tennis rackets, and remote-controlled television sets.)

Military largesse went to a select and remarkably stable group of core corporations, mostly involved in aerospace and telecommunications. Throughout the 1950s and 1960s, a hundred core corporations received two-thirds, by value, of all defense contracts. Ten firms received one-third. Ninety-six of the hundred largest defense contractors in 1957 were still among the hundred ten years later.[2] Their apparent permanence was due in part to the tendency of their top executives to be drawn from the ranks of Defense Department officials, whose generosity with taxpayers' money while in office was reciprocated once out of office. It was due as well to the not insignificant number of high-paying manufacturing jobs created by these contractors around the nation. By 1959, for example, 20 percent of California's nonagricultural work force was working, directly or indirectly, for major defense contractors; the figure was 22 percent in the state of Washington, 17 percent in Arizona, and 16 percent in Maryland.[3]

---

[2] William Baldwin, *The Structure of the Defense Market, 1955–1964* (Durham, N.C.: Duke University Press, 1967), p. 21.

[3] K. Kaysen, "The Corporation: How Much Power? What Scope?" in Edward S. Mason (ed.), *The Corporation in Modern Society* (Cambridge: Harvard University Press, 1959), pp. 86–89.

4

AMERICA at midcentury was not a major trading nation. Few war-devastated economies were capable of selling Americans much of anything (much of anything we couldn't purchase better or cheaper domestically, that is) or buying much of what we might have had to sell. Even by 1960, only 4 percent of the cars Americans purchased were built outside the United States, a bit more than 4 percent of the steel, less than 6 percent of televisions, radios, and other consumer electronic products, and only 3 percent of the machine tools. Nonetheless, America sought to extend the wonders of American capitalism to the rest of the world, as a further bulwark against the spread of Soviet communism. "Today the United States free market is the wonder of the world," preached *Fortune* magazine in the summer of 1955. "Its extension on an international scale would face the Soviets with an unbeatable combination of strength, and in the process reaffirm the basic libertarian principles on which this country has grown to greatness."[4]

America led the way toward a global capitalism modeled on American capitalism. In the early postwar years, the nation championed a system of fixed exchange rates to minimize currency fluctuations, an International Monetary Fund to ensure world liquidity, a World Bank to aggregate and direct development finance, and a General Agreement on Tariffs and Trade to ensure an open trading system. America funneled billions of dollars in aid to Western Europe and Japan in order to rebuild factories, roads, railways, and schools and targeted aid and know-how to developing nations. And it steadily reduced its tariffs on foreign imports. "The old imperialism—exploitation for foreign profit—has no place in our plans," said Harry Truman, in announcing his Point Four program of technological assistance to developing nations. "What we envisage is a program of development based on the concept of democratic fair-dealing." He might have added: "and the containment of the Soviet menace."

---

[4]*Fortune*, July 1955, p. 23.

The effort was an astounding success for all concerned. The years 1945 to 1970 witnessed the most dramatic and widely shared economic growth in the history of mankind. The world's gross national product grew from $300 billion to about $2 trillion. Allowing for inflation, real incomes tripled, world trade quadrupled. But here again, there was a convenient convergence between the nation's security objectives and the interests of America's core corporations. In helping to restore the world's leading economies and thus keep communism at bay, the new global system of trade and assistance created new opportunities for America's core corporations—far larger, richer, and more technologically advanced than any others—to expand and prosper. With the dollar as the currency upon which the system of fixed exchange rates was to be based, American bankers and core corporations could extend their reach at minimal risk. Under a World Bank controlled by Americans, development assistance could be focused precisely where America's core corporations saw the greatest opportunity. And so long as the recipients of America's foreign aid used it to buy American exports, core corporations could venture into global trade confident of receptive markets. Through such means, the playing field of global commerce was sufficiently tipped in America's direction so that by the mid-1950s even the National Association of Manufacturers could be persuaded to support tariff reduction.

Nor was it mere coincidence that the Central Intelligence Agency discovered communist plots where America's core corporations possessed, or wished to possess, substantial holdings of natural resources. When, in 1953, an anticolonial Iranian nationalist movement led by Mohammed Mossadegh challenged the power of the shah and seized the Anglo-Iranian Oil Company, the CIA secretly channeled millions of dollars to army officers dedicated to returning the shah to power; once their objectives had been fulfilled, generous access to Iranian oil was granted to Gulf, Texaco, Socony Mobil, and Standard Oil of New Jersey. That same year, Guatemala's duly elected President, Jacobo Arbenz Guzman, initiated a program of land reform which included confiscation of the United Fruit Company's plantations; the CIA then bankrolled right-wing revolutionaries who, in 1954, helped by CIA pilots and aircraft supplied by Nicaraguan dictator Anastasio Somoza, ultimately spared United Fruit so dismal a fate. Also in 1954, the United States became quietly involved in Indochina, another area rich in natural resources. In the battles that raged between the French colonial army and the Vietminh, America furnished euphemistically titled "technical advisers," CIA pilots, and 70 percent of the French military budget. Once the French were decisively defeated, President Eisenhower—fearful that the popular Ho Chi Minh, now in control of the northern part of Vietnam, would win a general election—refused to sign the Geneva Accords. He arranged instead for Ngo Dinh Diem, a staunch anticommunist in exile, to return from the United States to become Premier of South Vietnam. In 1965, when civil war in the Dominican Republic threatened American sugar plantations, Lyndon Johnson sent in 30,000 marines.

That relations with Iran, Vietnam, and Central America became less than cordial in subsequent decades may have had something to do with America's unflinching eagerness during this era to use foreign policy in the service of the core American corporation.

5

THE SCALE and technological superiority of America's core corporations extended the reach of American capitalism far more effectively than did the Department of Defense or the Central Intelligence Agency. Coca-Cola, Ford, General Motors, Heinz, National Cash Register, Sears, IBM, and scores of other core American corporations exported not only their products but, more important, their marketing and their know-how—in the form of manufacturing facilities, distribution outlets, and advertising around the world. And as the rest of the world's citizens acquired both a taste and a capacity to pay for the American goods produced in their midst, Americans enjoyed an ever-growing stream of dividends and royalties from all corners of the globe.

The American multinational corporation was not ungenerous to its foreign hosts, but it maintained tight control. Foreigners who became middle-level managers within such facilities typically exercised even less discretion over how they did their work than did their American counterparts. (General Motors, for example, routinely supplied its foreign managers with a 300-page manual detailing GM operating procedures.) Foreign nationals were rarely invited to share in the successes of the American operations they hosted. IBM chose to withdraw its investments from India rather than sell a minority interest in its operation to Indian partners.

Indeed, the very term "subsidiary," used to designate the foreign operations of core American corporations, suggested why foreign nationals felt uneasy about the relationship. They felt subordinate not only to America's economic interests but also, in view of Washington's repeated insistence that the foreign subsidiaries of American corporations not trade with the Soviet bloc, to America's Cold War strategies. The urgent tone of Jean-Jacques Servan-Schreiber's 1967 polemic *Le Défi Américain (The American Challenge)* summarized the prevailing mood in Europe and other regions increasingly dominated by American capitalism. Europe, he warned (in almost the very words some American commentators would employ two decades later to describe the Japanese challenge), was succumbing to the United States: "American industry spills out across the world primarily because of the energy released by the American corporation." That energy, in turn, derived from America's "highly organized economic system based on large units, financed and guided by national government." It was, in other words, a strategic coupling of national power and corporate power. "Most striking of all," he observed, "is the strategic character of American industrial penetration. One by one, U.S. corporations capture those sectors of the economy . . . with the highest growth rates."[5]

The choice was clear: ". . . building an independent Europe or letting it become an annex of the United States."[6] Servan-Schreiber, and most other Europeans, found the first alternative the more attractive of the two. And the way to build an independent Europe, it seemed, was to create national corporate champions that Europeans could call their own. In the 1960s, Britain proceeded to consolidate its automobile manufacturers into British Leyland, its steelmakers into British Steel, and its fledgling computer makers into ICL; France's automobile champion became

---

[5] Jean-Jacques Servan-Schreiber, *The American Challenge* (American ed.; New York: Penguin Books, 1969), p. 210.
[6] Ibid., p. 211.

Renault, its computer champion, Bull, and its steel champions, Unisor and Sacilor; Italy's chemical industry was concentrated in Montedison and steel into IRI; and so on. Some of these new national champions were owned outright by their governments while others were heavily subsidized. But however organized, the bargains between European nations and their core corporations were far more explicit than those between America and its own.

6

TO SUMMARIZE the terms of the national bargain at midcentury: First, the core American corporation would plan and implement the production of a large volume of goods. The large volume would create significant economies of scale, thus reducing the cost of producing each unit. By coordinating with other core corporations, prices could be set high enough to ensure substantial revenues. A large portion of the revenues would be reinvested in new factories and machinery, but a significant share would go to middle managers and production workers. Organized labor, in return, would eschew strikes and work stoppages that would interfere with high-volume production. Both sides would refrain from setting prices and wages so high as to spur inflation.

Government, meanwhile, would not intrude upon corporate decision-making. It would refrain from any kind of centralized economic planning, but would allow core corporations to undertake private planning by quietly coordinating their prices and output. To further aid core corporations in pursuit of high volume, government would smooth out the business cycle. The nation's youth would be appropriately prepared for the jobs awaiting them within this industrial system. Further, government would subsidize the purchase of new homes and build a national highway system, both further aids to mass consumption. Government also would contract with America's core corporations to defend the nation, thus indirectly providing them the funds to research and develop new commercial technologies. And government would encourage American companies to invest abroad, and protect their interests after they did so.

The system contained its own internal logic. Big Business, Big Labor, and the public at large would subsidize high-volume production in order to gain greater efficiencies of scale, which in turn would employ a growing middle class of Americans capable of buying the expanded output. It was truly a national bargain. The equation did not depend on domination of foreign markets, as had the older forms of mercantilism and imperialism. Foreign investment by American multinationals was understood, rather, as a means of hastening and expanding this virtuous circle (and thus, not incidentally, forestalling the spread of world communism).

The bargain thus rested on a tacit agreement by each party— business executives and investors, labor, and the public, as represented through government—to exercise restraint, sacrificing immediate gains for the sake of larger gains for all parties later on. It was a near-perfect illustration of what Alexis de Tocqueville had termed America's "principle of self-interest rightly understood," by which Americans were motivated to sacrifice for the general welfare not out of altruism or patriotism but because of the anticipated benefits they would enjoy from collective action. The national bargain was seldom discussed openly, of course. Its terms were revealed only when it seemed most in danger of coming unstuck, as when, in 1962, John F. Kennedy publicly denounced Roger Blough, the chairman of U.S. Steel, for raising steel prices and thus violating the wage-and-price agreement that had been worked out with the steelworkers union and other steel producers. Nor was it a perfect bargain. As noted, its terms did not extend to blacks or women, or to poorer nations that supplied America's core corporations with raw materials. Still, it delivered on its promises: For almost a quarter of a century, America's middle class expanded and prospered. Europe and Japan participated in the boom. Their own national bargains—more explicit than America's—were premised on the same logic of high-volume, standardized production.

6

The Presumed Problem

U.S. industry's loss of competitiveness over the past decade has been nothing short of an economic disaster.

BUSINESS WEEK (June 30, 1980)

IT WAS only a matter of time before American manufacturing know-how, arcing out into the postwar world, would come around full circle to where it began, like a giant boomerang. There had been foreshadowings. In 1953, RCA, Westinghouse, Du Pont, Armco Steel, and GE had all sold patents to the Japanese and helped start Japanese factories, prompting *Fortune* to ask, innocently enough, "[I]s it in the long-run interests of the United States? Will not revitalized Japanese industries cut into U.S. markets abroad, and increasingly invade our domestic market?"[1] But during those boom years of high-volume production, such concerns seemed farfetched to those who inhabited the highest reaches of American business, labor, and government.

Within a scant two decades, of course, Americans were to discover that foreigners could undertake high-volume production of standard goods—cars, televisions, household appliances, steel ingots, textiles—and sell them in the United States more cheaply (and sometimes at higher levels of quality) than America's core corporations. It was not just that foreign laborers were happy to work for a fraction of the soaring wages and benefits of Americans, or that foreigners had cheaper access to certain raw materials than did Americans. (Many of the far-flung subsidiaries of America's core corporations already were taking advantage of these attri-

---

[1] *Fortune*, April 1953, p. 188.

butes.) The truly humbling discovery was that they could build and manage modern factories as effectively as could the executives of America's national champions. Thanks to emerging efficiencies in global transportation and communications—cargo ships and planes, sealed containers capable of being moved from railroad to ship to plane to truck, overseas cables, and, eventually, satellites bouncing electric signals from one continent to another—they could ship the standardized goods back for sale in the United States at remarkably low cost. And as commodities became smaller and lighter (transistorized televisions, semiconductor chips), such costs dropped even faster. Between 1970 and 1988, for example, pounds shipped by vessel and air per real dollar of U.S. imports declined more than 4 percent a year.[2]

That almost anyone could undertake high-volume standardized production using state-of-the-art equipment, and could send the resulting products cheaply to almost any location on the globe, had one ineluctable consequence: By the late 1960s, America's core corporations could no longer set their prices. They were now subject to fierce foreign competition, not unlike the competition they first encountered a century before, at the dawn of high-volume production.

2

WHAT to do?[3] One strategy was to do precisely what they had done a hundred years before: try to keep cheap foreign products out of the American market. Thus, almost a century after America had erected its first great protectionist wall, the nation applied itself in earnest to building another. Construction was not from the ground up, however; American producers of textiles and apparel had insisted on strict quotas against foreign traders throughout the postwar era. Steelmakers did likewise in 1969, followed in rapid succession during the 1970s and 1980s by American manufacturers of televisions and other consumer electronic products,

---

[2] Figures from Alan Greenspan, "Goods Shrink and Trade Grows," *The Wall Street Journal*, October 24, 1988, p. 21.
[3] I have discussed the following three "endgame" strategies at greater length in *The Next American Frontier* (New York: Times Books, 1983), Chs. 8–10.

automakers, producers of machine tools, fabricators of semiconductors, and so on. By the end of the 1980s, almost a third of the standard goods manufactured in the United States, by value, were protected against international competition.[4]

America's core corporations insisted that they were simply protecting themselves against the "unfair" practices of foreign traders. The precise nature of this unfairness, however, was rarely stated with any specificity. It was said that foreigners were "dumping" their wares in the United States—a term conjuring up images of huge piles of substandard consumer durables and cheap novelty items littering American beaches. In fact, "dumping" described nothing more than foreign producers acting exactly as would any self-respecting competitor who wished to sell in large quantity: offer a cut-rate price from the very first sale onward, sometimes even taking a loss, in anticipation of making money later on after gaining scale efficiencies.[5] Alternatively, it was argued that foreign producers were being subsidized by their governments, hardly a stinging accusation in light of all the unrestrained largesse—research grants, defense contracts, outright bailouts—flowing from the U.S. government to American corporations.

Rarely did such alleged "unfairness" prompt the United States to erect unilateral quotas or tariffs, which, after all, would have violated the General Agreement on Tariffs and Trade. The more common tendency was for the foreign perpetrators to agree "voluntarily" to limit their exports to the United States—voluntarily, that is, in the narrow sense that they acquiesced in the full knowledge that they would suffer a worse fate—a more severe quota, directed only at them—were they to refuse to do so.

The protectionist strategy provided temporary relief to some of America's core corporations, but it was a stopgap which, in any

---

[4] This estimate is based on data from the International Trade Commission. It includes not only formal tariffs and quotas but also "voluntary" restraint agreements, antidumping levies, countervailing duties, and nontariff barriers such as regulatory standards barring foreign products from the United States market.

[5] In calculating whether a foreign company has dumped its goods in the United States, the Commerce Department insists that the foreign company must earn a profit of at least 8 percent. If the foreign company earns anything less than this, the Commerce Department assumes that it is selling the product at a loss, and thus illegally "dumping" it in the United States.

event, failed to restore the high and ever-rising revenues of twenty years before. For one thing, every time one industry gained protection, another industry, dependent on the first for material or components, found itself squeezed. Once the steel industry successfully warded off cheaper foreign steel, the Big Three American automakers discovered that they had to pay 40 percent more for it than did their global competitors, thus putting the American automakers at a greater competitive disadvantage and, paradoxically, making them all the more needful of protection. The same proved true for American apparel manufacturers when textiles were first protected, and American computer manufacturers when foreign semiconductors were blocked from the American market.

There was another difficulty: Foreign exports that were voluntarily limited had a remarkable knack of sneaking across the American border even when not inside other products. Sometimes they sneaked in via a third country that had not yet "voluntarily" agreed to hold back its exports; sometimes the foreign firm set up shop inside the United States and merely assembled the restricted item out of components shipped from back home. Thus, proliferating "voluntary" restraint agreements notwithstanding, between 1969 and 1979 the value of manufactured imports relative to domestic production in the United States surged from less than 14 percent to 38 percent. By 1986, for every $100 spent on goods produced in the United States, Americans were buying $45 worth of manufactured imports.[6]

Protectionist walls also ceded the rest of the world's markets to foreign producers, who could gain vast scale efficiencies by selling their goods everywhere but the United States. Protected behind their own borders, America's core corporations gained little; in the relatively lackluster American market, demand for many standardized products was slowing as population growth slowed. Meanwhile, by the 1970s many foreign markets were

---

[6]That year, according to the Department of Commerce, 66 percent of the televisions and radios purchased by Americans, 45 percent of all machine tools, 28 percent of all automobiles, and 25 percent of all computers were produced outside the United States. For a summary, see *U.S. News & World Report*, February 2, 1987, p. 18.

teeming, as their consumers were finally becoming able to indulge appetites for standard goods.

Nor, finally, did protection enhance the standard of living of most Americans. To the contrary, it caused them to pay extra for what they purchased. The "voluntary" export restraints on Japanese cars that temporarily helped the Big Three automakers maintain their profits (but not their work forces) through the 1980s cost American consumers about $1 billion a year more than they would have paid for cars had the American market been open.[7]

3

So a SECOND strategy was developed: If foreigners could do it cheaply, so, presumably, could America's core corporations. American executives began demanding sizable wage cuts from their American employees. Wielding the popular butcher metaphors of the 1970s and 1980s—cutting to the bone, getting lean and mean, hacking off the fat—they sought to "rationalize" their operations by closing inefficient factories and laying off workers. If none of these measures worked, they set up new factories abroad, in the very nations whose cheap sources of production were depressing corporate profits. The total value of American imports from American-owned factories abroad rose from $1.8 billion in 1969 to almost $22 billion by 1983, adjusted for inflation.[8] Unable to beat them, America's core corporations would try to join them.

But this strategy also failed to restore the profitability of most companies that tried it. Even when American producers successfully matched foreign costs of production, they still could not earn healthy profits. Whatever price they charged, foreign producers

[7] D. Tarr and M. Morke, *Aggregate Costs to the United States of Tariffs and Quotas on Imports*, Federal Trade Commission (Washington, D.C.: U.S. Government Printing Office, 1984), pp. 19–36.

[8] Figures from J. Grunwald and K. Flamm, *The Global Factory: Foreign Assembly in International Trade* (Washington, D.C.: Brookings Institution, 1985), pp. 14–20.

could always lure away customers by charging a still lower price and settling for an even smaller return. This painful lesson still eludes many: Perfect competition—the economist's Rosetta stone—eventually strips away all profits, causing even the best of businesses to fold.

4

A THIRD strategy was born, as futile as the other two: Unable to bar foreign products or to compete on the basis of price, some of America's core corporations sought to maintain profits through financial dexterity. Thus, beginning in the late 1960s and gathering momentum through the two succeeding decades, America's core corporations transformed themselves into financial holding companies for the efficient wielding of corporate assets. Initially they formed conglomerates of unrelated businesses, and then, when this ploy failed, sold them off. Such was the humbling fate of almost half the companies purchased by conglomerates between 1965 and 1975.[9] ITT's Harold Geneen acquired some two hundred companies in the late 1960s and 1970s and sold most of them in the 1980s, thereby enhancing the value of ITT's shares, adjusted for inflation, not one whit. Peter Grace, the indomitable head of W. R. Grace, who fulminated incessantly against government waste and inefficiency, embarked upon hundreds of acquisitions through the 1960s and 1970s, with the result that a dollar invested in his company at the start of his reign was worth less, by the close of the 1980s, than it would have if invested randomly in the Standard & Poor's 500.[10]

When, by the late 1970s, the conglomerate merger lost its allure, American corporations embarked upon the unfriendly take-

---

[9] Figures from W. T. Grimm and Company, *Merger Statistics Review 1985* (Chicago: Grimm, 1986), p. 92.

[10] By February 1990, Grace's stock was trading around $30 a share. The firm's estimated breakup value, according to *Business Week*, was twice that amount. Thus was Peter Grace, the scourge of government waste, diminishing the value of his shareholders' stock by half. Not even in government had there been waste on such a monumental scale. *Business Week*, February 19, 1990, p. 69.

over or the leveraged buyout, two ploys by which equity typically was exchanged for debt, thus reducing corporate income taxes (interest on debt is deductible, whereas dividend payments to shareholders are not). The tax advantages inherent in such transactions were clear; more dubious were the claimed efficiencies, synergies, and other stimulants. The primary result was for company ownership to circulate, as in a game of musical chairs. In one of the fastest and largest of such escapades, R. J. Reynolds acquired Nabisco in 1985, and then, three years later, sold it off after a leveraged buyout totaling $28 billion. Sometimes it was difficult to keep track of the comings and goings, from conglomeration to takeover to leveraged buyout. In the 1960s, Avis Rent-A-Car was a part of ITT's conglomerate empire. In the 1970s, ITT sold Avis to Norton Simon, which was taken over by Esmark. A year later, Esmark succumbed to the blandishments of Beatrice Foods. In 1986, Beatrice itself was taken over by a group of investors that included several former Esmark executives, who promptly dismembered Beatrice and sold Avis to its own managers. A mere fourteen months later, Avis's managers sold the erstwhile company to its employees. Who controls Avis now? Only God and a few investment bankers know for sure.

The problem, of course, was that such transactions did not alter the underlying system of production. Corporate headquarters proved an awkward location from which to play the stock market. The feverish buying and selling of assets, undertaken by corporate executives, ended up costing shareholders approximately three times more than a typical mutual fund manager would charge to look after a portfolio of stocks.[11]

5

THUS did the profits of America's core corporations wither. Measured on any scale—as the portion of total national income going to shareholders and other business owners or as the rate of return on investment—profits declined or stagnated from the mid-1960s

[11]See "Do Mergers Really Work?," *Business Week*, June 3, 1985, p. 88; "The Wasteful Games of America's Corporate Raiders," *The Economist*, June 1, 1985, p. 73.

onward. From a peak of nearly 10 percent in 1965, the average net after-tax profit rate of America's nonfinancial corporations dropped to less than 7 percent in 1980, a decline of more than one-third. This, it should be remembered, was at a time when a low American dollar should have made American exports relatively attractive to the rest of the world. Profits bounced back between 1982 and 1985, inspired by Ronald Reagan's vast military buildup, but then continued their downward slide.[12] The Dow Jones Industrial Average began its spurt in August 1982, but when adjusted for inflation the market's August 1987 peak (reached just before the sudden crash, or "correction," as Wall Streeters delicately put it) was below the old milestone of January 1966. The industrialized nations of Western Europe experienced a similar descent, as their major corporations also tried to adjust to the global changes.[13]

The presumed problem of America's "declining competitiveness" would be blamed for much of what seemed to ail America, including the nation's growing indebtedness to other nations, the increasing tendency of foreigners to purchase American assets, and the stagnation of average American incomes. "Certain American industries that once dominated world commerce . . . have lost much of their market share both at home and abroad; in a few industries . . . the American presence in the market has all but disappeared," warned the MIT Commission on Industrial Productivity in its 1989 report,[14] echoing the concerns of countless other reports, statements, and white papers issued by other commissions, study groups, task forces, advisory committees, caucuses, boards, delegations, and blue-ribbon panels.

This view of the problem, while not wholly inaccurate, was, by

---

[12]Calculations through 1986 from S. Bowles, D. Gordon, and T. Weisskopf, "Power and Profits: The Social Structure of Accumulation and the Profitability of the Postwar U.S. Economy," *Review of Radical Political Economics*, Vol. 18, Nos. 1 and 2 (Spring and Summer 1986), as revised.

[13]A. Glyn, A. Hughes, A. Lipietz, and A. Singh, "The Rise and Fall of the Golden Age," in S. Marglin and J. Schor (eds.), *The End of the Golden Age* (New York: Oxford University Press, 1989); T. P. Hill, *Profits and the Rate of Return* (Paris: Organization for Economic Cooperation and Development, 1979).

[14]M. Dertouzos, R. Lester, R. Solow, et al., *Made in America: Regaining the Productive Edge* (Cambridge: MIT Press, 1989), p. 1.

the last decade of the century, seriously misleading. It presumed the existence of entities—American corporations, American industries, even the American economy as a whole—whose vitality would have to be restored in order to improve American living standards. These entities, it was assumed, still intermediated between Americans and the world economy, such that their success was the prerequisite to increases in personal wealth. This was, of course, the picture of the American economy at midcentury, when the economic fates of most Americans were bound up together, within and around America's core corporations and industries.

This picture, however, is no longer correct. "American" corporations and "American" industries are ceasing to exist in any form that can meaningfully be distinguished from the rest of the global economy. Nor, for that matter, is the American economy as a whole retaining a distinct identity, within which Americans succeed or fail together. Thus, to assume that revitalization of these abstract entities will help Americans is to engage in a form of vestigial thought. The standard of living of Americans, as well as of the citizens of other nations, is coming to depend less on the success of the nation's core corporations and industries, or even on something called the "national economy," than it is on the worldwide demand for their skills and insights. This is the emerging reality to which I now turn.

Part Two
The Global Web

7

From High Volume to High Value

THE MODERN corporation at the close of the twentieth century bears only a superficial resemblance to its midcentury counterpart. The names and logos of America's core corporations are still emblematic of the American economy—General Electric, AT&T, General Motors, Ford, IBM, Kodak, American Can, Sears, Caterpillar Tractor, TWA, and so on, including even a few new giants virtually unknown at midcentury, like Texas Instruments, McDonald's, Xerox, and American Express. They still conjure up images of vast wealth and control over the wheels of commerce. They are still headquartered in formidable glass-and-steel buildings, as before, and their top executives still hobnob with politicians and celebrities, and write autobiographies congratulating themselves on their wisdom and daring.

But underneath, all is changing. America's core corporation no longer plans and implements the production of a large volume of goods and services; it no longer owns or invests in a vast array of factories, machinery, laboratories, warehouses, and other tangible assets; it no longer employs armies of production workers and middle-level managers; it no longer serves as gateway to the American middle class. In fact, the core corporation is no longer even American. It is, increasingly, a façade, behind which teems an array of decentralized groups and subgroups continuously contracting with similarly diffuse working units all over the world.

2

THE TRANSFORMATION has been less than smooth. No longer
able to generate large earnings from high-volume production of
standard commodities—and unable to restore profits by protecting the American market, cutting prices, or rearranging assets—
America's core corporations are gradually, often painfully, turning toward serving the unique needs of particular customers. By
trial and error, by fits and starts, often under great stress, and
usually without much awareness of what they are doing or why,
the firms that are surviving and succeeding are shifting from high
volume to high value. A similar transformation is occurring in
other national economies which have traditionally been organized
around high-volume production.

A few illustrations will help make the point.[1] In the United
States, as in other leading areas of the world economy, the fastest-
growing and most profitable part of steelmaking is no longer in
mammoth 5,000-employee integrated mills producing long runs
of steel ingots. It is in steels intended for particular uses: corrosion-
resistant steels (hot-dipped galvanized or electrogalvanized)
produced for specific automobiles, trucks, and appliances; iron
powder that can be packed and forged into lightweight and precisely balanced parts used in crankshafts and other high-stressed
parts of engines; alloys comprising steel mixed with silicon, nickel,
or cobalt, for turbine and compressor disks, spacers, seals, and
other high-temperature components of aircraft (McDonnell
Douglas now buys composite helicopter blades comprising seventeen different materials, for $50,000 each); and mini-mills, us-
ing electric-arc furnaces and scrap metal to serve particular
customers. A similar transformation is occurring in plastics, where
high earnings no longer flow from large batches of basic polymers
like polystyrene, but from special polymers created from unique
combinations of molecules which can withstand varying degrees
of stress and temperature and can be molded into intricate parts
(like those found in cellular telephones or computers). In chem-

---

[1] The following examples are gleaned from interviews with officers and employees of a wide range of corporations. A listing appears at the end of the
book, in "A Note on Additional Sources."

icals, the biggest profits likewise lie in specialty chemicals designed and produced for particular industrial uses.

Whether the industry is old or new, mature or high-tech, the pattern is similar. Leading tool and die casters make precision castings out of aluminum and zinc for computer frames, inserts, housings, and disk-drive components. The most profitable textile businesses produce specially coated and finished fabrics for automobiles, office furniture, rain gear, and wall coverings. The fastest-growing and most profitable semiconductor firms make specialized microprocessors and customized chips tailored to the particular needs of buyers. As computers with standard operating systems become commodities, the largest profits lie in the software that links computers to particular user needs. (In 1984, 80 percent of the cost of a computer was in its hardware, 20 percent in software; by 1990, the proportions were just the reverse.)

Traditional services are experiencing the same transformation. The highest profits in telecommunications derive from customized long-distance services like voice, video, and information processing; from "smart buildings" connecting office telephones, computers, and facsimile machines; and from specialized telecommunications networks linking employees in different locations. The fastest-growing trucking, rail, and air freight businesses meet shippers' needs for specialized pickups and deliveries, unique containers, and worldwide integration of different modes of transportation. The most profitable financial businesses offer a wide range of services (linking banking, insurance, and investment) tailored to the specific needs of individuals and businesses. As news becomes a commodity available on twenty-four-hour television, the fastest-growing news and wire service businesses similarly assemble unique packages of information tailored to subscribers' needs (customized newsletters, video news release services, eventually even home-computer-customized "videotext" newspapers). Again, from high volume to high value.

These businesses are profitable both because customers are willing to pay a premium for goods or services that exactly meet their needs and because these high-value businesses cannot easily be duplicated by high-volume competitors around the world. While competition among high-volume producers continues to compress profits on everything that is uniform, routine, and standard—that is, on anything that can be made, reproduced, or extracted in volume almost anywhere on the globe—successful businesses in advanced nations are moving to a higher ground based on specially tailored products and services. The new barrier to entry is not volume or price; it is skill in finding the right fit between particular technologies and particular markets. Core corporations no longer focus on products as such; their business strategies increasingly center upon specialized knowledge.

3

Look closely at these high-value businesses and you see three different but related skills that drive them forward. Here, precisely, is where the value resides. First are the problem-solving skills required to put things together in unique ways (be they alloys, molecules, semiconductor chips, software codes, movie scripts, pension portfolios, or information). Problem-solvers must have intimate knowledge of what such things might be able to do when reassembled, and then must turn that knowledge into designs and instructions for creating such outcomes. Unlike the researchers and designers whose prototypes emerged fully formed from the laboratory or drafting table ready for high-volume production, these people are involved in a continuing search for new applications, combinations, and refinements capable of solving all sorts of emerging problems.

Next are the skills required to help customers understand their needs and how those needs can best be met by customized products. In contrast to selling and marketing standardized goods— which requires persuading many customers of the virtues of one particular product, taking lots of orders for it, and thus meeting sales quotas—selling and marketing customized products requires having an intimate knowledge of a customer's business, where competitive advantage may lie, and how it can be achieved. The key is to identify new problems and possibilities to which the customized product might be applicable. The art of persuasion is replaced by the identification of opportunity.

Third are the skills needed to link problem-solvers and problem-identifiers. People in such roles must understand enough about specific technologies and markets to see the potential for new products, raise whatever money is necessary to launch the project, and assemble the right problem-solvers and -identifiers to carry it out. Those occupying this position in the new economy were typically called "executives" or "entrepreneurs" in the old, but neither term fully connotes their role in high-value enterprise. Rather than controlling organizations, founding businesses, or inventing things, such people are continuously engaged in managing ideas. They play the role of strategic broker.

4

IN THE high-value enterprise, profits derive not from scale and volume but from continuous discovery of new linkages between solutions and needs. The distinction that used to be drawn between "goods" and "services" is meaningless, because so much of the value provided by the successful enterprise—in fact, the only value that cannot easily be replicated worldwide—entails services: the specialized research, engineering, and design services necessary to solve problems; the specialized sales, marketing, and consulting services necessary to identify problems; and the specialized strategic, financial, and management services for brokering the first two. Every high-value enterprise is in the business of providing such services.

Steelmaking is becoming a service business, for example. When a new alloy is molded to a specific weight and tolerance, services account for a significant part of the value of the resulting product. Steel service centers help customers choose the steels and alloys they need, and then inspect, slit, coat, store, and deliver the materials. Computer manufacturers are likewise in the service business, where a larger and larger portion of every consumer dollar goes toward customizing software and then integrating and installing systems around it. IBM is a service company, although it appears annually on the list of the nation's largest industrial firms. In 1990 more than one-third of its profits came from designing software, up from 18 percent in the mid-1980s, and more than 20 percent came from integrating computer systems. Much of the rest was related to what it calls "sales and support," which involves helping customers define their data-processing needs, choose appropriate hardware and software, get it up and running, and then working out the bugs. Less than 20,000 of IBM's 400,000 employees were classified as production workers engaged in traditional manufacturing. The immensely successful IBM personal computer itself comprises a collection of services—research, design, engineering, sales, service; only 10 percent of its purchase price is for the physical manufacture of the machine.[2]

America's arcane system of national accounting still has separate categories for manufacturing and services—classifying, for example, computer software as a service (although it is reproduced like a manufactured item) and a computer as a manufactured good (although an ever-larger portion of the cost of a computer lies in computer services). The pharmaceutical industry is classified under "manufacturing," although a drug's production costs actually represent only a tiny fraction of the total costs, which mostly involve services like research and development, clinical trials, patent applications and regulatory clearances, drug detailing, and distribution. We are told, repeatedly, that nearly 80 percent of the new jobs created in the 1980s were in services, and that some 70 percent of private-sector employees now work in service businesses. But as the lines begin to blur between services and goods, such numbers are increasingly meaningless in terms of what is actually occurring in the economy and where the real value lies.

---

[2] From interviews with IBM officials and employees.

8

The New Web
of Enterprise

There was ... a mysterious rite of initiation through
which, in one way or another, almost every member of the
team passed. The term that the old hands used for this
rite ... was "signing up." By signing up for the project
you agreed to do whatever was necessary for success. You
agreed to forsake, if necessary, family, hobbies, and
friends—if you had any of these left (and you might not if
you had signed up too many times before).... Labor was
no longer coerced. Labor volunteered.

TRACY KIDDER,
The Soul of a New Machine (1981)

THE HIGH-VALUE enterprise has no need to control vast resources,
discipline armies of production workers, or impose predictable
routines. Thus it need not be organized like the old pyramids that
characterized standardized production, with strong chief executives presiding over ever-widening layers of managers, atop an
even larger group of hourly workers, all following standard operating procedures.

In fact, the high-value enterprise *cannot* be organized this way.
The three groups that give the new enterprise most of its value
—problem-solvers, problem-identifiers, and strategic brokers—
need to be in direct contact with one another to continuously
discover new opportunities. Messages must flow quickly and
clearly if the right solutions are to be applied to the right problems
in a timely way. This is no place for bureaucracy.

Anyone who has ever played the children's game Telephone—in which one person whispers a phrase to the next person in line, who then whispers the phrase to the next, and so on, until the last person announces aloud a phrase that invariably bears no resemblance to the original—knows what can happen when even the simplest messages are passed through intermediaries: "Have a nice day" turns into "Get out of my way." If problem-identifiers had to convey everything they were learning about the needs of their customers upward to top management through layers and layers of middle managers, while problem-solvers had to convey everything *they* were learning about new technologies upward through as many layers, and then both groups had to await top management's decisions about what to do—decisions which then had to travel back down through the same bureaucratic channels—the results would be, to say the least, late and irrelevant, and probably distorted.

Thus one of the strategic broker's tasks is to create settings in which problem-solvers and problem-identifiers can work together without undue interference. The strategic broker is a facilitator and a coach—finding the people in both camps who can learn most from one another, giving them whatever resources they need, letting them go at it long enough to discover new complements between technologies and customer needs, but also providing them with enough guidance so that they don't lose sight of mundane goals like earning a profit.

Creative teams solve and identify problems in much the same way whether they are developing new software, dreaming up a new marketing strategy, seeking a scientific discovery, or contriving a financial ploy. Most coordination is horizontal rather than vertical. Because problems and solutions cannot be defined in advance, formal meetings and agendas won't reveal them. They emerge instead out of frequent and informal communications among team members. Mutual learning occurs within the team, as insights, experiences, puzzles, and solutions are shared—often randomly. One solution is found applicable to a completely different problem; someone else's failure turns into a winning strategy for accomplishing something entirely unrelated. It is as if team members were doing several jigsaw puzzles simultaneously with pieces from the same pile—pieces which could be arranged to form many different pictures. (Such intellectual synergies can be found, on rare occasions, even in university departments.)

Instead of a pyramid, then, the high-value enterprise looks more like a spider's web. Strategic brokers are at the center, but there are all sorts of connections that do not involve them directly, and new connections are being spun all the time. At each point of connection are a relatively small number of people—depending on the task, from a dozen to several hundred. If a group was any larger it could not engage in rapid and informal learning.[1] Here individual skills are combined so that the group's ability to innovate is something more than the simple sum of its parts. Over time, as group members work through various problems and approaches together, they learn about one another's abilities. They learn how they can help one another perform better, who can contribute what to a particular project, how they can best gain more experience together. Each participant is on the lookout for ideas that will propel the group forward. Such cumulative experience and understanding cannot be translated into standard operating procedures easily transferable to other workers and other organizations. Each point on the "enterprise web" represents a unique combination of skills.

2

SPEED and agility are so important to the high-value enterprise that it cannot be weighed down with large overhead costs like office buildings, plant, equipment, and payroll. It must be able to switch direction quickly, pursue options when they arise, discover new linkages between problems and solutions wherever they may lie.

In the old high-volume enterprise, fixed costs such as factories, equipment, warehouses, and large payrolls were necessary in or-

---

[1] Information technologies have dramatically reduced the costs of coordinating even relatively large numbers of people without relying on standard operating procedures and other bureaucratic structures. See, for example, T. Malone, J. Yates, and R. Benjamin, "Electronic Markets and Electronic Hierarchies," *Communications of the ACM*, Vol. 30, No. 6 (June 1987).

der to achieve control and predictability. In the high-value enterprise, they are an unnecessary burden. Here, all that really counts is rapid problem-identifying and problem-solving—the marriage of technical insight with marketing know-how, blessed by strategic and financial acumen. Everything else—all of the more standardized pieces—can be obtained as needed. Office space, factories, and warehouses can be rented; standard equipment can be leased; standard components can be bought wholesale from cheap producers (many of them overseas); secretaries, routine data processors, bookkeepers, and routine production workers can be hired temporarily.

In fact, relatively few people actually work for the high-value enterprise in the traditional sense of having steady jobs with fixed salaries. The inhabitants of corporate headquarters, who spend much of their time searching for the right combinations of solutions, problems, strategies, and money, are apt to share in the risks and returns of their hunt. When a promising combination is found, participants in the resulting project (some at the center of the web, some at connecting points on the periphery) also may share in any profits rather than take fixed salaries.

With risks and returns broadly shared, and overhead kept to a minimum, the enterprise web can experiment. Experimentation was dangerous in the old high-volume enterprise because failures (like Ford's notorious Edsel) meant that the entire organization had to change direction—retool, retrain, redirect sales and marketing—at a huge cost. But experimentation is the lifeblood of the high-value enterprise, because customization requires continuous trial and error.

Sharing risks and returns has an added advantage. It is a powerful creative stimulus. If they are to spot new opportunities in technologies and markets, problem-solvers, -identifiers, and brokers must be highly motivated. Few incentives are more powerful than membership in a small group engaged in a common task, sharing the risks of defeat and the potential rewards of victory. Rewards are not only pecuniary. The group often shares a vision as well; they want to make their mark on the world.

At the web's outer edges, suppliers of standard inputs (factories, equipment, office space, routine components, bookkeeping, janitorial services, data processing, and so forth) contract to provide or do specific things for a certain time and for a specified price. Such arrangements are often more efficient than directly controlling employees.[2] Suppliers who profit in direct proportion to how hard and carefully they do their jobs have every incentive to find increasingly efficient ways of accomplishing their tasks. Consider the owner of a McDonald's franchise who works fifteen-hour days and keeps the outlet sparkling clean; or the machine operator who, owning the equipment and contracting to do jobs with it (and keep the profits), maintains the machine in perfect condition.[3]

3

ENTERPRISE webs come in several shapes, and the shapes continue to evolve. Among the most common are:

Independent profit centers. This web eliminates middle-level managers and pushes authority for product development and sales down to groups of engineers and marketers (problem-solvers and -identifiers) whose compensation is linked to the unit's profits. Strategic brokers in headquarters provide financial and logistical

---

[2] A number of studies have revealed a marked increase in outsourcing and the use of part-time workers during the 1980s. Part of the motive in the United States surely is to avoid paying employee benefits mandated by union contracts or legislation. But interestingly, the same pattern is observable in many other advanced economies where union contracts or legislated benefits are not affected. See I. W. Sengenberger and G. Loveman, *Smaller Units of Employment: A Synthesis of Research on Industrial Organization in Industrial Countries* (Geneva: International Institute for Labor Studies, 1988). Good surveys of the trend toward outsourcing and temporary work can be found in E. Appelbaum, "Restructuring Work: Temporary, Part-time, and At-home Employment," in H. Hartmann (ed.), *Computer Chips and Paper Clips: Technology and Women's Employment* (Washington, D.C.: National Academy Press, 1987); S. Christopherson, "Flexibility in the U.S. Service Economy and the Emerging Spatial Division of Labour," *Transactions of the British Institute of Geographics*, Vol. 14 (1989).

[3] This example is not hypothetical. A Finnish paper company, burdened by tree-harvesting machinery always in need of repair, sold the machines to its operators, and gave them contracts to do their old jobs. Productivity soared, as the operators now kept the machines in better condition and used them with far greater care than before. See *The Economist*, December 24, 1988, p. 16.

help, but give the unit discretion over how to spend money up to a certain amount. By 1990, Johnson & Johnson comprised 166 autonomous companies; Hewlett-Packard, some 50 separate business units. General Electric, IBM, AT&T, and Eastman Kodak, among others, were also adopting this approach. For much the same reason, large publishing houses were busily creating "imprints"—small, semiautonomous publishing houses within the structure of the parent firm, each comprising a dozen or so people with considerable responsibility for acquiring and publishing books on their own.

Spin-off partnerships. In this web, strategic brokers in headquarters act as venture capitalists and midwives, nurturing good ideas that bubble up from groups of problem-solvers and -identifiers and then (if the ideas catch on in the market) spinning the groups off as independent businesses in which the strategic brokers at headquarters retain a partial stake. Xerox and 3M have pioneered this form in the United States, but it is nothing new to the Japanese. Hitachi, for example, is actually more than 60 companies, 27 of which are publicly traded. Some venture-capital firms and leveraged-buyout partnerships are coming to resemble the same sort of web, in which risks and returns are shared between headquarters and the managers of the separate businesses.

Spin-in partnerships. In this web, good ideas bubble up outside the firm from independent groups of problem-solvers and -identifiers. Strategic brokers in headquarters purchase the best of them, or form partnerships with the independents, and then produce, distribute, and market the ideas under the firm's own well-known trademark. This sort of arrangement is common to computer software houses. In 1990, for example, over 400 tiny software-developing firms were purchased by big software companies such as Microsoft, Lotus, and Ashton-Tate. The software developers thus received a nice profit on their efforts, while the larger firms maintained a steady supply of new ideas.

Licensing. In this web, headquarters contracts with independent businesses to use its brand name, sell its special formulas, or otherwise market (that is, find applicable problems for) its technologies. Strategic brokers at the center of the web ensure that no licensee harms the reputation of the brand by offering inconsistent or poor quality, and also provide licensees with special bulk services like computerized inventory management or advertising.

Most of the ownership and control, however, is left in the hands of licensees. One example is franchises, which are among the fastest-growing businesses in every advanced economy, now selling everything from tax preparation and accounting services to hotel accommodations, cookies, groceries, printing and copying, health care, and bodybuilding. In 1988, American franchisees comprised 509,000 outlets and accounted for $640 billion in sales, amounting to more than 10 percent of the entire national product.[4]

Pure brokering. In the most decentralized kind of web, strategic brokers contract with independent businesses for problem solving and identifying as well as for production. This web is ideal for enterprises that need to shift direction quickly. By 1990, for example, Compaq Computers of Houston (which did not exist in 1982 but eight years later had revenues of $3 billion) was buying many of its most valuable components on the outside (microprocessors from Intel, operating systems from software houses like Microsoft, liquid-crystal screens from Citizen), and then selling the resulting machines through independent dealers to whom Compaq granted exclusive sales territories. The Apple II computer cost less than $500 to build, of which $350 was for components purchased on the outside.[5] Meanwhile, the Lewis Galoob Toy Company sold more than $50 million worth of tiny gadgets conceived by independent inventors and novelty companies, designed by independent engineers, manufactured and packaged by suppliers in Hong Kong (who contracted out the most labor-intensive work to China and Thailand), and then distributed in America by independent toy companies. Movie studios that once relied on their own facilities, crews, and exclusive stables of actors, directors, and screenwriters were contracting on a project-by-project basis with independent producers, directors, actors, writers, crews, and cinematographers, using rented space and equipment, and relying on independent distributors to get the films

---

[4] Figures from *Business Week*, November 13, 1989, p. 83.
[5] Apple initially got its microprocessors from Synertek, other chips from Texas Instruments and Motorola, video monitors from Hitachi, power supplies from Astec, and printers from Qume. See James Brian Quinn et al., "Beyond Products: Service-Based Strategy," *Harvard Business Review*, March–April 1990, pp. 58–60.

into appropriate theaters. Book publishers were contracting not only for authors but also for printing, graphics, artwork, marketing, and all other facets of production. Even automakers were outsourcing more and more of what they produced. (By 1990, Chrysler Corporation directly produced only about 30 percent of the value of its cars; Ford, about 50 percent. General Motors bought half its engineering and design services from 800 different companies.)

4

AMERICANS love to debate old categories. Does manufacturing have a future or are we becoming a service economy? Are big businesses destined to expire like prehistoric beasts, to be superseded by small businesses, or are big businesses critical to our economic future? Such questions provide endless opportunities for debate, not unlike the arguments of thirteenth-century Scholastics over how many angels could comfortably fit on a pinhead. Such debates are socially useful in that they create excuses for business seminars, conferences, and magazine articles and thus ensure gainful employment for many. But such debates are less than edifying. Debaters usually can find evidence to support whatever side they choose, depending on how they define their terms. Whether manufacturing is being replaced by a service economy depends on how "manufacturing" and "service" are defined; whether small businesses are replacing large depends equally on what these adjectives are taken to mean. In fact, all manufacturing businesses are coming to entail services, and all large businesses are spinning into webs of smaller businesses.

The federal government's Standard Industrial Classification system is as unhelpful and anachronistic here as before. It defines "establishment" as any business, including one that may be part of a larger company.[6] Thus, not surprisingly, official statistics show that the number of small "establishments" nearly doubled between 1975 and 1990, creating millions of new jobs—just as the high-volume, hierarchical corporation was transforming into a high-

---

[6] U.S. Office of Management and Budget, SIC Manual (1987), p. 12.

value, decentralized enterprise web. But even discounting this statistical sleight of hand, the shift from high-volume hierarchies to high-value webs would create the appearance of a dwindling core simply because core corporations no longer employ many people directly and their webs of indirect employment defy easy measurement.

As stated earlier, by most official measures, America's 500 largest industrial companies failed to create a single net new job between 1975 and 1990, their share of the civilian labor force dropping from 17 percent to less than 10 percent. Meanwhile, after decades of decline, the number of people describing themselves as "self-employed" began to rise.[7] And there has been an explosion in the number of new businesses (in 1950, 93,000 corporations were created in the United States; by the late 1980s, America was adding about 1.3 million new enterprises to the economy each year).[8] Most of the new jobs in the economy appear to come from small businesses,[9] as does most of the growth in research spending.[10] A similar transformation has been occurring in other nations.[11]

But to draw the natural conclusion from these data—that large businesses are being *replaced* by millions of tiny businesses—is to fall into the same vestigial trap as in the debate over "manufacturing" versus "services": both ignore the weblike relationships that are shaping the new economy. Here, the core corporation is no longer a "big" business, but neither is it merely a collection of

---

[7] In 1975, only 6.9 percent of the U.S. nonfarm work force was "self-employed"; by 1986, it was 7.4 percent. Data from *The State of Small Business: Report of the President* (Washington, D.C.: U.S. Government Printing Office, various issues).

[8] David L. Birch, "The Hidden Economy," *The Wall Street Journal*, June 10, 1988, p. 23R.

[9] Data from Douglas P. Handler, *Business Demographics* (New York: Dun & Bradstreet, Economic Analysis Department, 1988).

[10] According to the National Science Foundation, small firms with fewer than 500 employees doubled their share of America's corporate research and development spending during the 1980s, from 6 percent to 12 percent. National Science Foundation, Research Report (Washington, D.C.: National Science Foundation, November 1990), pp. 12–14.

[11] See, for example, "München Management," *The Economist*, October 14, 1989, p. 25.

smaller ones. Rather, it is an enterprise web. Its center provides strategic insight and binds the threads together. Yet points on the web often have sufficient autonomy to create profitable connections to other webs. There is no "inside" or "outside" the corporation, but only different distances from its strategic center.

The resulting interconnections can be quite complex, stretching over many profit centers, business units, spin-offs, licensees, franchisees, suppliers, and dealers, and then on to other strategic centers, which in turn are linked to still other groups. Throughout the 1980s, for example, IBM (which, as you recall, had jealously guarded its independence even to the point of departing India rather than sharing profits with Indian partners) joined with dozens of companies—Intel, Merrill Lynch, Aetna Life and Casualty, MCI, Comsat, and more than eighty foreign-owned firms—to share problem-solving, problem-identifying, and strategic brokering. Similarly, AT&T (which for seventy years had prided itself on having total control over its products and operating systems) found itself in a newly deregulated, unpredictable world of telecommunications, which required hundreds of alliances and joint ventures, and thousands of subcontracts.[12] Core corporations in other mature economies are undergoing a similar transformation. Indeed, as we shall see, their increasingly decentralized enterprise webs are becoming undifferentiated extensions of our own.[13]

The trend should not be overstated. Even by the 1990s there remain large corporations of bureaucratic form and function, which directly employ many thousands of workers and which own substantial physical assets. But these corporations are coming to be the exceptions. That they survive and prosper is despite, rather

---

[12] My interviews (see "A Note on Additional Sources") confirm the findings of other surveys. See, for example, R. Johnston and Paul Lawrence, "Beyond Vertical Integration: The Rise of the Value-Added Partnership," *Harvard Business Review*, July–August 1988; R. Miles, "Adapting to Technology and Competition: A New Industrial Relations System for the 21st Century," *California Management Review*, Winter 1988; and J. Badaracco, Jr., "Changing Forms of the Corporation," in J. Meyer and J. Gustafson (eds.), *The U.S. Business Corporation* (Cambridge, Mass.: Ballinger, 1988). See also Jordan D. Lewis, *Partnerships for Profit: Structuring and Managing Strategic Alliances* (New York: Free Press, 1990).

[13] For a description of the pattern in Europe, see D. J. Storey and S. Johnson, *Job Generation and Labour Market Changes* (London: Macmillan, 1987).

than because of, their organization. The most profitable firms are transforming into enterprise webs. They may look like the old form of organization from the outside, but inside all is different. Their famous brands adhere to products and services that are cobbled together from many different sources outside the formal boundaries of the firm. Their dignified headquarters, expansive factories, warehouses, laboratories, and fleets of trucks and corporate jets are leased. Their production workers, janitors, and bookkeepers are under temporary contract; their key researchers, design engineers, and marketers are sharing in the profits. And their distinguished executives, rather than possessing great power and authority over this domain, have little direct control over much of anything. Instead of imposing their will over a corporate empire, they guide ideas through the new webs of enterprise.

9

The Diffusion of
Ownership and Control

> In distinguishing between the interests of ownership and
> the powers of control, it is necessary to keep in mind the
> fact that, as there are many individuals having interests in
> the enterprise who are not customarily thought of as own-
> ers, so there may be many individuals having a measure of
> power over it who should not be thought of as in control.
>
> ADOLF A. BERLE AND GARDINER C. MEANS,
> *The Modern Corporation and Private Property* (1932)

THE IMAGE of the core corporation as owner and controller of
vast resources is thus, increasingly, a fictionalized representation,
reminding us of what the core corporation used to be but dis-
guising what it has become. The key assets of high-value enterprise
are not tangible things, but the skills involved in linking solutions
to particular needs, and the reputations that come from having
done so successfully in the past. No single group or participant
"controls" this enterprise as the high-volume enterprise was controlled. Nor does anyone "own" it in the traditional sense. Executives coordinate and broker; investors supply some of the money
needed to finance its activities, for which they will be rewarded,
like many other participants, with a portion of the profits. The
most skilled and talented problem-solvers and -identifiers, on
which so much depends, also are likely to receive a share of the
profits. They will have considerable discretion over what they do
and how they do it. Routine functions are, increasingly, contracted
out. Thus, power is diffused.

The formal organization chart has little relevance to the true sources of power in the high-value enterprise. Power depends not on formal authority or rank (as it did in the high-volume enterprise), but on the capacity to add value to enterprise webs. Problem-solvers, -identifiers, or brokers exercise leadership by creating ways in which others can add value as well. Thus do leaders emerge.

The process can be observed within Silicon Valley's high-tech companies, in the corporate suites of midtown Manhattan, in Hollywood movie studios, Madison Avenue advertising boutiques, law firms, consulting groups, investment banks, publishing houses, engineering companies, architectural firms, broadcasters, public relations companies, lobbying firms, and so on. As reputations for insightful problem-solving, -identifying, or brokering grow, informal leaders gain more credibility, and more followers. Eventually they and their followers receive a larger share of total profits, or they leave to start a separate business of their own. In this way, enterprise webs are reconfigured as new leaders emerge. Points at the periphery where a few threads once intersected evolve into new webs, centered on groups of people who create the most value and attract the most talented followers. Leadership is where the most value is created, nurtured, and developed.

Key strategic-brokering decisions about whom to contract with, and for what, increasingly occur at subterranean levels. Strategic brokers with day-to-day responsibility for spinning the enterprise webs often have unprepossessing titles like director of purchasing or procurement manager. They make thousands of small contracting decisions which, collectively, determine much of what the enterprise sells. Polaroid Corporation's director of purchasing, for example, spends about half of the corporation's annual revenues on everything from high-tech parts to janitorial services, purchased from more than 8,000 suppliers, through 95,000 contracts. Although not listed among Polaroid's twenty top officials in the firm's annual report, he is among the firm's most important strategists. On his decisions depends much of what the firm offers its customers, and at what price and quality. Within the informal organization, much of the power rests with him.

2

THE BUSINESS press, which conditions so much of how we think about the modern corporation, perpetuates the vestigial notion of centralized ownership and control. In the pages of *Fortune, Forbes, Business Week,* and *The Wall Street Journal,* and on the interminable business programs that belie the aesthetic promise of cable television, core corporations are discussed as if they were still large, hierarchical entities directed from the top down and acting en masse. This is misleading, to say the least.

A fanciful, but not farfetched, illustration: The Great American Corporation announces, and the business press dutifully reports, that the firm is introducing a new line of custom-tailored beanbags—in assorted weights, sizes, shapes, and consistencies (intended for bodybuilders of assorted weights, sizes, shapes, and consistencies). The news is of course relevant to Great American's top strategic brokers and its shareholders, the value of whose stocks will rise or fall depending on how many aspiring bodybuilders flock to retail stores, aerobics centers, and bodybuilding clinics to buy the new beanbag. But the announcement creates the false impression that there is an immense single entity called the Great American Corporation which is solely, or even largely, responsible for the beanbag, and that the primary effects of the beanbag's success or failure in the market will fall upon Great American's shareholders.

In fact, the custom-tailored beanbag is more likely to be the combined output of a complex enterprise web. Typically, the beanbag was conceived by one group—call it Company A, which is formally a division of Great American but functions quite independently. The beanbag was design-engineered by another group that specializes in turning ideas into products that can be produced cheaply and efficiently—call it Company B, which is legally distinct from the Great American Corporation but closely tied to it, since most of Company B's designs are purchased by Great American. The beanbag was fabricated and assembled by Company C, whose employees operate state-of-the-art equipment in Taiwan and Hong Kong. It was packaged by Company D, distributed by Company E, and marketed by Company F. Companies G and H have lent money to the project and already have sold the debt instruments to several other companies. Companies I and J are selling the beanbags through their franchised health salons and physical-fitness centers. Company K is handling all legal matters, while Company L is doing the advertising. Company M owns the factory where the beanbag is assembled, and Company N owns the machines. Companies O and P have exclusive contracts to market the beanbags in their regions of the country, while Company Q has purchased the rights to make and sell the beanbag in Europe and will be contracting with Companies R, S, T, U, and V to market and distribute it there. Company W, meanwhile, is keeping the accounts and managing the cash flow, while Companies X, Y, and Z are taking care of all travel, communication, and logistics. People in some of these groups receive salaries directly from the Great American Corporation; others will share in any profits from the beanbag (and receive nothing should the product fail); still others operate under long-term contracts with the company and are paid a flat fee for their services.

What, then, *is* the Great American Corporation? It is a weblike combination of all of these groups, plus some outside investors—Great American's shareholders—who also will get a portion of any profits, and the strategic brokers in headquarters who negotiated all these contracts and put the deal together (a not inconsiderable feat, for which they will receive a handsome reward should the custom-tailored beanbag become next year's health fad).

To attribute the beanbag to the "Great American Corporation" disguises where the real value lies in this web. In fact, the profits flowing to Great American's shareholders are likely to be small relative to the returns to other participants who have added considerably more value than money and assumed much of the risk. Suppose that Company A consists of two dozen people who specialize in developing ideas for new bodybuilding products. Strategic brokers in Great American recently lured them away from a competitor, for whom they had devised immensely popular bodybuilding concepts. The lure consisted of high salaries plus a share in any profits resulting from their ideas. Thus one important (although generally untold) story buried within the story about "Great American's" new custom-tailored beanbag is the talented group in Company A that came up with the idea for it, and how much they stand to gain if the product succeeds. The prevailing description similarly obscures where the real power resides in this web. The idea merchants of Company A exert at least as much authority, and have as much control over the final product, as do the executives back at headquarters.

The verbs and the possessives used to describe what is occurring—as in "The Great American Corporation is introducing a new product," or "Great American's custom-tailored beanbag"—suggest the same structure of ownership and control as in the high-volume enterprise. But when applied to the high-value enterprise, with its widely shared ownership and control, this grammar perpetrates a subtle but pervasive deception.

3

A RELATED illusion arises in reports about core corporations buying companies or selling subsidiaries, as in "The Great American Corporation is selling its Company A to the Big General Corporation." The image that comes to mind is one of factories, equipment, and people being passed from one owner and controller to another, as in the transfer of any property. In the old high-volume enterprise, where control was lodged at the top and almost everyone else implemented top management's plans, such transfers of assets did in fact resemble sales of property. But in the high-value enterprise, the transfer signifies little more than a change in how problem-solving and -identifying are combined with strategic brokering and finance.

In this case, Big General's strategic brokers and investors do not actually gain "ownership" or "control" over much of anything. Recall that the key assets of Company A are skilled and talented people, rather than property that can be bought or sold. While the past successes of this group may have resulted in tradeable assets like patents, copyrights, and trademarks, to which Big General can now claim legal title, their *future* insights cannot be owned or traded. Whatever the potential value of *these* conceptual assets, their real owners will continue to be the people in whose heads they reside. Such assets cannot be extracted from their heads without their acquiescence, nor can their commitments be commanded. Even if the Thirteenth Amendment to the Constitution did not bar involuntary servitude, there is no way to enslave people into creativity. Their future insights and commitments can be purchased, but if they are unhappy with the deal, they are unlikely to be very insightful and creative. Ultimately they will depart for friendlier and more lucrative environs.

Thus, regardless of which corporation they are working for, they will command a return on their contribution (sometimes in the form of a share in any eventual profits) reflecting the real value they are capable of adding to the enterprise. Rather than describe the transaction as the Great American Corporation "selling *its*" Company A to the Big General Corporation, one might more accurately say that the talented problem-solvers and -identifiers of Company A exchanged Great American's strategic brokers for Big General's. If the latter do a better job than the former, Company A's problem-solvers and -identifiers will earn more money, as will Big General's investors. But if they do worse, the talented people comprising Company A may seek a different partner (or leave Company A altogether).

High-value enterprises can no more be "acquired" than can the skilled and talented individuals who comprise them. On more than one occasion this fact has surprised investors and strategic brokers who thought they had made such a purchase only to have it disappear like cotton candy as soon as it touched their lips. (Had they known it was an enterprise web, and not a hard commodity, maybe they would not have tried to swallow it.) In 1986, General Electric assumed that it had "acquired" Kidder, Peabody, the financial-services house. But when GE tried to exert control over its new acquisition—imposing stricter reporting requirements and tighter cost accounting—many of Kidder, Peabody's most skilled personnel departed for more congenial surroundings. GE was left with little more than Kidder, Peabody's good, but fading, reputation.[1]

4

THE KEY industrial struggle in the high-volume economy of the late nineteenth century and the first half of the twentieth—a strug-

---

[1]Steve Swartz, "GE Finds Running Kidder, Peabody & Co. Isn't All That Easy," *The Wall Street Journal*, January 27, 1989, p. 1.

gle that preoccupied Karl Marx, Andrew Carnegie, and John L. Lewis, among many others—was between those who owned the machines and those who ran them. Each side wanted a larger share of the revenues. An accommodation of sorts was achieved in the 1950s, by which management acceded to labor's demand for ever-higher wages in return for labor's cooperation in producing an ever-higher volume of goods—thus lowering the unit costs of such goods while creating a larger number of middle-class Americans with the discretionary income to buy them. Government played an important supporting role in this accommodation. Such was the national bargain, until the global economy began to intercede.

In the high-value enterprise, however, the claims of both routine labor and financial capital increasingly are subordinated to the claims of those who solve, identify, and broker new problems. Consequently, a steadily diminishing share of every dollar (or pound, mark, or yen) spent in an advanced economy has gone to production workers. Profits, similarly, have been squeezed. Those who conceptualize problems, however, have commanded ever-higher salaries and fees. In 1920, more than 85 percent of the cost of an automobile went to pay routine laborers and investors. By 1990, these two groups received less than 60 percent, with the remainder going to designers, engineers, stylists, planners, strategists, financial specialists, executive officers, lawyers, advertisers, marketers, and the like. Today, not more than 3 percent of the price of a semiconductor chip goes to the owners of raw materials and energy, 5 percent to those who own the equipment and facilities, and 6 percent to routine labor. More than 85 percent is for specialized design and engineering services and for patents and copyrights on past discoveries made in the course of providing such services.

The pattern can be observed in the economy as a whole. Through the postwar era, the wages of production workers in the United States steadily declined as a percentage of gross national product, from 11.6 percent in 1949 to 4.6 percent in 1990.[2] Over

---

[2] Figures through 1983 from Census data as calculated by W. Johnson, A. Packer, et al., *Workforce 2000: Work and Workers for the 21st Century* (Indianapolis: Hudson Institute, 1987), p. 27, Fig. 1-11, projected through 1990.

Over the same period, the share of total manufacturing value (as "man-the same interval, corporate profits also declined as a percentage of gross national product. In the mid-1960s, corporate profits (adjusted for inventory gains and losses and for depreciation) reached 11.7 percent of GNP, and then fell to 6.9 percent in the 1969–70 recession. Subsequent percentages were lower at both expansionary heights and recessionary lows. At the end of the 1980s, profits claimed only 5.3 percent of GNP.[3] As the portions of GNP going to routine labor and to investors steadily dwindled, the portion going to problem-solvers and -identifiers and strategic brokers steadily grew.

5

THE SUBORDINATION of routine labor has had consequences which will be explored in later chapters. The increasing subordination of capital, meanwhile, has caused confusion among investors, to say the least. "Owning" a company no longer means what it once did. Members of the accounting profession, not otherwise known for their public displays of emotion, have fretted openly about how to inform potential investors of the true worth of enterprises whose value rests in the brains of employees. They have used the term "goodwill" to signify the ambiguous zone on corporate balance sheets between the company's tangible assets and the value of its talented people. But as intellectual capital continues to overtake physical capital as the key asset of the corporation, shareholders find themselves on shakier and shakier ground. Much "goodwill" can disappear with the departure of valued employees.

Of course, certain intellectual assets will remain even after talented employees depart—among them, patents and copyrights, which are the legal legacies of past insights. But in the high-value economy, such intellectual property often loses its value quite quickly. After all, patents and copyrights guard only discoveries

---

ufacturing" is defined in government statistics) represented by the wages of production workers dropped from 40 percent to 24 percent. Ibid., p. 26, Fig. 1-10.
[3] Figures from U.S. Department of Commerce, *Survey of Current Business* (Washington, D.C.: U.S. Government Printing Office, various issues).

made at a particular point in time. They do not protect the initial finding that a specific problem exists which consumers are eager to remedy (such as how to record television programs for viewing at a later and more convenient time); nor do they protect many subsequent insights about how to improve upon a given solution (such as a lightweight camcorder that doubles as a videocassette recorder). Yet these sorts of discoveries—that a market exists and that there are various ways to serve it—are often more valuable even than the original patented or copyrighted invention. Problem-solvers, -identifiers, and brokers who may have played no part in the original product typically rush to take advantage of new markets that have been uncovered and stimulated by the discovery. Thus it is often the case that greater rewards flow to quick and clever followers than to brilliant and original inventors. Old solutions to old problems, although legally protected, are rapidly outmoded and replaced.

A familiar brand name is another form of intangible goodwill appearing on the corporate balance sheet. General Electric, RCA, Westinghouse, Kodak, Sears, BankAmerica, General Motors, Procter & Gamble, Ford, Walt Disney, IBM, American Express —the names give comfort, suggesting solid and reliable institutions. That such institutions are becoming decentralized webs of contractors, subcontractors, licensees, franchisees, partnerships, and other temporary alliances—spun by small groups of strategic brokers—has not dimmed consumer loyalty, because consumers are largely unaware of the transformation. Here is another economic consequence of vestigial thought—this time among consumers. A product with a GE trademark is assumed to be "made" by General Electric in the traditional sense of GE employees under the control of GE managers in GE factories. The reassurance itself is a tradeable commodity.

In fact, the trademarks and brand names of many core corporations are now among their most valuable assets. The names can be marketed on their own. They illuminate the skylines of cities. They appear, tastefully, at the beginnings and ends of public television programs, when a dignified voice notifies the viewer of the corporation's magnanimous beneficence. They are found in full-page magazine advertisements, superimposed on serene landscapes or classic paintings, often without a product in sight. It is the perfect tautology: The emblem represents the corporation, and the corporation represents the emblem. In the public's mind, IBM is an abstraction having to do with computers, Charlie Chaplin, and a conservative Swiss-modernist logo in blue and white, suggesting power and authority.[4]

When a corporate name becomes too closely associated with a failing industry or product, an identity alteration can help recapture the dwindling value. The old, plodding U.S. Steel rechristens itself as the sleek, contemporary USX. Or perhaps an image alteration is in order, by which advertisers and marketers recast not products but impressions. Thus does Philip Morris pay $600,000 to the National Archives for the privilege of advertising the Bill of Rights alongside the Philip Morris brand, in hopes that the American public will somehow come to associate its cigarettes with the Founding Fathers.

Ironically, an investment in corporate imagery may pay off even if the core corporation has no direct relation to the product being marketed: The comforting trademark has independent worth. Thus the GE emblem adds value to a microwave oven designed, fabricated, and assembled by Samsung in South Korean factories that GE officials have rarely entered; the uplifting Walt Disney signature and cheery Mickey Mouse, to cigarette lighters and T-shirts shipped from Thailand; the reassuring American Express logo, to maps, vacation guides, tours, and lodgings provided by people whose only relationship to American Express is a contract entitling them to use the name; the Kodak name, to photocopiers and videotapes made by Canon and Matsushita, respectively.[5]

But even the most inspiring trademark cannot retain its value forever. Memories fade. New products connected to new brands gain followings. The old trademark may appear on products of low quality which damage its reputation. Or consumers eventually

---

[4]See Ken Carls, "Corporate Coats of Arms," *Harvard Business Review*, May–June 1989.

[5]Since some foreign labels have recently become more prestigious and reassuring than their American counterparts, the tables have turned: A Minolta trademark now appears on instant cameras made by Polaroid. A Polaroid executive explained that "Minolta's good name . . . would lend a positive brand identification to instant photography." *The Wall Street Journal*, July 6, 1990, p. D2.

discover that they no longer need reassurance, and can purchase the same product at lower cost without subsidizing the core corporation and its advertising agencies. Matsushita's videotape is as good as Kodak's. Thus, like patents and trademarks, comforting brand names lose their value as they age. Even this form of goodwill is a depreciating asset.

6

IN THE high-value enterprise, only one asset grows more valuable as it is used: the problem-solving, -identifying, and brokering skills of key people. Unlike machinery that gradually wears out, raw materials that become depleted, patents and copyrights that grow obsolete, and trademarks that lose their ability to comfort, the skills and insights that come from discovering new linkages between technologies and needs actually increase with practice.

The more complex the task, the better it serves as preparation for a more complicated task the next time. One puzzle leads to another. Strategic brokers who successfully locate just the right combination of technical and marketing skills to develop software for mechanical engineers gain insight into what's needed to develop more complex user interfaces for aerospace engineers. Producing musical recordings that send audiences into paroxysms of ecstasy lays the groundwork for producing even more euphoric recordings later on. Developing and marketing specialty chemicals is prerequisite for high-performance ceramics and single-crystal silicon. And so forth.

The old high-volume enterprise benefited from experienced employees, of course. Senior laborers often knew the machines and materials so well that they could spot trouble before it occurred. But there, growth depended fundamentally upon everlarger economies of scale. Those who invested in the factories and machines that made such large scale possible could thus command an ever-larger share of any resulting profits. In the high-value enterprise, however, growth depends on the cumulative experience of key employees. Accordingly, more and more of the enterprise's value—along with its authority and rewards—shifts to those whose problem-solving, -identifying, and brokering skills gain in sophistication.

Conventional economic theory is premised on the assumption of diminishing returns. As a resource gets used up, its price increases; the price rise in turn encourages buyers to conserve the resource and hunt for cheaper substitutes, which ultimately bring the price down again. The high oil prices of the 1970s, for example, motivated consumers to conserve energy and encouraged oil companies to find more oil—both initiatives eventually causing oil prices to drop in the 1980s. One of the great advantages of a price system, as all economists will attest, is that it tends to balance itself automatically.

But human capital operates according to a different principle. Because people learn through practice, the value of what they do usually increases as they gain experience. This system is not self-correcting, in the sense that those who first gain the experience eventually lose whatever premium price they command in the market when others catch up with them. To the contrary, people fortunate enough to have had an excellent education followed by on-the-job experience doing complex things can become steadily more valuable over time, making it difficult for others ever to catch up.[6] In fact, their increasing advantage may extend beyond a single generation, as their extra earnings are invested in their children's education and training. Such widening divergences may be endemic to a global economy premised on high-value skills rather than on routine labor or capital. I shall return to this issue in later chapters.

---

[6]On the contrast between the conventional economic view and this more dynamic approach, see W. Brian Arthur, "Positive Feedbacks in the Economy," *Scientific American*, February 1990, p. 92.

10
The Global Web

THE NEW organizational webs of high-value enterprise, which are replacing the old core pyramids of high-volume enterprise, are reaching across the globe. Thus there is coming to be no such organization as an "American" (or British or French or Japanese or West German) corporation, nor any finished good called an "American" (or British, French, Japanese, or West German) product.

The old American multinational corporation was controlled from its American headquarters. Its foreign subsidiaries were indeed subsidiary—as foreign workers and customers were often reminded. Whether they extracted raw materials and sent them back to the United States for processing, or distributed and sold American-made products in their own markets and sent the revenues back to America—even if they manufactured the products according to specifications set by headquarters in America before marketing and distributing them and then sending back the revenues—it was clear that the subsidiaries served the interests of their American parent. Ownership and control were indisputably American. There was no doubt about which nationality was at the top of the pyramid. And regardless of how much of the final product was made abroad, the most complicated work—design and fabrication of the most intricate parts, and strategic planning, financing, and marketing—was done in the United States, by Americans. Such financial and technological dominance prompted many Europeans, and then East Asians, to respond by creating their own national champions.

But this kind of top-down control and centralized ownership is impossible in the weblike organizations of the high-value enterprise. Here, power and wealth flow to groups that have accumulated the most valuable skills in problem-solving, problem-identifying, and strategic brokering. Increasingly, such groups are to be found in many places around the globe other than the United States. As the world shrinks through efficiencies in telecommunications and transportation, such groups in one nation are able to combine their skills with those of people located in other nations in order to provide the greatest value to customers located almost anywhere. The threads of the global web are computers, facsimile machines, satellites, high-resolution monitors, and modems—all of them linking designers, engineers, contractors, licensees, and dealers worldwide.[1]

Of course, many nations still try to inhibit the flow of knowledge and money across their borders. But such inhibitions are proving increasingly futile, partly because modern technologies have made it so difficult for nations to control these flows. By the last decade of the twentieth century, governments could successfully block at their national borders few things other than tangible objects weighing more than three hundred pounds. Much of the knowledge and money, and many of the products and services, that people in different nations wish to exchange with one another are now easily transformed into electronic blips that move through the atmosphere at the speed of light. In 1988, some 17,000 leased international telephone circuits carried engineering designs, video images, and data instantaneously back and forth between problem-solvers, -identifiers, and brokers working together on different continents. The threads of the emerging global webs are barely visible, thus often elusive.

2

IN THE older high-volume economy, most products—like the corporations from which they emanated—had distinct nationalities. Regardless of how many international borders they crossed, their

---

[1] See, for example, Calvin Sims, "Global Communications Net Planned by GE for Its Staff," *The New York Times*, May 31, 1989, p. C1; Woody Hochswender, "How Fashion Spreads Around the World at the Speed of Light," *The New York Times*, May 13, 1990, p. E5.

country of origin—the name of which was usually imprinted right on them—was never in doubt. Most of the work that went into these products was done in one place, simply because economies of scale necessitated a central location. Into the large, centralized factory would go raw materials like coal or cotton, or commodities like steel or cotton fabric; out would come standard products like automobiles or dresses.

But in the emerging high-value economy, which does not depend on large-scale production, fewer products have distinct nationalities. Quantities can be produced efficiently in many different locations, to be combined in all sorts of ways to serve customer needs in many places. Intellectual and financial capital can come from anywhere, and be added instantly.

Consider some examples: Precision ice hockey equipment is designed in Sweden, financed in Canada, and assembled in Cleveland and Denmark for distribution in North America and Europe, respectively, out of alloys whose molecular structure was researched and patented in Delaware and fabricated in Japan. An advertising campaign is conceived in Britain; film footage for it is shot in Canada, dubbed in Britain, and edited in New York. A sports car is financed in Japan, designed in Italy, and assembled in Indiana, Mexico, and France, using advanced electronic components invented in New Jersey and fabricated in Japan. A microprocessor is designed in California and financed in America and West Germany, containing dynamic random-access memories fabricated in South Korea. A jet airplane is designed in the state of Washington and in Japan, and assembled in Seattle, with tail cones from Canada, special tail sections from China and Italy, and engines from Britain. A space satellite designed in California, manufactured in France, and financed by Australians is launched from a rocket made in the Soviet Union.[2] Which of these is an

---

[2]Sometimes, of course, geographic specialization of this sort allows economies of scale *within* particular stages of production. Tail cones for jet aircraft, for example, can be produced in large volume within Canada, to be combined in unique ways with other mass-produced components in order to create a wide variety of aircraft. But even under these circumstances, much of the value of the final product derives from the problem-solving, -identifying, and brokering skills entailed in putting such modules together in unique ways.

American product? Which a foreign? How does one decide? Does it matter?

3

IN SUCH global webs, products are international composites. What is traded between nations is less often finished products than specialized problem-solving (research, product design, fabrication), problem-identifying (marketing, advertising, customer consulting), and brokerage (financing, searching, contracting) services, as well as certain routine components and services, all of which are combined to create value.

When an American buys a Pontiac Le Mans from General Motors, for example, he or she engages unwittingly in an international transaction. Of the $10,000 paid to GM, about $3,000 goes to South Korea for routine labor and assembly operations, $1,750 to Japan for advanced components (engines, transaxles, and electronics), $750 to West Germany for styling and design engineering, $400 to Taiwan, Singapore, and Japan for small components, $250 to Britain for advertising and marketing services, and about $50 to Ireland and Barbados for data processing. The rest—less than $4,000—goes to strategists in Detroit, lawyers and bankers in New York, lobbyists in Washington, insurance and health-care workers all over the country, and General Motors shareholders—most of whom live in the United States, but an increasing number of whom are foreign nationals.

The proud new owner of the Pontiac is not aware of having bought so much from overseas, of course. General Motors did the trading, within its global web. This is typical. By the 1990s, most "trade" no longer occurred in arm's-length transactions between buyers in one nation and sellers in another, but between people within the same web who are likely to deal repeatedly with each other across borders. They may be part of the same multinational corporation, collecting salaries from one source, or they may be working in different companies that share in any profits from the joint venture, or they may simply contract with one another to perform specific services for a preestablished fee. The West German engineers who designed the Pontiac Le Mans may be on GM's payroll; or they may be on the payroll of West German–

owned Siemens AG, within a joint venture between Siemens and
GM; or Siemens may simply license GM to use automotive designs
developed by its engineers. Regardless of the precise legal form
it takes, the economics are similar: West German design engineers
have added value to a global web, for which they are compensated.
The exact amount of compensation may vary, but the reward is
likely to approximate whatever value these West German engineers added to this global enterprise web.

Such cross-border links now comprise most international trade
among advanced economies. Less than half of America's declining
trade balance in the 1980s was due to imports of finished products
like cars, videocassette recorders, fax machines, or any of the other
wonderful gadgets that American consumers demand. Most of
the imports were parts of such items, plus the engineering, design,
consulting, advertising, financial, and management services which
would find their way into them. In fact, in 1990 more than half
of America's exports and imports, by value, were simply the transfers of such goods and related services *within* global corporations.[3]

This sort of trade is hard to pin down. When, as now, traders
deal repeatedly with one another across borders—exchanging
services that are priced not in an open market but among divisions
of the same global corporation, or within complex employment
contracts, profit-sharing agreements, and long-term supply
arrangements—determinations about what it is that one "nation"
has paid out to another "nation" can be no better than fair ap-
proximations. Thus trade statistics are notoriously imprecise, subject to wide swings and seemingly inexplicable corrections. The
truth is that these days no one knows exactly, at any given time,
whether America's (or any other nation's) international trade is
in or out of balance, by how much it is out of balance, or what
the significance of such an imbalance might be.

For the same reason, it is becoming impossible to tell with any
precision how much of a given product is made where. National
governments seeking to levy income taxes on parts of global webs
are often baffled. What was earned on work performed within
the nation? Armies of international tax attorneys have been kept

---

[3]By one estimate, 92 percent of U.S. exports and 72 percent of U.S. imports
(in 1987) occurred within global corporations. See Amir Mahini, "A New
Look at Trade," *The McKinsey Quarterly*, Winter 1990, p. 42.

busy for years, Internal Revenue Service regulation writers have done overtime, Ministers of Finance from around the world have met endlessly, with no final resolution in sight. As more and more enterprises become parts of global webs whose internal accounting systems record the transfers of intermediate goods and related services, earnings and revenues can appear in all sorts of places (often, not coincidentally, where taxes are lowest). Exactly who earns what and where is a question for which there is, apparently, no straightforward answer.

4

GLOBAL webs often cloak themselves in whatever national garb is most convenient. When operating within a nation whose market is protected from foreign competition, they characterize themselves as loyal citizens, even occasionally demanding more protection. In 1987, for example, the Hyster Company, an American-owned manufacturer of forklift trucks (used to shuttle heavy materials around factories and warehouses) headquartered in Portland, Oregon, accused several Japanese-owned firms of pricing their forklifts sold in America below what they charged in Japan, prompting the Commerce Department to impose special duties on the forklift imports. In response, the Japanese firms began to make forklifts in the United States. Hyster cried foul, arguing that the competing forklifts were still "Japanese," since many of their parts came from Japan. What Hyster carefully did not reveal, however, was that its own "American" forklifts contained even more foreign parts than those they were accusing of being "Japanese." What looked like foreign "dumping" in the United States was in reality nothing more than one global web charging a lower price in the United States for its globally made forklifts than that charged by another global web.[4]

---

[4]After investigating the allegation of illegal dumping, Commerce Department officials discovered that "strictly speaking, there was no such thing as a U.S. forklift, or a foreign forklift for that matter." Nevertheless, to get on with the case, the officials decided to define a "U.S. forklift" as one whose frame was made in the United States. Henceforth, all a manufacturer had to do to avoid antidumping duties in the United States was to use an Amer-

Changing national costumes can be relatively easy. Consider, for example, how effortlessly global webs manipulate Pentagon regulations requiring that the agency purchase "American" military supplies unless foreign goods are substantially cheaper. Such rules are, of course, justified as necessary for national defense and as being in the interest of American workers (who, it is supposed, are more deserving than foreign workers of such privileges as laboring in dangerous munitions factories). But since most weapons systems use components that are designed and fabricated all over the world, the practical effect of these regulations has been to encourage American companies to front for foreign designers and fabricators. The U.S. government considers a firm to be "American" if it is incorporated in the United States, so it is a relatively easy matter for an "American" firm to assign the work to its far-flung global web. In reality, the Pentagon has no idea who is making what and where.[5] Bull HN, an amalgam of French-owned Bull, American-owned Honeywell, and Japanese-owned NEC, repeatedly reassures the Pentagon that it is still an American company, entitled to all the pecuniary advantages of citizenship, even though it designs and makes gadgets for the Pentagon all over the world.

When there are greater advantages to being seen as "foreign," on the other hand, even the most native of goods and services are magically transformed into alien products. Is a particular American firm still operating a firm in South Africa? No longer, says the corporate director of public relations reassuringly. The company has pulled out. Closer inspection reveals a somewhat less heartening reality. The corporation has merely changed the legal form of its web, which still extends deeply into that nation. Instead of owning its South African subsidiary outright, it now licenses it

---

ican-made frame—even if everything else in the forklift truck was produced abroad. See Anne E. Brunsdale, Chair, U.S. International Trade Commission, "Global Industries and U.S. Trade Laws," Western Cargo Conference, October 13, 1989.

[5] The Defense Department has acknowledged the problem. "It is hard to know what percentage of [Department of Defense] purchases from companies located in the United States are actually purchases from U.S. subsidiaries of foreign firms." Draft Report, *Task Force on Ownership and Control*, Defense Manufacturing Board, Office of the Under Secretary of Defense, February 1, 1990, p. 8.

to make and sell the same product. Revenues flowing from South Africa to the American strategic brokers and investors remain identical.[6]

Such costume changes can be breathtakingly quick. Consider the Ford Motor Company's instant 1990 alteration in light of Environmental Protection Agency (EPA) regulations. The EPA had required that every automaker's fleet of "American-made" cars achieve a certain minimum average fuel economy. Any foreign cars made or imported by the American firm would have to meet the same standard when these cars' fuel economy ratings were averaged together. By not allowing American automakers to average their small, fuel-efficient imports with their far more profitable American gas guzzlers, the EPA had wanted to encourage American automakers to retain small-car production in the United States. In 1989, however, Ford—displaying a talent for regulatory innovation-as-circumvention—concocted a brilliant idea: By increasing the foreign-made parts in its American gas guzzlers just a tad, Ford could qualify the big clunkers as "foreign-made," thus permitting them to be averaged with all the high-mileage Ford imports. Presto! Overnight, Ford's remarkably inefficient "foreign-made" Mercury Marquises and LTD Crown Victorias could be sold in America without first having to be balanced by smaller (and far less profitable) high-mileage cars made in the United States. Ford's clever costume change did not serve the cause of energy conservation, but it did save the company a heap of money.

Official decisions about how much of a product must be produced within the nation in order for it to qualify as "domestic" rather than "foreign"—and how to measure such things—have consumed millions of hours of legal time and herculean efforts by regulators here and abroad. Must 50 percent of its value orig-

---

[6]In response to the U.S. government's Anti-Apartheid Act of 1986, which barred American corporations from making any new investment in their South African subsidiaries after November 1986, General Motors sold its South African subsidiary to its South African executives for $40 million. According to the agreement, GM would continue to supply the newly independent company with components, designs, and spare parts, largely through GM's Opel subsidiary in West Germany. Glenn Adler, "Withdrawal Powers: GM and Ford Disinvest from South Africa," New York University, Center for Labor-Management Policy Studies, November 1989.

inate here in order for it to be deemed a domestic product? Sixty percent? Should the cost of advertising and marketing the product be included in the tally? What about interest payments to banks located within the nation? And so on. With each passing day, the rule books get thicker, the regulations more complex, the inspections and accounting ledgers more picayune.

Such decisions have required delicate diplomatic maneuvers as well. In the 1980s French bureaucrats limited Japanese automobile imports to 3 percent of the French market, but then faced the awesome task of explaining to Margaret Thatcher why Nissan Bluebirds, assembled in Britain, 80 percent of whose parts came from Europe, would be subject to the quota (the bureaucrats failed). When in 1989 Taiwan tried to apply its ban on Japanese car imports to Toyotas assembled in the United States, it was the Bush administration's turn to express outrage—and Taiwan backed down. In a remarkably facile, though somewhat less successful turnabout, the administration then attempted to beat back a European Community ruling that Ricoh copiers assembled in California were really "Japanese" and therefore subject to special import duties.

The notion that products have national origins is so deeply ingrained that governments, and the publics they represent, are unable to adjust to the emerging reality. Preoccupied with vestigial concerns, they continue to focus on the wrong question: Is it a "foreign" or a "domestic" product? The answer they find is perplexing and elusive, predicated on refined measurements, subtle discriminations, and bureaucratic and legal manipulations. Unfortunately, all of these contortions accomplish little more than distracting attention from a far more relevant question: For any given product, which nation's workers have gained what sort of experience, equipping them to do what in the future? I shall return to this more fundamental question in later chapters.

11

The End of
the National Champion

I was asked the other day about United States competitiveness and I replied that I don't think about it at all. We at
NCR think of ourselves as a globally competitive company
that happens to be headquartered in the United States.

GILBERT WILLIAMSON, president,
NCR Corporation (1989)

THE ASSUMED vehicle for improving the competitive performance of the United States has been the American corporation.
After all, it was the core American corporation that mobilized and
directed the vast army of American workers toward higher and
higher productivity, expanded the American middle class, and
demonstrated to the rest of the world the raw economic power
of the nation. "Engine Charlie" Wilson had summed up the prevailing view in 1952 when he saw no inherent difference between
what was good for General Motors and what was good for the
United States.

Like American products, however, the "American" corporation
is becoming disconnected from America. We still call them "American" corporations because most of their shares are held by American citizens, their top strategic brokers are Americans, and their
world headquarters are located here. Yet they are fast becoming
parts of global webs in which much of the value of what they sell
comes from other places around the world—including, importantly, high-value problem-solving and -identifying. Meanwhile,
ever more of the value of what other nations' corporate champions
sell around the world is coming from the United States.

In fact, as American-owned firms go abroad and foreign-owned firms come to the United States, the two kinds of enterprise webs are beginning to look very much alike in terms of where they derive most of the value inherent in their products and services. The nationality of a firm's dominant shareholders and of its top executives has less and less to do with where the firm invests and with whom it contracts around the world.

2

DIRECT evidence of this transformation is found in the armies of foreign workers now employed by so-called American corporations. By 1990, for example, 40 percent of IBM's world employees were foreign, and the percentage was growing. IBM Japan boasted more than 18,000 Japanese employees and annual sales of more than $6 billion, making it one of Japan's major exporters of computers. Or consider Whirlpool. After cutting its American work force by 10 percent, shifting much of its production to Mexico, and buying Dutch-owned Philips's appliance business, Whirlpool employed 43,500 people in forty-five countries—most of them non-Americans. Or Seagate Technology, a California-based world leader in the production of hard-disk drives. In 1990, the company had 40,000 employees, 27,000 of whom worked in Southeast Asia.

All told, more than 20 percent of the output of American-owned firms was produced by foreign workers outside the United States—and the percentage was rising quickly. Overseas capital spending by American corporations accelerated from the early 1980s onward, increasing by 24 percent in 1988 alone. In 1989 it was 13 percent above the record level of 1988, and in 1990, 16 percent higher than that (even while their capital spending in America increased at an anemic 6.7 percent). Intent on a strong presence in Europe after European economic union, American corporations led the world in snapping up European companies —investing $5.2 billion in just the last six months of 1989.[1] Even

---

[1] Figures from U.S. Department of Commerce, Bureau of Economic Analysis, "Foreign Direct Investment by U.S. Companies," various issues; see also Translink's *European Deal Review* (February 1990).

America's major utilities were getting into the global race. By 1990, Bell South, the largest provider of basic telephone services in the United States, had operations in more than twenty countries—developing cellular telephone networks in Argentina and France, cable systems in France, management software in India, voice and data system designs in China, and digital network technical assistance in Guatemala. And Bell Atlantic spent $1.5 billion to acquire New Zealand's telephone company, the Telecom Corporation.[2]

This pattern has not been confined to America's traditional core corporations. Consider the Molex Corporation, headquartered in a suburb of Chicago, with 1989 sales of about $572 million worth of connectors used to link wires in cars and computer boards; most of these connectors are made in Molex's forty-six overseas factories spread over twenty countries, employing more than 6,000 foreign workers. The Loctite Company, headquartered in Newington, Connecticut, with annual sales of about $457 million worth of adhesives and sealants, employed 3,500 people in 1989, fewer than a third of whom were Americans.[3] Family-owned Swan Optical Corporation, of Long Island City, New York, is touted as one of only six surviving American makers of eyeglass frames. Swan's factories, however, are in Hong Kong, mainland China, and Italy. Alan Glassman, Swan's president, describes the company's strategy as "hopping and skipping and jumping to everywhere we can find a competitive labor market."[4] Swan is far from unique: During the decade of the 1980s, America's most profitable small and middle-sized companies (as classified by the Department of Commerce) increased their overseas investments an average of 20 percent each year.[5]

Of course, some of this worldwide activity is nothing more than high-volume standardized production transplanted abroad in order to meet low-cost foreign competitors head-on. And, as has

---

[2] From interviews with Bell South officials and company reports.

[3] From *China Trade*, March 1990; see also *Business Week*, April 13, 1987, p. 63.

[4] "Enter the Mini-Multinational," *Northeast International Business*, March 1989, p. 13.

[5] This from a survey of 100 profitable middle-sized and smaller companies: "Winning in the World Market," American Business Conference, November 1987.

been noted, profits from this "if you can't beat them, join them" strategy are apt to be small since there are no barriers to entry. Any firm around the world can follow precisely the same low-wage route. Nonetheless, by the close of the 1980s, American-owned corporations directly employed 11 percent of the industrial work force of Northern Ireland, mass-producing everything from cigarettes to computer software, much of which ultimately ended up on store shelves in the United States.[6] On the other side of the world, 200 American-owned corporations employed more than 100,000 Singaporeans to fabricate and assemble electronic components for export to the United States. In fact, Singapore's largest private employer was General Electric, which also accounted for a large share of that nation's growing exports. Taiwan, meanwhile, counted AT&T, RCA, and Texas Instruments among its largest exporters. And with the opening up of Eastern Europe, American corporations suddenly had access to workers happy to labor for wages comparable to those earned by workers in the Philippines, but with the important difference that Eastern Europeans worked only a few hundred miles from one of the largest and most lucrative markets in the world. In 1989, GE plunked down $150 million for a Hungarian light bulb factory, with the result that hundreds of Hungarians now find themselves working for the same company that once employed Ronald Reagan. Capitalism, unlike other ideologies, is indifferent to the beliefs or pedigrees of its practitioners so long as they contribute to the bottom line.

3

A GROWING portion of this new global activity of American-owned corporations, however, entails high-value problem-solving and -identifying outside the United States.[7] It is from these efforts that

---

[6] *The New York Times*, April 18, 1988, p. A32.

[7] Professor Michael Porter premises much of his argument about the competitive advantage of nations on the supposition that a corporation's home nation is "where the core product and process technology are created and maintained," and thus "where its most productive jobs are located" and "most advanced skills" are nurtured. *The Competitive Advantage of Nations* (New

the global web earns most of its profits, because skills and insights cannot be easily replicated. Italian stylists help GM produce a sleek-looking sports car, German design engineers ensure that its engine is dependable, and Japanese manufacturing engineers confirm that it can be reliably assembled at a low cost. Researchers in many nations help American-owned corporations discover new products, applications, and refinements. According to National Science Foundation figures, American-owned corporations increased their overseas spending on research and development by 33 percent between 1986 and 1987, compared with a 6 percent increase in R&D spending in the United States.[8] Beginning in 1987, Eastman Kodak, W. R. Grace, Du Pont, Merck, Procter & Gamble and Upjohn all opened new R&D facilities in Japan. At Du Pont's Yokohama laboratory, more than 180 Japanese scientists and technicians have been working at developing new materials technologies. IBM's Tokyo Research Lab, tucked away behind the far side of the Imperial Palace in downtown Tokyo, houses a small army of Japanese engineers who have been perfecting image-processing technology. In IBM's Kanagawa lab in Yamato City, 1,500 Japanese researchers have been developing advanced hardware and software.

American firms have not confined their pioneering research work to Japan. In the late 1980s two European researchers at IBM's Zurich laboratory announced major breakthroughs into superconductivity and microscopy—earning both of them Nobel Prizes. One of Procter & Gamble's major new products of the 1980s—Liquid Tide—was the handiwork of the company's European researchers. By 1990, Hewlett-Packard's West German researchers were making significant strides in fiber-optic technologies; its Australian researchers, in computer-aided engineering software; its Singaporean researchers, in laser printers.

York: Free Press, 1990), p. 97. Porter's assumption would have been correct as late as the 1970s, but more recent evidence suggests otherwise, as I will show. See also John Cantwell, note 21, *infra*.

[8] *Highlights*, National Science Foundation, Washington, D.C., March 9, 1990, Table 2. Even after adjusting for devaluation of the U.S. dollar, R&D spending of American-owned companies rose faster abroad than in the United States. National Science Foundation, *Science and Technology Update* (Washington, D.C.: U.S. Government Printing Office, 1989).

Motorola's Hong Kong researchers were designing special semi-conductor chips. Monsanto's Oxford University researchers were devising new carbohydrate molecules. Apple Computer chose Singapore as its research center for developing video screens of the future.[9]

American firms were seeking high-value problem-solving even in Eastern Europe and the Soviet Union. Strategic brokers at Du Pont's headquarters in Wilmington, Delaware, were sponsoring viral research at the Institute of Organic Chemistry and Biology in Czechoslovakia. Brokers at Monsanto were paying $500,000 to a team of Soviet biological scientists at the Shemyakin Institute in Moscow in return for the right to market their discoveries in the West. "This is a way for us to increase our biotechnical research with some of the finest minds on earth," a Monsanto official told *The New York Times*.[10]

The emerging American company knows no national boundaries, feels no geographic constraints. In 1989, within the first six months of its cosmopolitan life, the Momenta Corporation, headquartered in Mountain View, California, had raised almost $13 million from Taiwanese and American investors. A small band of American engineers were designing Momenta's advanced computer, all of whose components would be engineered and produced in Japan, and thereafter assembled in Taiwan and Singapore. Global financing was "one of the only ways we [could] be assured of the $40 million we needed," said the Iranian-born strategic broker who organized the company. And global production was the optimal way to "make use of the best technology that is available to the company."[11]

Of course, those directly employed by American corporations abroad contribute only a small fraction of the total "foreign" value

[9]David Sanger, "Singapore's Aim: High-Tech Future," *The New York Times*, May 15, 1990, pp. D1, D8.
[10]A top-level scientist at a major American corporation would cost at least $250,000, including salary, benefits, and overhead. The same caliber of talent could be had in the East for one-tenth the cost. J. Holusha, "Business Taps the East Bloc's Intellectual Reserves," *The New York Times*, February 20, 1990, pp. A1, D5.
[11]Quoted in John Markoff, "Silicon Valley Is Changing Programs," *The New York Times*, January 14, 1990, p. D24.

added to these firms' products. The greater share is added through foreign supply contracts, licensing agreements, and joint ventures in which some of the brokers and much of the high-value problem-solving and -identifying is performed outside the United States by people who draw salaries from foreign-owned companies.[12] In the 1980s, Corning Glass abandoned its national pyramidlike organization in favor of a global web—making optical cable, for example, through its European partner, Siemens AG, and medical equipment with Ciba-Geigy. Such foreign alliances generated almost half of Corning's earnings in 1990.[13] AT&T also has turned itself into a global web: Japan-owned NEC helps AT&T supply and market memory chips; Dutch-owned Philips helps AT&T make and market telecommunications switching equipment and application-specific integrated circuits; Japan-owned Mitsui helps it with value-added networks. IBM, meanwhile, has combined with Mitsubishi for value-added networks, with Siemens for disk drives, and with both Siemens and Italtel for switching equipment. The new high-value webs extend to the Soviet Union. In 1989, Chrysler's Gulfstream Aerospace subsidiary announced plans to make a new supersonic corporate jet with the help of its partner, the Soviets' Sukhoi Aerospace, which would develop the prototype from Gulfstream's designs and handle the manufacturing engineering; Britain's Rolls-Royce would design the engine, to be manufactured by the Soviet firm Lyulka.

---

[12] The following examples are drawn from interviews and company reports. A number of recent surveys have confirmed the trend. See, for example, David J. Teece et al., "Joint Ventures and Collaborative Arrangements in the Telecommunications Equipment Industry," in D. Mowery (ed.), *International Collaborative Ventures in U.S. Manufacturing* (Cambridge, Mass.: Ballinger, 1988); D. Morris and M. Hergert, "Trends in International Collaborative Agreements," *Columbia Journal of World Business*, Summer 1987, pp. 15–21; and Ashoka Mody, "Changing Firm Boundaries: An Analysis of Technology-Sharing Alliances," The World Bank, Industry and Energy Department, Working Paper, Industry Series Paper No. 3, February 1989, pp. 2–4.

[13] Company reports.

4

THE CHIEF executives of American-owned corporations continue to rail against what they claim to be unfair foreign competition, of course. This is a necessary pose. It confirms their patriotism, and reassures the American public that the captains of American industry are still at the national helm. Self-righteous fulmination about the heavy burdens borne by American corporations relative to their foreign competitors may even elicit a sympathetic tax break or subsidy from the U.S. government. But most of this is for the cameras. Beyond politics and public relations, within the sanctity of the corporate boardroom, the American chief executive is wheeling and dealing worldwide, oblivious to national borders. Lee Iacocca, for example, the irrepressible chairman of Chrysler Corporation, has worked up quite a lather about Japanese automobile imports. Mr. Iacocca, you may recall, was instrumental in convincing Congress in 1979 to guarantee Chrysler Corporation $1.2 billion in new loans so that Chrysler could avoid bankruptcy and continue to make cars in the United States. He helped force a "voluntary restraint agreement" on Japan's exports of cars to the United States. And in television commercials, he told Americans to abandon their "inferiority complex" vis-à-vis the Japanese. By the start of the 1990s, however, Chrysler cars contained the highest percentage of foreign-made parts of any of the Big Three—including the most complex components, like engines and transaxles. In addition, Chrysler owned 12 percent of Mitsubishi Motors and, through Mitsubishi, a part of South Korea's Hyundai Motors—both of which supplied Chrysler customers with Dodge Colts, Chrysler Conquests, Dodge Vistas, Eagle Summits, and other exhilaratingly named vehicles. It was even rumored that the firm, finding itself once again in financial difficulty, would merge with Mitsubishi, or possibly Fiat.

Other "American" automakers were similarly disengaging from America. By 1990, Ford owned 25 percent of Mazda, and both companies owned shares of South Korea's Kia Motors; Mazda and Kia supplied Ford with small cars and parts. Ford also bought components from Japan's Yamaha Motor Company (Ford television commercials boasting of the "hot engine" in the Ford Taurus failed to mention its Japanese pedigree). Ford had increased its capital spending in Europe by 37 percent since the start of the 1980s, while reducing its spending in the United States by 17 percent. Along the way, it bought the very symbol of highbrow British elegance—the Jaguar. Ford's plan is to design, engineer, and assemble small cars in Europe for export around the world. Not to be outdone, General Motors bought more than 40 percent of Japan's Isuzu, which has supplied it with over 300,000 small cars annually; it bought half of South Korea's Daewoo Motors, which has supplied another 80,000 cars; and it bought 50 percent of Sweden's Saab. GM also joined with Japan's Fanuc to make robots. And by the start of the 1990s GM was investing in European factories at a furious pace, even as it, too, closed many of its American plants.[14]

When pressed to justify these linkages, the chief executives of American-owned firms typically claim they are necessary in order for the corporation to learn as much as possible about new manufacturing techniques and technologies wherever they arise around the globe. This justification is misleading, however, because it suggests that the desired know-how is somehow absorbed by the American corporation's American employees, who can then utilize it in the future. But the fact that foreign know-how finds its way into products sold under an American firm's trademark is no reason to suppose that any Americans played a substantial role in getting it there. By their very nature, global webs can utilize new knowledge and insights efficiently without any American learning a thing.

5

AN EVEN more dramatic development has been the arrival of foreign-owned corporations in the United States at a rapidly increasing pace. In 1977, foreign investment equaled about 2 percent of the total net worth (by book value) of all the nonfinancial corporations in the United States; by 1988, it equaled 9 percent,

---

[14] In 1990, even though it was building half as many passenger cars as the North American Division, GM-Europe accounted for almost all GM's total profits from automobile manufacturing. *Time*, February 19, 1990, p. 68.

and was expected to reach 15 percent by 1995.[15] As recently as 1977, foreign-owned firms accounted for only about 5 percent of American manufacturing (as "manufacturing" is formally classified in government statistics) and 3 percent of American manufacturing employment; by 1990, foreigners owned more than 13 percent of America's manufacturing assets (including half of all American-based companies involved in consumer electronics) and employed more than 8 percent of America's manufacturing workers—comprising some 3 million Americans.[16] In 1990, Mitsubishi alone employed more than 3,000 Americans to assemble televisions in Santa Ana, California, test and assemble semiconductors in Durham, North Carolina, fabricate automobile parts in Cincinnati, Ohio, and put together televisions and cellular mobile telephones in Braselton, Georgia. And as the Big Three automakers abandoned America, Japanese automakers rapidly filled the gap. Between 1987 and 1990 alone, the Big Three laid off 9,063 American autoworkers, while the Japanese hired 11,050.[17] These were no mere assembly operations; by 1992, Japanese-owned automakers planned to make or buy within the United States at least 75 percent of the content of their American cars—a higher percentage than American-owned automakers.[18]

In fact, many of these foreign-owned companies have been vigorously exporting from the United States. By 1990 Sony was exporting audiotapes and videotapes to Europe from its Dothan, Alabama, factory and shipping audio recorders from its Fort Lau-

---

[15] Data on foreign stock from "Foreign Direct Investment in the United States, Detail for Position and Balance of Payments Flows," 1988 *Survey of Current Business*, U.S. Department of Commerce, August 1989; on the net worth of nonfinancial corporations, from Federal Reserve Board, "Balance Sheets for the U.S. Economy 1949–1988," April 1989.

[16] Assets and employment of foreign manufacturing affiliates estimated from Bureau of Economic Analysis, U.S. Department of Commerce, "Foreign Direct Investment in the United States: Operations of U.S. Affiliates of Foreign Companies," various issues; assets of U.S. manufacturing companies from U.S. Bureau of the Census and Federal Trade Commission.

[17] Figures from Joseph White, "Chrysler to Shut St. Louis Plant, Third Since 1987," *The Wall Street Journal*, February 21, 1990, p. 14.

[18] Robert Z. Lawrence, *Japanese-Affiliated Automakers in the United States: An Appraisal* (Washington, D.C.: Brookings Institution, 1989), pp. 41–53.

derdale, Florida, plant. Sharp was exporting 100,000 microwave ovens annually from its factory in Memphis, Tennessee; Dutch-owned Philips Consumer Electronics Company, 30,000 televisions from its Greeneville, Tennessee, plant to Japan; Toshiba America, projection televisions from its Wayne, New Jersey, plant to Japan; Matsushita, cathode-ray tubes from Ohio; and Honda was laying plans to export 50,000 cars to Japan from Ohio. In all, by 1990, more than a quarter of American exports bore the labels of foreign-owned companies; Japanese-owned companies alone accounted for over 10 percent of America's total exports. (Note that this figure, of course, does not reveal how much of these exported products comprise work that originated outside the United States.)[19]

Importantly, foreign-owned companies have been doing an ever-larger amount of their high-value research and design in the United States. In fact, during the 1980s foreign-owned corporations invested more money in the United States on research and development for each of their American workers than did American-owned corporations.[20] By 1990, more than 500 American scientists and engineers worked for Honda Motors in Torrance, California; another 200 worked in Ohio. At Mazda's new $23 million R&D center in Irvine, California, hundreds of American designers and engineers undertook long-term automotive research. Nissan employed 400 American engineers at its engineering center in Plymouth, Michigan; Toyota, 140 at its technical research center in Ann Arbor. At Philips's research center in Sunnyvale, California, American computer engineers designed the world's fastest computer chip.

In addition, foreign-owned companies were financing research in American universities and laboratories. According to a General Accounting Office study, 496 foreign-owned firms financed American academic research in 1988, for which the firms got an

---

[19] Calculated from Bureau of Economic Analysis, "Foreign Direct Investment in the United States, Detail for Position and Balance of Payments Flows," *Survey of Current Business* (August, various years, projected to 1990).

[20] From E. Graham and P. Krugman, *Foreign Direct Investment in the United States* (Washington, D.C.: Institute for International Economics, 1990), pp. 58–59, Table 3-3.

early look at unpublished findings and a chance to buy patents from the universities.[21] At the Massachusetts Institute of Technology alone, 130 foreign-owned companies joined 161 American companies to provide more than $4 million of research funding each year.[22] At leading American research laboratories, such as Battelle Memorial Institute and SRI International, most research was funded by foreign firms, mainly Japanese-owned.

Meanwhile, foreign-owned corporations, like their American counterparts, are relying ever more on developing nations for high-volume, standardized production. This is the case even for Japanese-owned firms, which have mastered high-volume manufacturing engineering. Intense and increasing competition from South Korea and the rest of Southeast Asia has squeezed profit margins on standardized production in Japan, forcing Japanese firms to shift to low-wage nations. Thus by 1990, for example, Japanese microwave ovens and color televisions actually issued from factories in Thailand, Malaysia, and mainland China. Most of these products were exported back to Japanese consumers (largely explaining why Japanese manufactured imports shot up in the late 1980s),[23] but a growing percentage found their way

---

[21] U.S. General Accounting Office, *Foreign Sponsorship of U.S. University Research* (Washington, D.C.: U.S. Government Printing Office, 1989). Research by John Cantwell suggests that, in general, global corporations do *not* concentrate their research and development in their home country. See J. Cantwell, *Technological Innovation and Multinational Corporations* (London: Blackwell, 1989).

[22] American scientists and inventors have continued to supply a large portion of the world's inventions. (Americans authored over a third of the world's scientific articles in 1987; the Japanese, 7 percent; the West Germans, 6 percent.) Foreign-owned companies eagerly purchase them; American-owned corporations do so as well, often transferring them to foreign production sites to be transformed into products for sale to the rest of the world. The fees and royalties flowing to the United States in payment for new inventions substantially exceeds the fees and royalties flowing in the opposite direction. See National Science Foundation, *Science and Technology Update* (Washington, D.C.: U.S. Government Printing Office, annual issues); also John Alec, "Report on Foreign Purchases of U.S. Technology," U.S. House of Representatives, Task Force on Technology Policy, Committee on Science, Space, and Technology, October 22, 1989.

[23] Manufactured goods (as defined) amounted to 22 percent of Japan's total import bill in 1980; by 1989, they comprised 61 percent of Japanese imports.

back to the United States. Many Mitsubishi automobiles, some of which were sold in the United States under the Chrysler trademark, were actually assembled by workers in Thailand.

6

WHAT'S the difference between an "American" corporation that makes or buys abroad much of what it sells around the world, and a "foreign" corporation that makes or buys in the United States much of what it sells? And how to differentiate either of them from a joint venture between the two, involving making or buying here and there? The mind struggles to keep the players straight. In 1990, Japan's NTT was purchasing digital switches made in Canadian-owned Northern Telecom's factory in North Carolina. If you found that one too easy, try this: Beginning in 1991, Japan's Mazda would be producing Ford Probes at Mazda's plant in Flat Rock, Michigan. Some of these cars would be exported to Japan and sold there under Ford's trademark. A Mazda-designed compact utility vehicle would be built at a Ford plant in Louisville, Kentucky, and then sold at Mazda dealerships in the United States. Nissan, meanwhile, was designing a new light truck at its San Diego, California, design center. The trucks would be assembled at Ford's Ohio truck plant, using panel parts fabricated by Nissan at its Tennessee factory, and then marketed by both Ford and Nissan in the United States and in Japan. Who is Ford? Nissan? Mazda?

The trend is worldwide. National champions everywhere are becoming global webs with no particular connection to any single nation. As American corporations increasingly produce or buy from abroad, and foreign-owned firms increasingly produce in or buy from America, the two sets of global webs are coming to resemble each other—regardless of their nominal nationality. The same trend is observable between the global webs of other nations: In 1990 alone, Daimler-Benz, West Germany's largest industrial group, announced that it was expanding its business ties with Mitsubishi, one of Japan's largest; and Sweden's Volvo disclosed

---

See Yoshi Tsurumi, "From Brinkmanship to Statesmanship," *World Policy Journal*, Winter 1989–90.

plans to merge with France's Renault, forming Europe's fourth-largest industrial group.[24] Even tiny Singapore was creating global corporations of its own. Weng Kok Siew, president of Singapore Technologies, described its worldwide strategy in words that could describe that of any other global web: "We plan to manufacture in any country in the world where there is an advantage—to make things in Thailand where the cost is low, in Germany because the market is big, to do R and D in Boston."[25]

All such variations are differing legal formulations of essentially the same global web. Closely examine each and you begin to see a similar pattern: high-volume, standardized production occurs mainly in low-wage countries (save for what must be assembled in higher-wage nations where the final products are to be sold, either because it's cheaper to assemble the parts there or because of protectionist barriers); high-value problem-solving, -identifying, and brokering occurs wherever useful insights can be found around the world. Thus is the high-value global enterprise evolving into an international partnership of skilled people whose insights are combined with one another and who contract with unskilled workers from around the world for whatever must be standardized and produced in high volume.

In its purest and most advanced form, the global partnership sells its high-value insights directly on the open market. Consider McKinsey, the distinguished consulting firm, which by 1990 comprised over 2,500 problem-solvers, -identifiers, and brokers worldwide, most of them non-Americans. (Years ago, when McKinsey's foreign clients sought the secrets of America's economic success, the firm sold them its American management expertise; today, not surprisingly, it sells McKinsey expertise instead.) Other global "insight partnerships" include those that

[24] At the time of the announcement, Renault was still officially "owned" by the French government. But as Renault gradually merged into a global web, even its explicit government connection became less relevant to its business decisions about where to do what around the world. Everywhere, state-owned enterprises were in eclipse. See Raymond Vernon, "The Eclipse of the State-Owned Enterprise: Causes and Consequences," Center for Business and Government, John F. Kennedy School of Government, 1989.
[25] Sanger, op. cit.

sell expertise about information technology, like Arthur Andersen, with over 46,000 employees worldwide (of whom only 18,000
are Americans); global advertising and marketing, like the WPP
Group (including what were formerly America's J. Walter Thompson and Ogilvy & Mather), with 21,500 employees in 50 countries;
civil engineering (Bechtel, with 29,000 employees in 33 nations);
financial services (Morgan Stanley, with 6,000 employees spread
out over 18 countries); legal services (Baker & McKenzie, with
3,500 staff employees and 1,500 lawyers in 50 cities around the
world, of whom fewer than a third are Americans), and so on:
advanced research, public relations, agricultural engineering, software engineering, architecture, and, not least, investment banking
(global partnerships in this last category having grown 5 percent
larger and more profitable since you began reading this para-
graph).

Many of these insight partnerships have as many employees,
and earn as much money, as more traditional corporations that
produce tangible things. In fact, the jobs within these partnerships
are identical to the jobs of problem-solvers, -identifiers, and brokers within enterprise webs of the sort noted before, except that
their insights are sold worldwide to people described as "clients"
rather than subcontractors, licensees, franchisees, or joint-venture
partners. The distinction is chiefly semantic. Global insight partnerships specializing in particular problem-solving, -identifying,
and brokering are becoming important points of intersection in
rapidly expanding global webs.

7

SEVERAL implications of this transformation should be noted. One
is that national savings increasingly flow to whoever can do things
best, or cheapest, wherever located around the world. "National
competitiveness" is thus less dependent on the quantity of money
that a nation's citizens save and invest than it is on the skills and
insights they potentially contribute to the world economy. Even
were Americans to save enough to finance every investment they
might want to undertake in the United States, and thus have no
reason to borrow money from abroad, flows of global capital into

the United States would remain large, and probably increase—as foreigners invested more and more of their savings in global webs that threaded their way to America, and as Americans continued to invest much of their savings in global webs that threaded their way abroad. More on this later.

A related conclusion is that much of America's stubborn trade imbalance during the 1980s was due not to the predations of foreign nations and corporations, insistent on selling more to us than we sold to them, but to American-owned firms making things abroad (or, more precisely, contracting with foreigners to supply them with particular goods and services, which the firm then sold in the United States). This cosmopolitan practice accounted, for example, for more than one-third of Taiwan's notorious trade surplus with the United States during the 1980s, and more than 20 percent of the U.S. trade imbalances with Mexico, Singapore, South Korea, and even Japan.[26] In fact, American-owned firms were doing so much abroad, and foreign-owned so much here, that by 1990 American consumers intent on improving the nation's trade balance would have done better to buy a Honda than a Pontiac Le Mans.

There is no reason to blame the top executives of American-owned corporations for this confusing state of affairs. The stream of books exhorting managers to one-minute excellence notwithstanding, many of the strategic brokers in American headquarters have done a commendable job maintaining their companies' shares of world exports. Having adjusted to the tribulations of the 1970s by focusing on high value over high volume, their firms' overall portion of world exports was by the 1980s almost identical to (by some measures, even higher than) their share in 1966—about 17 percent. They maintained this export share by moving much of their operations outside the United States—adding value in other nations, and then exporting from abroad. During the same period, exports from the United States (as opposed to American-owned corporations) steadily declined as a share of world

---

[26]Calculated from Amir Mahini, "A New Look at Trade," *The McKinsey Quarterly*, Winter 1990. See also DeAnne Julius, *Global Companies and Public Policy* (London: RIIA Pinter, 1990); M. Barker, "U.S. Merchandise Trade Associated With U.S. Multinational Companies," *Survey of Current Business*, U.S. Department of Commerce, May 1986.

exports.[27] In other words, the top executives of American-owned corporations have done reasonably well at what they are paid to do, even if they have not done very well by American workers.

The picture that emerges contrasts sharply with the lingering image of the core American corporation as national champion. While most of its financing still comes from the United States, much of the rest—both high-value problem-solving and problem-identifying and what remains of high-volume production—occurs, increasingly, outside the country. Some of the profits return to Americans, of course, but this profit stream is narrowing relative to the ever-growing stream of returns to problem-solvers, -identifiers, and brokers around the world. That the strength of the American economy is synonymous with the profitability and productivity of American corporations is thus an axiom on the brink of anachronism.

-----

[27] Calculations from Robert E. Lipsey and Irving Kravis, "The Competitive and Comparative Advantage of U.S. Multinationals, 1957–1983," Working Paper No. 2051, National Bureau of Economic Research, November 1986.

12

The Coming Irrelevance
of Corporate Nationality

> Two identical cars roll off the same assembly line in Amer-
> ica. A Japanese nameplate goes on one, an American
> nameplate goes on the other. And people prefer the car
> with the Japanese nameplate! This has got to stop.
>
> LEE IACOCCA,
> Chrysler advertisement (1990)

> Merchants have no country. The mere spot they stand on
> does not constitute so strong an attachment as that from
> which they draw their gain.
>
> THOMAS JEFFERSON (1806)

BY THE 1990s, many of America's core corporations had fallen
into foreign hands—RCA, CBS Records, American Can, Columbia Pictures, Doubleday, Mack Truck, Allis-Chalmers, Firestone, Goodyear, Giant Food, Grand Union, A&P, Blooming-
dale's, Pillsbury, National Steel. The list seemed to grow longer
by the day. And as it grew, many Americans became increasingly
concerned.

The concern is understandable. Our habit of equating the success of the American economy with that of the American corporation, and the success of foreign economies with that of their
corporations, makes us fearful when foreigners seem to be laying
claim to more and more of our assets—regardless of how many
foreign assets are already owned by Americans. (In fact, by 1991,
the total value of foreign-owned assets in America was still less

than the market value of American-owned assets abroad.[1]) And our assumption that national wealth depends on the assets that a nation's citizens own and control causes us to worry for the future of the nation.

These fears are relatively new to the United States (at least in the twentieth century), but not to other nations. Canadians have long fretted over the dominance of corporations owned and controlled by foreigners—in particular, by citizens of the United States. Western Europeans have been similarly upset by the power of the American-owned multinational. But now, as the Japanese, West Germans, and others appear to be "buying up" America, we are experiencing similar trepidation.[2]

Such concerns, however, are the product of outmoded thinking. They are based on a picture of national corporations and industries which is no longer accurate. As corporations of all nations are transformed into global webs, the important question—from the standpoint of national wealth—is *not* which nation's citizens own what, but which nation's citizens learn how to do what, so they are capable of adding more value to the world economy and therefore increasing their own potential worth. This latter issue *is* a cause for concern, to which I will return. But first I want to put to rest the concerns about foreign ownership.

2

CONSIDER first who gets the profits. It does matter, of course, whose citizens are entitled to the stream of earnings from a com-

---

[1] Because all such assets are measured at book value (what they cost) rather than market value (what they would sell for if they were sold today), assets purchased years ago—as were a substantial percentage of current American-owned assets abroad—are likely to be undervalued relative to more recently purchased assets. Current market values can only be estimated, but most estimates place the value of American-owned assets abroad, as of 1990, above the value of foreign-owned assets in the United States.

[2] Most attention focused on the Japanese. But by 1990, British holdings in the U.S. far exceeded Japanese. In the first half of 1990 alone, the British purchased $7.9 billion of American assets; the French, $5.7 billion; the Japanese, only $3.8 billion. *The New York Times*, July 17, 1990, p. D2.

pany, in the form of shares. All else being equal, a profitable American-owned company is better for Americans than a profitable foreign-owned company, for the obvious reason that Americans get the profits. But all else is seldom equal. Increasingly, American citizens also own shares of stock in companies whose dominant shareholders are foreign, and foreigners likewise own more and more stock of companies whose majority shareholders are American. The typical American investor may gain higher returns from owning, say, one-third of the shares of two successful Japanese firms than by owning a majority of the shares of a single, somewhat less successful American firm.

Following this logic, Americans in 1989 were investing about 10 percent of their portfolios in foreign securities, and the percentage was increasing precipitously. That year, cross-border equity investments by Americans, British, Japanese, and West Germans increased by 20 percent over 1988.[3] Rather than bar such investments, governments were beginning to encourage them. The Japanese and British removed most barriers to the free flow of capital across their borders at the start of the 1980s; France and Italy, in 1986. Some governments still prevented foreigners from buying a majority of the shares of companies headquartered within their borders, but nonnationals could participate nonetheless via a baffling array of mutual funds.[4] Meanwhile, twenty-four-hour electronic-trading networks linking New York, London, Tokyo, and Bonn were transforming the very meaning of a "national" stock exchange. Already Wall Street brokers such as Morgan Stanley, Merrill Lynch, and Goldman Sachs were members of the Tokyo Stock Exchange. And within a few years, a

---

[3] By 1989, cross-border equity investing climbed to $1.6 trillion, or about 14.5 percent of world stock turnover. One transaction out of seven involved a foreign investor, and over 7 percent of the aggregate value of the world stock market was held by foreign investors. See "Cross Border Investments," Salomon Brothers, July 1990.

[4] By the start of the 1990s, American investors could invest overseas through global mutual funds (investing anywhere around the globe), international funds (investing only outside the United States), regional funds (focusing on Europe or Asia), single-country funds (specializing in the stocks of companies headquartered in certain countries), and depository receipts (representing claims on foreign shares held in safekeeping for U.S. investors by financial institutions).

single global clearinghouse for internationally traded equity shares will cause cross-border equity investments to surge even further. Gone forever are the days when an American President could avoid financial panic simply by waiting to deliver unpleasant news to the nation until after the New York Stock Exchange had closed for the day. Today's news, good and bad, is instantly received and reacted to by the world's financial markets.

Cross-border investing is undertaken quietly, without fanfare. The average American investor, assigning his or her savings to a mutual fund, insurance fund, or pension plan, is unaware of owning small portions of companies with foreign-sounding names, headquartered in exotic places. But the people who manage the funds, and who compete furiously to be able to show that they are more successful than other fund managers, are increasingly scouring the globe to find good investment prospects for their clients. Between 1985 and 1990, the bullish U.S. stock market rose 147 percent, but it still lagged behind fourteen other international stock markets, as measured in total returns in U.S. dollars.[5] In consequence, net American purchases of foreign shares of stock surged from $4.2 billion in 1985 to $13.7 billion in 1989.[6] A 1989 survey of pension fund managers revealed that most of them planned to be investing a quarter of their portfolios in foreign securities during the 1990s.[7]

In sum, the total return to American investors from their equity investments no longer depends on the success of firms whose dominant shareholders happen to be Americans. It depends, rather, on two other factors: first, and most obviously, on the total amount that Americans invest (regardless of where the companies they invest in are headquartered and who owns most of them); second, on the care and wisdom with which such worldwide portfolios of investments have been compiled.

---

[5] A dollar invested in the Austrian stock market in 1985 would have returned $6.97 by 1990; Belgium, $5.51; Spain, $5.11; Japan, $4.66. *Morgan Stanley Capital International Study*, January 1990.

[6] Securities Industry Association, 1990.

[7] L. Birinyi, Jr., *International Equity Analysis* (New York: Salomon Brothers, 1989).

3

QUITE apart from who gets the profits, there has been a concern about who controls the corporation. Even if foreign executives hire Americans and give them good-paying jobs, can we be assured that they will continue to do so? They might suddenly withdraw their investments from the United States and leave us stranded, or so the often implied argument goes.

This argument is based on a curious assumption, however. It presupposes that American-owned corporations—in contrast to foreign-owned corporations—will subordinate their shareholders' interests to what is good for the United States. By this view, an American-owned corporation is more likely than a foreign-owned corporation to refrain from shifting production abroad, even when profits depend on it. This is a charming, but, again, naïvely vestigial thought, harking back to midcentury, when the core American corporation had tacit obligations (enforced by the threat of both strikes and government intrusions) to balance the needs of the American public against the faintly audible demands of shareholders, and when, more often than not, these interests neatly coincided.

By the last decade of the century, however, global competition had altered the tacit rules of American capitalism. No longer could American corporations count on the quiet cooperation of other American producers in the same industry to maintain prices and thus generate healthy earnings. Nor were shareholders as content as before to let executives manage as they wished. The dispersed individual shareholders of yore had been supplanted by the professional investment manager, willing to shift funds quickly from one corporation to another depending on whose share prices were rising or falling at the moment. The "corporate statesman" had gone the way of the Edsel. American capitalism was now organized relentlessly around profits, not patriotism. When profitability requires that production be shifted from an American factory to a foreign one, the American executive hesitates not.

In fact, the top executives of American corporations are among the loudest in the world in declaring that their job is to maximize shareholder returns, not to advance public goals. "The United States does not have an automatic call on our resources," noted a top executive of Colgate-Palmolive in 1989. "There is no mind-set that puts this country first."[8] American corporate executives do worry about the strength of the American economy, but only insofar as the American market is a source of their corporate revenues—and in this respect they are no different from the executives of foreign-owned firms who sell their goods in the American market. Says one top IBM executive, "IBM has to be concerned with the competitiveness and well-being of any country or region that is a major source of IBM revenue."[9]

This is not to suggest that the top executives of American-owned corporations are lacking in patriotism. The transformation of their companies into global enterprise webs may even disturb them. "[T]o the extent a company can keep its best stuff at home, it will do so," claimed Motorola's vice president for international strategy, with obvious conviction.[10] That Motorola goes abroad for the semiconductors, pagers, and many of the advanced electronic systems that find their way into the products Motorola sells in the United States and around the world may trouble this worthy gentleman. But were the top executives of Motorola or any other American-owned firm to sacrifice profits for the sake of the national interest by making or buying things in America that they could make or buy better and more cheaply elsewhere, the executives would be vulnerable to takeover by financial entrepreneurs with fewer patriotic scruples who could thus assure shareholders a higher return on their investment. Alternatively, such public-spirited executives would be liable for breach of fiduciary responsibility to their shareholders.

Nor, in this new global economy, is it clear, in any event, how the top executives of American-owned corporations could be made to take on such national responsibilities. Regulations governing how corporations should operate in the United States are applicable to *all* firms doing business here, regardless of the nationality of their shareholders. The American system has no special means of alerting the top executives of American-owned (as

---

[8]Quoted in L. Uchitelle, "U.S. Businesses Loosen Link to Mother Country," *The New York Times*, May 28, 1989, p. A1.
[9]Quoted in L. Uchitelle, "Global Strategies vs. National Ties," *The New York Times*, March 26, 1990, p. D2.
[10]Ibid.

opposed to foreign-owned) corporations to the existence of public goals, or of mandating that they pursue these goals. In fact, were American-owned corporations subject to special burdens and obligations, they would be put at a distinct disadvantage relative to foreign-owned companies doing business in the United States, who would be free to maximize their profits—a point which the top executives of American-owned companies have not been reluctant to stress repeatedly before Congress and government agencies.[11]

4

THE RAPID globalization of the American-owned corporation does not inhibit America's top corporate executives from conspicuous displays within the United States of good corporate citizenship or proclamations of deep and abiding commitment to the public interest. Sensible executives recognize the value of highly visible donations to local schools and hospitals, contributions to finding cures for dread diseases, and sponsorship of British television programs on Public Broadcasting. All improve the corporation's public image and thus help sell its products. (That the corporation's lobbyists in Washington and state capitals simultaneously demand tax breaks of far greater magnitude—which imperil the financing of public schools, hospitals, medical research, public television, and much else—is beside the point. Corporate munificence is a high-profile affair. Lobbying for huge tax breaks is, conveniently, far less so.)

Naturally, foreign-owned firms doing business in America are equally desirous of cultivating a good public image in the United States. In fact, they may be even more motivated, given the widespread presumption that because of their nationality they are not good American citizens. In recent years Japanese companies have

---

[11]The interested reader is invited to examine the periodic debates over the Foreign Corrupt Practices Act, which bars American corporations from bribing foreign officials, or debates over regulations preventing American corporations from exporting certain militarily sensitive technologies to the Soviet Union and its allies.

hired scores of American public relations specialists to advise them on which American charities to support and to what degree.[12] Natural disasters on American soil present wonderful opportunities for high-visibility generosity. In 1989, following Hurricane Hugo and the San Francisco Bay earthquake, several Japanese firms purchased full-page advertisements in American newspapers solemnly announcing their donations to the victims. At the present rate of giving, according to "Corporate Philanthropy Report," by 1994 Japanese corporations are expected to be contributing about $1 billion to American charities, which will comprise about 8 percent of total corporate donations in the United States.[13]

American-owned corporations operating abroad feel a similar compulsion to act as good citizens in their host countries. Whatever the genuine motivations of its American executives, the firm cannot afford to be seen as playing favorites by promoting American interests; allowing such a perception to arise would needlessly jeopardize its relationships with foreign workers, consumers, and governments. Some of America's top managers have been quite explicit on this point. "IBM must be a good citizen everywhere it does business," said Jack Kueler, IBM's president.[14] Robert H. Galvin, chairman of Motorola, is even blunter: Should it become necessary for Motorola to close some of its factories, it would not close its Southeast Asian plants before it closed its American ones. "We need our Far Eastern customers," said Galvin in a burst of cosmopolitanism, "and we cannot alienate the Malaysians. We must treat our employees all over the world equally."[15]

The cosmopolitan corporation, eager to avoid the appearance of national favoritism and desirous of a familiar and reliable image wherever it does business, also hires and promotes citizens of many nations to its executive ranks. The ineluctable trend is toward multinational and multilingual teams of

---

[12] At this writing, the Japanese government has even allowed Japanese-owned corporations to deduct charitable contributions made in the United States from their taxable income in Japan.

[13] See Craig Smith, editor of "Corporate Philanthropy Report," quoted in *The Chronicle of Higher Education*, November 8, 1989, p. A-34.

[14] Telephone interview, March 6, 1988.

[15] Uchitelle, "U.S. Businesses Loosen Link to Mother Country."

strategic brokers at the center of global webs—drawn from Europe, North America, the Far East, and other major markets. IBM prides itself on having eleven different nationalities represented among its highest officer ranks and three among its directors. Sony is not too far behind. Corporations that are reluctant to consider foreign nationals for top positions have difficulty recruiting the best talent from around the world into their enterprise webs, for the obvious reason that talented people will not join an organization that holds out no promise of promotion.[16]

Just as empty is the concern that foreign-owned companies might leave the United States stranded by suddenly abandoning their American operations. The typical argument suggests that foreign-owned firms might withdraw because of profit or foreign-policy considerations. But either way, the bricks and mortar would remain in the United States, as would the equipment. So, too, would the accumulated learning gained by the firm's American employees. Under such circumstances, capital from another source surely would rush in to finance these attractive assets. An American (or another foreign) company would simply buy the facilities. Most important, the American work force would remain, with its skills and capabilities intact and ready to work.

After all, the American government retains jurisdiction over assets located within the United States. Unlike foreign assets held by American-owned companies, which are subject to foreign control and, occasionally, foreign expropriation, foreign-owned assets in the United States are secure against sudden changes in the policies of foreign governments. During World War II, Ford's German subsidiary dutifully produced trucks for the Nazis.[17] What is in the United States is indubitably under America's political control, should the need arise; what is outside, indubitably is not.

---

[16] As of 1990, most other Japanese corporations are still far behind Sony in this respect. Directors and top officers of Japanese corporations are uniformly Japanese. This insularity is a handicap to the Japanese in global commerce, and will become more so.

[17] R. Vernon, "Multinational Enterprise and National Security," *Adelphi Papers*, 74 (London: Institute for Strategic Studies, 1985).

5

WHY, THEN, do foreigners come here? If ownership and control are less and less potent, why do they nevertheless purchase American assets? Because they think they can make better use of American assets—including American workers—than can American firms.

It is true, of course, that the dollar dropped relative to foreign currencies in the late 1980s, turning American assets suddenly into cheap bargains. But this is no explanation for the surge of foreign investors. The cheaper dollar simultaneously reduced the value of the profits expected to be generated by the American assets—thus canceling out any perceived bargain. The fact is that foreign investment in the United States increased steadily throughout the 1970s and 1980s, whether the dollar was high or low, whether America was a creditor or a debtor. The two leading foreign investors in the United States during most of the 1970s and 1980s were the British and the Dutch—not the Japanese and the West Germans, whose trade surpluses were the counterparts of America's trade deficits. Even by 1990, the total of British investment in the United States was still twice that of the Japanese.

Nor are foreign-owned firms coming to America mainly because they fear that the United States otherwise will close off its market to their exports. Most foreign investments in the United States are unrelated to products that have been protected or are likely to be in the future. And even when related, the investments appear to be motivated by economic rather than political concerns. For example, when in 1988 Nissan's sales in the United States dropped sharply, the firm could have cut production in its American factories and fully supplied the American market from its quota of Japanese-made imports. But it chose not to. In fact, it did just the opposite—slashing its Japanese imports by more than 50,000 cars, while reducing its American-made output by only 7,000. Even when it was allowed to supply the American market from Japan, Nissan preferred to manufacture automobiles in the United States.[18]

---

[18] Robert Z. Lawrence, *Japanese-Affiliated Automakers in the United States* (Washington, D.C.: Brookings Institution, 1989).

Regardless of the value of the dollar or the likelihood of protectionist barriers around the U.S., a foreign-owned firm will come to the United States only if it can make a profit here—that is, only if it has an advantage over American-owned firms already operating in the United States which will more than compensate the foreign firm for the extra cost of operating far from home. So the main reason why foreigners bring their money and strategic-brokering skills to the United States is the same reason Americans invest their money and strategic-brokering skills abroad: because they think they can utilize the *other* nation's assets and its workers better than that nation's investors and managers can—rendering the assets and workers more productive than before.[19]

With regard to American assets and workers, the evidence suggests that many foreigners have judged correctly. For example, the increasing dominance of Japanese automakers within the United States is due largely to the fact that they have been able to utilize American workers to make a higher-quality car, in less time, than can American-owned automakers. Although the 1990 *Consumer Reports* ranks most Japanese cars higher in quality than American cars, it finds no difference between the quality of Japanese cars produced in the United States and the quality of Japanese cars made in Japan.[20] Further, Japanese automotive factories in the United States are almost as productive as they are in Japan, and far more productive than American-owned factories. John Krafcik of MIT's International Motor Vehicles Program found that Americans working in Japanese-owned plants could assemble a car in about 19.5 hours—just a bit more than the 19.1 hours averaged by Japanese workers, but far less than the 26.5 hours averaged by American workers in American-owned factories.[21] After Toyota took over the management of General Motors' factory in Fremont, California, in 1984, productivity soared by 50

---

[19]There is one strategic advantage to operating within your competitor's backyard, even if you run a slight loss in doing so: You thereby prevent your competitor from charging a high price in its home market with which it might otherwise subsidize cutthroat pricing abroad. Of course, if your foreign competitor already competes fiercely in its home market, there is no particular reason to embark on such a costly strategy.

[20]*Consumer Reports*, May, 1990.

[21]John F. Krafcik, "The Triumph of the Lean Production System," *Sloan Management Review* 41, Vol. 30, No. 1 (Fall 1988).

percent over what it had been under GM's managers. Absenteeism had been as high as 25 percent under GM management; under Toyota, absenteeism fell to 3 to 4 percent.[22] A similar transformation occurred when Japan's Bridgestone took over Firestone's ailing U.S. tire factories.[23] In both instances, notably, the work force remained the same; the only pertinent difference was the exchange of American management and capital for Japanese.

American workers have benefited considerably from all this, even if American-owned companies have not. Foreign-owned firms pay their American workers higher wages than American-owned firms in the same industry.[24] The Japanese also have been spending about $1,000 more on training each American worker than is spent by American employers in the same industry.[25] Were American workers able to choose the more reliable set of strategic brokers and investors on which to depend for their future well-being—American executives and Wall Street financiers, on the one hand, or Japanese executives and Tokyo bankers, on the other—they would not be unwise to opt for the latter.

Foreigners whose strategic-brokering skills are superior to those of Americans can earn healthy profits in the United States in ways other than buying up American companies or opening

---

[22] H. Shimada and J. P. MacDuffie, "Industrial Relations and 'Humanware': Japanese investments in Automobile Manufacturing in the United States," briefing paper for the 1987 International Motor Vehicles Program, Massachusetts Institute of Technology, 1987, p. 91.

[23] Between 1989 and 1992, Bridgestone planned to invest more than $1 billion in its U.S. factories, to develop the next generation of radial passenger tires. "The order of magnitude is close to twice what Firestone could have invested as an independent company," John J. Nevin, Firestone's chairman, told *The New York Times*. See John P. Hicks, "Foreign Owners Are Shaking Up the Competition," *The New York Times*, May 28, 1989, p. D9.

[24] In 1986 (the last year for which such data are available), the average American employee of a foreign-owned manufacturing firm earned $32,887, while the average American employee of an American-owned manufacturer earned $28,945. See Bureau of Economic Analysis, *Foreign Direct Investment in the U.S.: Operations of U.S. Affiliates* (Washington, D.C.: U.S. Department of Commerce, 1988), for data on foreign companies; for U.S. companies, U.S. Bureau of the Census, *Annual Survey of Manufacturing Statistics for Industry Groups and Industries, 1986* (Washington, D.C.: U.S. Government Printing Office, 1987).

[25] Lawrence, op. cit.

their own factories in America, of course. They can, for example, sell their management insights directly. In years to come we can expect more American-owned corporations to hire Japanese companies to run their American factories and laboratories, in return for which the Japanese will receive a share of the resulting profits. (This was precisely the agreement between General Motors and Toyota for managing GM's Fremont facility.) One virtue of this arrangement is that it may reduce the discomfort felt by many Americans who cling to the vestigial view of the economy. No longer are foreigners perceived to be "taking over" American assets; instead, they are more accurately perceived as helping Americans to become more productive. Of course, the underlying transaction is virtually identical; whether the Japanese own the facility outright or manage it for a share in the final profits proportional to the value they add to the operation, they will earn roughly the same amount.

6

THE SHIFT from high volume to high value also bears upon the issue of foreign ownership and control and whether it should be a matter of public concern. As has been observed, whatever degree of power resided in ownership and control of the high-volume firm has been substantially diminished in the high-value enterprise. Because the high-value enterprise is based on insights, the highest returns and the greatest leverage belong to skilled people within the web (including key licensees, partners, or subcontractors) rather than to shareholders or executives occupying formal positions of authority. Top executives may play an important role in organizing the overall web, of course, but most key decisions occur at lower and more decentralized points. So long as key problem-solvers, -identifiers, and brokers are Americans residing in the United States, it is of little significance which nation's citizens formally own, or preside at the top of, the enterprise. By the same token, if these key people are not Americans, it is of little help to the nation that the formal owners and top executives of the enterprise are. Whoever in the web possesses the most valuable skills and insights will receive the largest rewards, whether in the form of salaries, bonuses, licensing fees, or partnership shares.

To illustrate the point, consider Sony's purchases in 1988 and 1989 of CBS Records and Columbia Pictures, respectively—in what appeared to be a double-barreled assault on American popular culture. But what, exactly, did Sony buy? Very little, apart from the right to resell old recordings and films and the title to some real estate and equipment. The future earnings of CBS Records and Columbia Pictures—their potential value in the world economy—depends far more on the talents and insights of American vocalists, sound technicians, directors, producers, actors and actresses, cinematographers, designers, songwriters, scriptwriters, advertisers and marketers, and hundreds of other creative people.

The talented Americans who had before worked for CBS Records did not suddenly lose their skills and insights when Sony bought the two companies; nor did their talents become any less valuable than they were before the transaction. The sale did not put Bruce Springsteen—one of CBS's star vocalists, who had once belted out "Born in the USA"—under the ownership and control of the Japanese. Springsteen was as autonomous, and at least as valuable, after the transaction as he was before. The only change in his life was that more of the financial capital and strategic brokering linking him to the world market now came from Japan. Springsteen had, in effect, exchanged Laurence Tisch (the financial entrepreneur who had taken over CBS several years before) for Akio Morita (Sony's chairman). If Morita and other Japanese strategic brokers did a better job than Tisch and company of linking Springsteen to the world market, the singer's world audience would be larger and more appreciative than previously, and his compensation would increase accordingly. In fact, by 1990, CBS Records was surging forward—as its Japanese strategic brokers spent far more on promotions, MTV videos, and other tie-ins than had their tightfisted predecessors. It may well be asked: Did Sony buy Springsteen or did Springsteen buy into Sony?

When in the following year Sony paid $3.4 billion to the American shareholders of Columbia Pictures for the privilege of rescuing this lackluster studio from the economic doldrums, it obtained, of course, the rights to resell *The Wizard of Oz* and many other old Hollywood favorites. But Columbia Pictures' key assets were its relationships with a large number of talented people—among them, Peter Guber and Jon Peters, who, having produced

Batman and *Rain Man*, were considered the hottest moviemaking team in Hollywood. Guber and Peters did not come easy or cheap, however. The producers' relationship with Columbia had apparently soured, causing them to jump ship and sign on with Warner Bros., a competing studio. So in order to recapture this dynamic duo, Sony first had to pay Warner Bros. to break their contract, then strike a blockbuster deal with Guber and Peters—buying their production company for $55 million, agreeing to give them and their partners an additional $2.75 million for each of the next five years plus a share of studio profits, plus shares of a one-time $50 million bonus, plus a share in any increase in Columbia Pictures' assessed value. In considering Sony and its pricey American talent, the same question arises: Exactly who bought whom? The "human capital" of Columbia Pictures, which is its most valuable asset, continues to be firmly under the "control" of Americans.

7

ARE FOREIGNERS buying up America's technology? Should we be concerned? The same logic applies. When foreign money and strategic brokerage are added to American problem solving and identifying, the result may be better for Americans than before. Consider three small American high-tech companies that were purchased by foreigners in 1989: After a twelve-year, $200 million effort to become the world's leader in photovoltaic technology, Arco Solar (a subsidiary of Atlantic Richfield, the large American oil company) was sold to West Germany's Siemens; Atlantic Richfield did not want to continue investing in Arco Solar without more assurance that big profits were imminent. Some of the stock of International Fuel Cells Corporation of South Windsor, Connecticut, the world leader in fuel-cell technology, was sold to Japan's Toshiba and Tokyo Electric, after its parent, United Technologies, refused to sink any more money into it. And Materials Research of Orangeburg, New York—a semiconductor equipment firm—was sold to Sony, after Wall Street's best offer was still well below the firm's book value. Clearly, there are no grounds for blaming the West Germans or Japanese for making these purchases, since the American owners were eager to sell.

Should, then, these transactions trouble us? While they surely exemplify the shortsightedness of American finance and strategic brokerage, we should be clear about who gains and loses by them.

Superficially, it appears as if foreigners are buying up America's leading-edge technologies, leaving the nation in the lurch. But this is not true. America is not losing these technologies. Look closely at Arco Solar, International Fuel Cells, and Materials Research, and what do you find? Groups of American problem-solvers and -identifiers—scientists, inventors, technicians, marketers—who have been accumulating potentially valuable insights about how to produce highly efficient solar energy, fuel cells, and semiconductor equipment, respectively. By "acquiring" them, the foreign-owned firms did not destroy this cumulative learning. That would have wiped out the value of these investments. Nor did the foreign firms enslave these Americans and ship them back to West Germany and Japan, or impound their notes and send *them* back. These problem-solvers and -identifiers had no intention of leaving the United States, and the potential value of their learning continues to reside in their heads, not in their notes. Indeed, these people remain here in the United States and continue to improve on their inventions here.

The only thing that has changed is that most of the money they need in order to pay for their laboratories and equipment and the fabrication and testing of their inventions, and their salaries, now comes from West Germany and Japan instead of the United States. And, importantly, it comes with fewer and less urgent demands for short-term profits. After Sony bought Materials Research, for example, the American president of the company finally felt free to pursue long-term research. "I'm no longer concerned with quarterly profits," he said, with great relief. "I can think of projects that take two years. It's a wonderful way to live."[26]

---

[26]Quoted in *The Wall Street Journal*, August 16, 1989, p. B4. Similar relief was expressed by the president of Genentech, America's largest biotechnology company, when the firm was sold to Switzerland's Roche Holdings Ltd. at the start of 1990. "We have so much we want to do. The quarterly pressures of the stock market, though real and understandable, inevitably inhibit the brain trust here on this 30 acres." Quoted in *The Wall Street Journal*, February 5, 1990, p. A3.

To be sure, West German and Japanese investors will share in whatever profits these gadgets bring in from around the world, rather than the shareholders of Atlantic Richfield, United Technologies, or various venture-capital funds. Further, it will be a few German and Japanese strategic brokers at the center of these webs, rather than Americans in the corporate headquarters of Atlantic Richfield or United Technologies, who help find people around the world to manufacture, market, and distribute the inventions.

But to view these transactions as losses of American technology is to indulge, once again, in vestigial thought. The primary value in these technologies lies in the skills and insights needed to create and refine them. These skills and insights are still American; Americans continue to develop the technologies, and are well compensated for doing so. That some of the profits now go to investors and strategic brokers outside the United States should not cause Americans great alarm. American investors and strategic brokers are simultaneously working the other side of the same street, busily combing the rest of the world for good investment prospects and opportunities to contract with people of all nations to solve and identify new problems, as well as to undertake high-volume, standardized production.

What, then, does it mean to "lose" American technology? Not what is commonly supposed. New inventions are constantly disseminated around the world from American laboratories, in the form of blueprints, codes, specifications, and instructions. They reach design engineers in Rome, fabricators in Kuala Lumpur, assemblers in Hong Kong, and markets in London as fast as they reach St. Louis. This is true regardless of who—Japanese, West Germans, or Americans—"owns" the firm: Strategic brokers working with Arco Solar, International Fuel Cells, and Materials Research will ship the inventions to whoever around the world can produce and market them cheapest and best. New information quickly becomes part of worldwide webs.

What remains behind are the skills and insights necessary to *continue* to invent. These are a nation's key technological assets. They are lost only if insufficiently nurtured and developed. In these three cases, had foreigners not stepped in to provide financing and brokering, the accumulated learning might well have been squandered.

8

To CLAIM that corporate nationality is becoming irrelevant is emphatically not to argue that, in the global economy toward which we are rapidly heading, national economic interests have ceased to exist or ceased to matter. The distinction is important. The Japanese, South Koreans, Taiwanese, West Germans, and Dutch, among many others, are acutely aware of their national economic interests, although they continue to invest beyond their borders. In so doing, each nation is striving to enhance the well-being and security of its citizens. Accordingly, each is trying to increase the potential value of what their citizens can contribute to global webs of enterprise.

Such an ambition should not be regarded as a threat to the well-being and security of Americans. To the contrary, these efforts add to the total wealth of the world. America should pursue the same worthy goal. It is just that the corporation has become an awkward means of achieving it. Nations can no longer substantially enhance the wealth of their citizens by subsidizing, protecting, or otherwise increasing the profitability of "their" corporations; the connection between corporate profitability and the standard of living of a nation's people is growing ever more attenuated. The following chapter should help illuminate the difference.

13

The Perils
of Vestigial Thought

When I want to keep my dividends up, you will discover
that my want is a national need.

ANDREW UNDERSHAFT, in *Major Barbara*,
by G. B. Shaw (1905)

TWO POINTS bear repeating. First: The standard of living of a
nation's people increasingly depends on what they contribute to
the world economy—on the value of their skills and insights. It
depends less and less on what they own—on the profitability of
companies in which they have major stakes. Second: The skills
involved in problem-solving, problem-identifying, and strategic
brokering improve with experience. People learn by doing. Together, the two points suggest a simple truth. A foreign-owned
firm (or, more precisely, a group of foreign investors and strategic
brokers) that contracts with Americans to solve or identify complex problems helps Americans far more than does an American-
owned firm that contracts with foreigners to do the same.

This truth may be simple, but it has been lost on policy makers
and on the American public. Nowhere has the power of vestigial
thought been more evident than among Washington officials who
are determined to restrict foreign ownership of American assets
and limit government largesse to corporations that fly the American flag. Here is one illustration of the tendency: In 1986, Fujitsu,
the large Japanese electronics company, announced that it would
buy Fairchild Semiconductor Corporation—one of Silicon Valley's
preeminent high-technology firms. Fairchild needed cash in order
to stay competitive, so its executives had approached Fujitsu. But

the proposed sale was greeted with dismay in Washington. Fairchild's designers and engineers fashioned high-speed electronic circuits on tiny silicon chips which guide the operations of all sorts of weapons systems. Between a third and a half of Fairchild's production was sold to American defense contractors. Thus, Pentagon officials worried that the proposed sale would put critical technology into the hands of the Japanese. Officials in the Commerce Department were concerned that the deal would give Fujitsu control over related chip technologies that are used in many American products, from automobiles to telecommunications equipment, at a time when American competitiveness was thought to be in jeopardy. So worried were officials of the Reagan administration that—Adam Smith neckties and free-market rhetoric notwithstanding—they suggested to Fujitsu that it might think it wise to reconsider the purchase. And so courteous was Fujitsu that it withdrew its offer.

Niceties aside, this was a mistake. Not only could Fujitsu have been an important source of capital for Fairchild, but its Japanese engineers were ahead of Fairchild's in knowing how to produce many complex memory chips. Making advanced memory chips was a skill that Fairchild's American engineers needed to develop. The purchase would not have destroyed whatever learning Fairchild's engineers had accumulated to date; it would have supplemented it. Nationality of ownership should have been irrelevant. Ironically, Fairchild was not even an "American" company at the time. It had been bought in 1979 by Schlumberger, the French oil field services firm.

2

CENTRAL to such handwringing in Washington has been concern over American dependence on Japanese firms producing microelectronic devices that lie at the heart of military weapons systems as well as cars, televisions, and almost every other complex gadget imaginable. Throughout the 1980s, hundreds of commissions and panels issued solemn warnings about Japan's surging strength in microelectronics. Typical was a National Security Council report in April 1987 warning of the American military's increasing reliance on Japanese firms, as well as issuing ominous forecasts about the American economy in general. "By the turn of the century, microelectronics will certainly have major direct effects upon the performance of industries which will directly account for perhaps a quarter of GNP, and which have powerful effects upon military capabilities, economy-wide productivity, and living standards. These include automobiles, industrial automation, computer systems, defense and aerospace products, telecommunications, and many consumer goods. . . . If the United States loses competitive advantage in these industries, its productivity, living standards, and growth will suffer severely." The immediate danger, according to the NSC report, was that Japanese high-tech firms could withhold their advanced chips and related technologies from American firms that had become dependent on them, and could thus "impede the ability of the United States to compete in almost any area of manufacturing."[1]

Note the slippery logic. When the National Security Council (NSC) warned of "Japan's" growing strengths and the "United States" losing competitive advantage, it was referring, presumably, to Japanese and American corporations. But recall that American-owned firms are researching, designing, and fabricating some of the highest of their high technologies in Japan, while Japanese-owned firms are doing ever more of their complex work in the United States. Consequently, there is coming to be less difference between the two, in terms of where their work forces are located around the world and what sort of work they do. America is surely more "secure," in the sense of access to critical technologies in the event of war, by having Americans learn to do complex things on American soil (even if the firm they work for happens to be owned by the Japanese) than by having foreign citizens learn to do complex things on foreign soil (even if the firm they work for is owned by Americans). If the United States wants to be assured, for purposes of national security, of possessing a critical technology on American soil, the logical step would be to encourage global en-

---

[1] National Security Council, *Draft Report on Military Dependency on Foreign Technologies*, April 1987, pp. 5–6. See also *Defense Semiconductor Dependency*, Report of the Defense Science Board Task Force, Office of the Under Secretary of Defense for Acquisition, February 1987, p. 1. "[A] direct threat to the technological superiority deemed essential to U.S. defense systems exists."

terprise webs to design and develop it in the United States—not to bar foreign firms or investors from America.

Should the United States nevertheless be concerned about the possibility that a foreign-owned firm in America might withhold a critical technology if its home government instructed it to do so? European governments became dramatically aware of this possibility in 1982, when, in response to Poland's imposition of martial law, the Reagan administration prohibited the European subsidiaries of American-owned firms from fulfilling contracts to build a gas pipeline to Europe from the Soviet Union. The risk is real, but it is reduced considerably by the fact that no global corporation wants a reputation for unreliability. The American subsidiaries that obeyed Washington's command in 1982 saw their subsequent European business decline precipitously, as Europeans shifted to other vendors who could be counted on in a pinch. Even the reputations of American subsidiaries not directly involved were tarnished; the possibility that Washington might try to impose its will on them rendered them less reliable as well, in the eyes of their European customers. As a result, American-owned corporations suffered considerable losses, and the Reagan administration bore much of the responsibility. Such consequences operate as a powerful disincentive upon governments that might otherwise try to assert control over the global operations of enterprises headquartered within their nations. As global corporations are transformed into ever more decentralized webs, moreover, the capacity of governments to assert such control is greatly diminished. A subsidiary that markets or distributes what its parent company produces is clearly dependent on headquarters, and thus susceptible to foreign control; a more independent firm, working within an enterprise web and contracting with strategic brokers at the center, is far less so.[2]

Despite all this, the NSC report, and several others which followed, prompted Congress, in 1988, to make official what had been only informal resistance to foreign ownership. The Omnibus Trade Act, signed into law that year, allowed the United States

---

[2] For a lucid discussion of a nation's stake in maintaining control over its defense base, see Theodore H. Moran, "The Globalization of America's Defense Industries: What's the Threat? How Can It Be Managed?," School of Foreign Service, Georgetown University, October 1989.

government to block foreign investors from obtaining a controlling interest in an American company. A high-level Committee on Foreign Investment in the United States, comprising the heads of eight federal agencies and chaired by the Secretary of the Treasury, could thereafter decide that a proposed purchase threatened to "impair the national security."

On the surface, this requirement seems quite sensible. Why *shouldn't* high-level officials screen out purchases that threaten national security? Probe a bit deeper and the problem becomes apparent. What does "national security" mean? Congress did not say. In principle, a nation sacrifices a bit of "security" when it becomes dependent on foreigners for anything. Albania, which refuses trade with the West and eschews money, technology, and everything else the rest of the world has to offer, is quite secure, in its own curious way. Then again, its citizens transport their wares in oxcarts and live in hovels. Complete security is equivalent to autarky. But autarky deprives a nation's citizens of all of the advantages of economic interdependence with the wider world. You cannot have it both ways.

Upon what evidence, then, should the committee base its decision? On how much money the foreigners are willing to sink into a risky American venture, which, presumably, American financiers have shunned? Or on how desperate Americans are for this foreign aid? Or, perhaps, on how much wealthier the foreigners will be in the event that the venture succeeds? If foreigners are not dissuaded from pursuing American investments by the sheer uncertainty and complexity of such a proceeding, they may still lose heart when they consider the fees they will have to pay Washington lawyers to help them run this gauntlet.[3]

Other nations have erected their own barriers to foreign investment, of course, based on similarly misguided notions about national security and the meaning of corporate "ownership" in the global economy. Many of these barriers are falling, however. By the start of the 1990s, places as diverse as Mexico and China, which had long limited foreign direct investment, were actively courting it. Even Japan's traditional wariness of foreign investors

---

[3] According to one government official involved with the committee, "We could become the ultimate takeover defense." *The Wall Street Journal*, March 8, 1989, p. A16.

was starting to give way, although slowly. In any event, that other nations handicap themselves by discouraging foreign investment is not a compelling argument for following their lead.

3

THE SAME confusion mars government efforts to spur America into "technologies of the future," such as advanced semiconductors and high-definition television. Recall that through the postwar era the Pentagon has quietly been in charge of helping American corporations move ahead with technologies like jet engines, airframes, transistors, integrated circuits, new materials, lasers, and optic fibers. This tacit, however benign, industrial policy accelerated under the Reagan administration, as America's military buildup proceeded apace. And even as the Cold War thawed, Pentagon funding of high technology remained among its most important sources of capital. The Pentagon and the 600 national laboratories that work with it and with the Department of Energy are the closest thing America has to Japan's well-known Ministry of International Trade and Industry.[4]

This system worked reasonably well when American corporations represented the American economy. In the 1950s, the 1960s, and even the 1970s, there was reason to equate the technological advances of American firms with American economic prowess. But by the 1980s the equation was breaking down, with the result that the subsidies now given to American corporations to develop new technologies have less and less bearing on what Americans learn to do.

Consider the fingernail-sized chips on which ever tinier electronic circuits are etched. By the end of the 1980s, Japanese-owned firms were making most of the world's memory chips,

---

[4] At this writing, the Bush administration has displayed somewhat less interest in, if not hostility toward, several of the Pentagon's more overt efforts to target certain high technologies of the future, like high-definition television. Support for these efforts remains strong in Congress, however. And even if the administration were to reduce or eliminate some of these efforts, the Pentagon (and its sister agency, the Department of Energy) would continue to subsidize much of America's high-technology research and development.

which worried American officials no end.[5] Intent on strengthening America's chip-making abilities, they decided to provide $100 million a year to Sematech, a consortium of American semiconductor companies that would add their own resources as well, in order to design state-of-the-art equipment necessary for making the next generation of chips. Sematech's membership included Texas Instruments, Motorola, IBM, AT&T, and eight others. No foreign-owned firms, however, would be allowed to join. "We must re-establish our technological lead," said an administration official. According to the president of one of the companies involved in Sematech, "[t]his is our last chance. If we lose the ability to make this equipment in America, we might as well fold up the tent."[6]

In evaluating national policy, however, one is immediately confronted by the question posed by Tonto after the Lone Ranger exclaims, "We're surrounded!" To wit: "What you mean *we*, kemo sabe?" When American government and corporate officials use the pronoun "we," they are usually referring to American corporations. Yet, as we have seen, American corporations only tangentially embody "we" Americans.

Even as Sematech got underway, its members were weaving global webs. Texas Instruments (or, more accurately, the strategic brokers in TI's world headquarters) had decided to build a new $250 million semiconductor fabrication plant in Taiwan, which by 1991 would produce four-megabit memory chips and other integrated circuits. (TI's plant in Kywhyu, Japan, already made the firm among the largest semiconductor chip producers in Japan.) TI also had joined with Hitachi to design and produce "superchips" that would store 16 million bits of data. The strategic brokers in Motorola's world headquarters, meanwhile, had decided to seek the help of Toshiba's researchers and design engineers to produce a future generation of chips. Other American chip makers were forging similar global semiconductor links:

---

[5] "If this vital industry is allowed to wither away, the Nation will pay the price measured in millions of jobs across the entire electronics field, technological leadership in many allied industries such as telecommunications and computers, and the technical edge we depend on for national security." *A Strategic Industry at Risk*, National Advisory Committee on Semiconductors, November 1989.

[6] Interview.

AT&T with Japan's NEC and Mitsubishi Electric; Intel with Japan's NMB Semiconductor Company and Matsushita Group; IBM with West Germany's Siemens.

In other words, Sematech's noble nationalist intentions notwithstanding, the consortium was in fact little more than a partnership among several emerging global webs whose future would be only tangentially related to the future skills of Americans. Even if Sematech became a roaring success, relatively few Americans would be making advanced chips in the United States.

Ironically, just as Sematech was getting organized, the largest advanced-chip fabrication facility in the United States was being built by a Japanese company which hadn't been allowed to join. In June 1989, Japan's NEC announced that it would erect a $400 million facility in Rosevale, California, for making four-megabit memory chips and other advanced devices not yet in production anywhere.

Or consider high-definition television (HDTV). Since 1970, hundreds of Japanese design engineers have been trying to perfect ways to broadcast and receive far clearer television pictures than possible with current technology; for most of this time, Americans have not been trying. But beginning in 1988, several members of Congress and high-level administration officials decided that America should dive headlong into HDTV. Thus, the Pentagon began to funnel some $30 million annually to American firms wanting to develop it. Japan's Sony, Dutch-owned Philips, and France's Thompson all sought to be involved in this effort, but the Bush administration declined to issue an invitation. Robert Mosbacher, Secretary of Commerce, noted that the subsidies were strictly for American companies. "It is vitally important for *us* to be in the forefront of this emerging technology," he explained.[7]

But here again, the question arises: Whom did Mosbacher mean by "us"? Even if an American version of high-definition television were successfully launched, there is no reason to assume that many of the new televisions would be designed and manufactured in the United States. By 1989, Zenith Electronic Corporation was the only remaining American-owned television

---

[7] News conference, December 18, 1988. Emphasis added. The Bush administration subsequently expressed less enthusiasm for this project. See above, note 4.

manufacturer. It employed about 2,500 Americans, but many of its televisions were assembled in Mexico.

Zenith's American employees were not, however, the only Americans involved in designing and making televisions in the United States that year. In fact, more than 15,000 Americans were so engaged. The only difference between them and those who worked for Zenith was that the former group worked for Japanese-owned Sony and Matsushita, Dutch-owned Philips, and French-owned Thompson. Furthermore, some of these Americans were involved in researching and developing high-definition television. Philips, for example, had built a $100 million facility in the United States for making HDTV components and had teamed up with America's NBC and French-owned Thompson to develop an HDTV system for the United States. Matsushita also had created a U.S. research institute for HDTV; Sony was developing a prototype HDTV in San Jose, California. Meanwhile, several thousand other Americans were busy designing advanced computer chips for Japanese and European HDTV; they, too, were selling their skills and insights directly to the Japanese and the Europeans.

The point is that many Americans were gaining valuable experience in HDTV technologies—experience which, presumably, would be the foundation for whatever HDTV industry America would possess in future years. Indeed, their emerging skills and insights *were* America's HDTV industry. Paradoxically, however, because they did not work for American-owned corporations, none of these Americans was eligible to participate in the U.S. government program.

4

GOVERNMENT policy makers apparently view technologies as things that a nation's citizens "own," like gold mines, machines, or other tangibles. Thus, bolstering "our" technologies has seemed equivalent to enlarging the assets of American-owned firms, wherever on the earth these firms happen to be designing, making, and marketing their newfangled products, or whomever in the world they may contract with to supply such services. Policy makers have failed to understand that a nation's real technological assets are the capacities of its citizens to solve the complex problems of the future—which depend, in turn, on their experience in solving today's and yesterday's. Thus NEC's move to Rosevale for four-megabit semiconductors is of more lasting value to the nation than any operation that Texas Instruments, Motorola, or AT&T opens in some other nation. NEC's investment will build the technological experience of American engineers, technicians, and manufacturing workers more than an AT&T plant in Spain will build the technological experience of any Americans indirectly involved in that project. So, too, with Philips's HDTV components facilities in America, or Matsushita's HDTV research institute.

Money, plants, information, and equipment are footloose, along with corporate logos. Brains, however, are far less mobile internationally. Government policy makers should be less interested in helping American-owned companies earn hefty profits from new technologies than in helping *Americans* become technologically sophisticated. It makes perfect sense, then, to encourage Sony, Philips, Thompson, NEC, or any other global company to train Americans to design and make advanced semiconductors, high-definition televisions, complex parts for jet aircraft, and other exotica of the future. Invite them in; we need the training. By the same token, make government subsidies for technological development available to any corporation, regardless of the nationality of its owners—so long as the company agrees to undertake research, development, and fabrication in the United States, using American scientists, engineers, and technicians. To make the link even more explicit, the amount of government assistance could be tied to the number of Americans involved in the research, development, and engineering.

5

THE RECURRENT demand that foreigners open their markets to American companies suggests the same confusion. Periodically, the U.S. Trade Representative threatens to retaliate against a foreign nation that excludes an "American" product. At first glance, such threats seem appropriate. Why let them exclude us? But here again, it is necessary to examine carefully who is "us." American trade officials see their job as representing the interests of

companies that happen to carry the American flag—without regard to where they undertake actual production. And yet, there
is less reason to be concerned with opening foreign markets to
American-owned companies (which may be adding most of their
value overseas) than with opening those markets to companies
that employ Americans—even if the companies happen to be
foreign-owned.

To take one example: In early 1989 Carla Hills, U.S. Trade
Representative in the Bush administration, accused Japan of excluding Motorola from the lucrative Tokyo market for cellular
telephones and pagers. Japan duly loosened its restrictions. Oddly
enough, primary among the beneficiaries of Mrs. Hills's tough
talk were engineers and production workers in Kuala Lumpur,
Malaysia—where Motorola designed and made many of its pagers
and obtained several of its cellular phone components. Other beneficiaries were Motorola's shareholders, both in the United States
and abroad. These people were not unworthy of Mrs. Hills's attention; her unwitting concern for their welfare was commendable. But Mrs. Hills might better have expended her scarce
political capital urging the Japanese to reduce barriers to goods
and services actually produced in the United States, through which
Americans could accumulate hands-on expertise.

Even as Mrs. Hills made her charges, thousands of Americans
were making cellular telephone equipment in the United States
for export. Some of the components they designed or fabricated
found their way into telephones sold in the Tokyo market. But
the companies these Americans worked for were not of concern
to Mrs. Hills because they had Japanese names and received most
of their financing (and some strategic-brokerage services) from
Japan—even though more American labor was being exported
to Japan through them than would be exported through Motorola
once all trade barriers were removed.[8]

---

[8] Another high priority of the Trade Representative was to force Japan to
allow large American retail chains, like Toys-R-Us, to establish businesses
there. But almost all of the Toys-R-Us inventory consisted of items designed
and fabricated in Southeast Asia and Latin America. Were Japan to open
its market to Toys-R-Us, the only American beneficiaries would be a relatively small group of strategic brokers at its American headquarters, plus
whatever portion of the firm's investors were American citizens.

More important than reducing foreign barriers to the exports of American companies is discouraging other governments from invoking domestic-content rules against the labors of Americans. Such rules induce global corporations (American-owned and foreign-owned alike) to increase the amount of work they do within such countries, rather than in, say, the United States. Domestic-content rules cause little hardship to American companies already operating abroad, but they deprive some Americans of the opportunity to compete for jobs here—jobs that produce valuable skills, knowledge, and experience. A European requirement that European television broadcasters limit non-European programming, for example, would not impinge too drastically on American-owned global media companies, most of whom are already safely inside the European Community, hiring Europeans to perform a variety of creative functions. (By 1990, Walt Disney was building a studio near London, and MTV was initiating a European venture with British press magnate Robert Maxwell.) But such a requirement surely would reduce the amount of American input included in the television programs that such American-owned (as well as Japanese-owned and European-owned) global media companies sold in Europe, and thus block the capacity of Americans to add value to the world entertainment market.

Lack of access by American-owned corporations to foreign markets is, of course, a problem. But it becomes a crucial problem for Americans only to the extent that both American-owned and foreign-owned companies are forced to make products within the foreign market—products they otherwise would have made in the United States. When American trade negotiators establish priorities for how they will spend their limited political clout on reducing foreign trade barriers, they would do well to pay less attention to corporate nationality and more attention to the work actually performed by Americans. By this logic, a foreign trade barrier to Ricoh copiers made in the United States may be more injurious to the national interest than a ban on Kodak copiers made in Korea and Japan.[9]

---

[9] Protectionist domestic-content rules are different from the public-private bargains suggested earlier, through which a government funds technology specifically on condition that its own citizens produce it. While it is perfectly appropriate for government to exact such a quid pro quo from corporations

6

By THE last decade of the twentieth century, the assumed linkage between the profitability of American-owned corporations and the competitiveness of Americans led U.S. government officials to accept some remarkable propositions. One was that America would become more competitive if American-owned global corporations in the same industry could combine to produce their output jointly. Thus, in 1990, Congress and the administration backed a relaxation of antitrust law to permit joint production agreements. According to the administration's Economic Policy Council, the change "would be a strong statement of the administration's support of American efficiency and competitiveness."[10] The presumed logical connection between giant combinations of American firms and the nation's efficiency and competitiveness was not articulated, however. Not even the voluble chief executives of the nation's two largest media empires were able to pinpoint the connection when reassuring Congress that the merger of Time Inc. and Warner Communications would be good for America. "Our union will make America better able to challenge foreign media companies," the chairman of Time Inc. told the congressmen, who nodded in solemn agreement.[11] Why such a merger would help the United States in particular, relative to what the nation gained from Rupert Murdoch's News Corporation (which included 20th Century-Fox, Fox Broadcasting, TV Guide, and Harper & Row), or West Germany's Bertelsmann's media empire (including RCA Records and Bantam, Doubleday, and Dell), or France's Hachette (Woman's Day and Grolier's Encyclopedia), or Sony (CBS Records and Columbia Pictures), remained a mystery. American writers, editors, directors, musicians, and cinematog-

---

accepting particular subsidies from the public, there is no justification for conditioning market access itself upon local production. The costs of such a restriction fall not only upon domestic consumers but upon all those outside the nation who, in consequence, are unable to market their skills.

[10] Quoted in The Wall Street Journal, January 22, 1990, p. A4.

[11] U.S. House of Representatives, Committee on the Judiciary, Hearings Before the Subcommittee on Economic and Commercial Law, March 14, 1989.

raphers were involved in all these global media companies, as were their foreign counterparts.

Meanwhile, otherwise sensible people expressed outrage that foreign-owned firms had the audacity to hire red-blooded Americans—among them, former U.S. government officials—to lobby in Washington on their behalf. The efforts of Japanese-owned corporations were deemed especially pernicious. "Americans first have to decide what is in their national interest. But the effect of Japan's influence campaign is to make [that] debate impossible," complained a columnist for *The New Republic*.[12] The unstated premise behind such indignation was that American-owned corporations were the only trustworthy participants in Washington policy debates—because, presumably, their myriad lobbyists and ex-government officials represented the interests of "us" Americans.

Of course, American firms engaged in precisely the same lobbying tactics abroad. Cleveland-based TRW's vice president for the Asia-Pacific region noted proudly that the firm was "developing an extensive network with [Japanese] politicians, political analysts, political reporters, and other government relations personnel [through which the firm could] participate in the development of legislative initiatives and policies of interest to TRW."[13] Translated from corporate bureaucratese, this meant that TRW was influencing the Japanese government. Other American-owned firms had insinuated themselves even more deeply into the Japanese government. By 1990, the president of IBM Japan sat on Japan's Industry Structural Council, which advises Japan's Ministry of International Trade and Industry on its industrial policies.

Ironically, it was precisely because Washington policy debates were so often dominated by American-owned corporations that U.S. government officials engaged in such dubious practices as inhibiting foreign ownership, restricting research and development subsidies to American-owned firms, pushing foreign nations to open their borders to the products of American-owned firms

---

[12] John Judis, "Yen for Power," *The New Republic*, January 22, 1990. See also Pat Choate, *Agents of Influence* (New York: Knopf, 1990).

[13] "How TRW Plays the Game," *Japan Economic Journal*, May 19, 1990, p. 6.

(rather than of Americans), and allowing American-owned firms to merge into huge global combines. One remedy for these antics was to do just the reverse of what was being recommended: Instead of muffling the voices of foreign corporations, open the public debate even more widely than before to their views. An even better solution, no less evenhanded but surely more effective: Bar former U.S. government officials from lobbying their former agencies on behalf of any client, regardless of the client's putative nationality.

7

THE FOREGOING criticisms are not intended to comfort the defenders of laissez-faire orthodoxy, who urge that government play no constructive role at all in improving the economic prospects of citizens. The point, rather, is that efforts to increase the profitability of American-owned corporations are the wrong vehicle for achieving this end. Habituated to an older economy in which corporate nationality mattered, policy makers have been more concerned about who owns what than about which nation's work force learns to do what. Getting our priorities straight requires a fundamental change in our thinking. The problem is not that American-owned corporations are insufficiently profitable; it is that many Americans are not adding sufficient value to the world economy to maintain or enhance their standard of living. It is to this critical issue that I now turn.

Part Three

The Rise of
the Symbolic Analyst

14

The Three Jobs
of the Future

THE USUAL discussion about the future of the American economy
focuses on topics like the competitiveness of General Motors, or
of the American automobile industry, or, more broadly, of American manufacturing, or, more broadly still, of the American economy. But, as has been observed, these categories are becoming
irrelevant. They assume the continued existence of an American
economy in which jobs associated with a particular firm, industry,
or sector are somehow connected within the borders of the nation,
so that American workers face a common fate; and a common
enemy as well: The battlefields of world trade pit our corporations
and our workers unambiguously against theirs.

No longer. In the emerging international economy, few American companies and American industries compete against foreign
companies and industries—if by *American* we mean where the
work is done and the value is added. Becoming more typical is
the global web, perhaps headquartered in and receiving much of
its financial capital from the United States, but with research,
design, and production facilities spread over Japan, Europe, and
North America; additional production facilities in Southeast Asia
and Latin America; marketing and distribution centers on every
continent; and lenders and investors in Taiwan, Japan, and West
Germany as well as the United States. This ecumenical company
competes with similarly ecumenical companies headquartered in
other nations. Battle lines no longer correspond with national
borders.

So, when an "American" company like General Motors shows healthy profits, this is good news for its strategic brokers in Detroit and its American investors. It is also good news for other GM executives worldwide and for GM's global employees, subcontractors, and investors. But it is not necessarily good news for a lot of routine assembly-line workers in Detroit, because there are not likely to be many of them left in Detroit, or anywhere else in America. Nor is it necessarily good news for the few Americans who are still working on assembly lines in the United States, who increasingly receive their paychecks from corporations based in Tokyo or Bonn.

The point is that Americans are becoming part of an international labor market, encompassing Asia, Africa, Latin America, Western Europe, and, increasingly, Eastern Europe and the Soviet Union. The competitiveness of Americans in this global market is coming to depend, not on the fortunes of any American corporation or on American industry, but on the functions that Americans perform—the value they add—within the global economy. Other nations are undergoing precisely the same transformation, some more slowly than the United States, but all participating in essentially the same transnational trend. Barriers to cross-border flows of knowledge, money, and tangible products are crumbling; groups of people in every nation are joining global webs. In a very few years, there will be virtually no way to distinguish one national economy from another except by the exchange rates of their currencies—and even this distinction may be on the wane.

Americans thus confront global competition ever more directly, unmediated by national institutions. As we discard vestigial notions of the competitiveness of American corporations, American industry, and the American economy, and recast them in terms of the competitiveness of the American work force, it becomes apparent that successes or failures will not be shared equally by all our citizens.

Some Americans, whose contributions to the global economy are more highly valued in world markets, will succeed, while others, whose contributions are deemed far less valuable, fail. GM's American executives may become more competitive even as GM's American production workers become less so, because the functions performed by the former group are more highly valued in the world market than those of the latter. So when we speak of the "competitiveness" of Americans in general, we are talking only about how much the world is prepared to spend, *on average*, for services performed by Americans. Some Americans may command much higher rewards; others, far lower. No longer are Americans rising or falling together, as if in one large national boat. We are, increasingly, in different, smaller boats.

2

IN ORDER to see in greater detail what is happening to American jobs and to understand why the economic fates of Americans are beginning to diverge, it is first necessary to view the work that Americans do in terms of categories that reflect their real competitive positions in the global economy.

Official data about American jobs are organized by categories that are not very helpful in this regard. The U.S. Bureau of the Census began inquiring about American jobs in 1820, and developed a systematic way of categorizing them in 1870. Beginning in 1943, the Census came up with a way of dividing these categories into different levels of "social-economic status," depending upon, among other things, the prestige and income associated with each job. In order to determine the appropriate groupings, the Census first divided all American jobs into either business class or working class—the same two overarching categories the Lynns had devised for their study of Middletown—and then divided each of these, in turn, into subcategories.[1] In 1950, the Census added the category of "service workers" and called the resulting scheme America's "Major Occupational Groups," which it has remained ever since. All subsequent surveys have been based on this same set of categories. Thus, even by 1990, in the eyes of the Census, you were either in a "managerial and professional specialty," in a "technical, sales, and administrative support" role, in

---

[1] See Alba M. Edwards, *U.S. Census of Population, 1940: Comparative Occupation Statistics, 1870–1940* (Washington, D.C.: U.S. Government Printing Office, 1943).

a "service occupation," an "operator, fabricator, and laborer," or in a "transportation and material moving" occupation.

This set of classifications made sense when the economy was focused on high-volume, standardized production, in which almost every job fit into, or around, the core American corporation, and when status and income depended on one's ranking in the standard corporate bureaucracy. But these categories have little bearing upon the competitive positions of Americans worldwide, now that America's core corporations are transforming into finely spun global webs. Someone whose job falls officially into a "technical" or "sales" subcategory may, in fact, be among the best-paid and most influential people in such a web. To understand the real competitive positions of Americans in the global economy, it is necessary to devise new categories.[2]

Essentially, three broad categories of work are emerging, corresponding to the three different competitive positions in which Americans find themselves. The same three categories are taking shape in other nations. Call them *routine production services, in-person services,* and *symbolic-analytic services.*

Routine production services entail the kinds of repetitive tasks performed by the old foot soldiers of American capitalism in the high-volume enterprise. They are done over and over—one step in a sequence of steps for producing finished products tradeable in world commerce. Although often thought of as traditional blue-collar jobs, they also include routine supervisory jobs performed by low- and mid-level managers—foremen, line managers, clerical supervisors, and section chiefs—involving repetitive checks on subordinates' work and the enforcement of standard operating procedures.

Routine production services are found in many places within

---

[2] Because much of the information about the American work force must be gleaned from the old categories, however, the only way to discover who fits into which new category is to decompose the government's data into the smallest subcategories in which they are collected, then reorder the subcategories according to which new functional group they appear to belong in. For a similar methodology, see Steven A. Sass, "The U.S. Professional Sector: 1950 to 1988," *New England Economic Review,* January–February 1990, pp. 37–55.

a modern economy apart from older, heavy industries (which, like elderly citizens, have been given the more delicate, and less terminal, appellation: "mature"). They are found even amid the glitter and glitz of high technology. Few tasks are more tedious and repetitive, for example, than stuffing computer circuit boards or devising routine coding for computer software programs.

Indeed, contrary to prophets of the "information age" who buoyantly predicted an abundance of high-paying jobs even for people with the most basic of skills, the sobering truth is that many information-processing jobs fit easily into this category. The foot soldiers of the information economy are hordes of data processors stationed in "back offices" at computer terminals linked to worldwide information banks. They routinely enter data into computers or take it out again—records of credit card purchases and payments, credit reports, checks that have cleared, customer accounts, customer correspondence, payroll, hospital billings, patient records, medical claims, court decisions, subscriber lists, personnel, library catalogues, and so forth. The "information revolution" may have rendered some of us more productive, but it has also produced huge piles of raw data which must be processed in much the same monotonous way that assembly-line workers and, before them, textile workers processed piles of other raw materials.

Routine producers typically work in the company of many other people who do the same thing, usually within large enclosed spaces. They are guided on the job by standard procedures and codified rules, and even their overseers are overseen, in turn, by people who routinely monitor—often with the aid of computers—how much they do and how accurately they do it. Their wages are based either on the amount of time they put in or on the amount of work they do.

Routine producers usually must be able to read and to perform simple computations. But their cardinal virtues are reliability, loyalty, and the capacity to take direction. Thus does a standard American education, based on the traditional premises of American education, normally suffice.

By 1990, routine production work comprised about one-quarter of the jobs performed by Americans, and the number was declining. Those who dealt with metal were mostly white and male; those who dealt with fabrics, circuit boards, or information were mostly black or Hispanic, and female; their supervisors, white males.[3]

In-person services, the second kind of work that Americans do, also entail simple and repetitive tasks. And like routine production services, the pay of in-person servers is a function of hours worked or amount of work performed; they are closely supervised (as are their supervisors), and they need not have acquired much education (at most, a high school diploma, or its equivalent, and some vocational training).

The big difference between in-person servers and routine producers is that *these* services must be provided person-to-person, and thus are not sold worldwide. (In-person servers might, of course, work for global corporations. Two examples: In 1988, Britain's Blue Arrow PLC acquired Manpower Inc., which provides custodial services throughout the United States. Meanwhile, Denmark's ISS-AS already employed over 16,000 Americans to clean office buildings in most major American cities.) In-person servers are in direct contact with the ultimate beneficiaries of their work; their immediate objects are specific customers rather than streams of metal, fabric, or data. In-person servers work alone or in small teams. Included in this category are retail sales workers, waiters and waitresses, hotel workers, janitors, cashiers, hospital attendants and orderlies, nursing-home aides, child-care workers, house cleaners, home health-care aides, taxi drivers, secretaries, hairdressers, auto mechanics, sellers of residential real estate, flight attendants, physical therapists, and—among the fastest-growing of all—security guards.

In-person servers are supposed to be as punctual, reliable, and tractable as routine production workers. But many in-person servers share one additional requirement: They must also have a pleasant demeanor. They must smile and exude confidence and good cheer, even when they feel morose. They must be courteous and helpful, even to the most obnoxious of patrons. Above all, they must make others feel happy and at ease. It should come as no

---

[3] For an illuminating discussion of routine jobs in a high-technology industry, see D. O'Connor, "Women Workers in the Changing International Division of Labor in Microelectronics," in L. Benerici and C. Stimpson (eds.), *Women, Households, and the Economy* (New Brunswick, N.J.: Rutgers University Press, 1987).

surprise that, traditionally, most in-person servers have been women. The cultural stereotype of women as nurturers—as mommies—has opened countless in-person service jobs to them.[4]

By 1990, in-person services accounted for about 30 percent of the jobs performed by Americans, and their numbers were growing rapidly. For example, Beverly Enterprises, a single nursing-home chain operating throughout the United States, employed about the same number of Americans as the entire Chrysler Corporation (115,174 and 116,250, respectively)—although most Americans were far more knowledgeable about the latter, including the opinions of its chairman. In the United States during the 1980s, well over 3 million *new* in-person service jobs were created in fast-food outlets, bars, and restaurants. This was more than the *total* number of routine production jobs still existing in America by the end of the decade in the automobile, steelmaking, and textile industries combined.[5]

Symbolic-analytic services, the third job category, include all the problem-solving, problem-identifying, and strategic-brokering activities we have examined in previous chapters. Like routine production services (but *unlike* in-person services), symbolic-analytic services can be traded worldwide and thus must compete with foreign providers even in the American market. But they do not enter world commerce as standardized things. Traded instead are the manipulations of symbols—data, words, oral and visual representations.

Included in this category are the problem-solving, -identifying, and brokering of many people who call themselves research scientists, design engineers, software engineers, civil engineers, biotechnology engineers, sound engineers, public relations executives, investment bankers, lawyers, real estate developers, and even a few creative accountants. Also included is much of the work done by management consultants, financial consultants, tax consultants, energy consultants, agricultural consultants, armaments consultants, architectural consultants, management information specialists, organization development specialists, strategic

---

[4]On this point, see Arlie Russell Hochschild, *The Managed Heart: The Commercialization of Human Feeling* (Berkeley: University of California Press, 1983).
[5]U.S. Department of Commerce, Bureau of Labor Statistics, various issues.

planners, corporate headhunters, and systems analysts. Also: advertising executives and marketing strategists, art directors, architects, cinematographers, film editors, production designers, publishers, writers and editors, journalists, musicians, television and film producers, and even university professors.

Symbolic analysts solve, identify, and broker problems by manipulating symbols. They simplify reality into abstract images that can be rearranged, juggled, experimented with, communicated to other specialists, and then, eventually, transformed back into reality. The manipulations are done with analytic tools, sharpened by experience. The tools may be mathematical algorithms, legal arguments, financial gimmicks, scientific principles, psychological insights about how to persuade or to amuse, systems of induction or deduction, or any other set of techniques for doing conceptual puzzles.

Some of these manipulations reveal how to more efficiently deploy resources or shift financial assets, or otherwise save time and energy. Other manipulations yield new inventions—technological marvels, innovative legal arguments, new advertising ploys for convincing people that certain amusements have become life necessities. Still other manipulations—of sounds, words, pictures—serve to entertain their recipients, or cause them to reflect more deeply on their lives or on the human condition. Others grab money from people too slow or naïve to protect themselves by manipulating in response.

Like routine producers, symbolic analysts rarely come into direct contact with the ultimate beneficiaries of their work. But other aspects of their work life are quite different from that experienced by routine producers. Symbolic analysts often have partners or associates rather than bosses or supervisors. Their incomes may vary from time to time, but are not directly related to how much time they put in or the quantity of work they put out. Income depends, rather, on the quality, originality, cleverness, and, occasionally, speed with which they solve, identify, or broker new problems. Their careers are not linear or hierarchical; they rarely proceed along well-defined paths to progressively higher levels of responsibility and income. In fact, symbolic analysts may take on vast responsibilities and command inordinate wealth at rather young ages. Correspondingly, they may lose authority and income if they are no longer able to innovate by building on their cumulative experience, even if they are quite senior.

Symbolic analysts often work alone or in small teams, which may be connected to larger organizations, including worldwide webs. Teamwork is often critical. Since neither problems nor solutions can be defined in advance, frequent and informal conversations help ensure that insights and discoveries are put to their best uses and subjected to quick, critical evaluation.[6]

When not conversing with their teammates, symbolic analysts sit before computer terminals—examining words and numbers, moving them, altering them, trying out new words and numbers, formulating and testing hypotheses, designing or strategizing. They also spend long hours in meetings or on the telephone, and even longer hours in jet planes and hotels—advising, making presentations, giving briefings, doing deals. Periodically, they issue reports, plans, designs, drafts, memoranda, layouts, renderings, scripts, or projections—which, in turn, precipitate more meetings to clarify what has been proposed and to get agreement on how it will be implemented, by whom, and for how much money. Final production is often the easiest part. The bulk of the time and cost (and, thus, real value) comes in conceptualizing the problem, devising a solution, and planning its execution.

Most symbolic analysts have graduated from four-year colleges or universities; many have graduate degrees as well. The vast majority are white males, but the proportion of white females is growing, and there is a small, but slowly increasing, number of blacks and Hispanics among them. All told, symbolic analysis currently accounts for no more than 20 percent of American jobs. The proportion of American workers who fit this category has increased substantially since the 1950s (by my calculation, no more than 8 percent of American workers could be classified as symbolic

---

[6] The physical environments in which symbolic analysts work are substantially different from those in which routine producers or in-person servers work. Symbolic analysts usually labor within spaces that are quiet and tastefully decorated. Soft lights, wall-to-wall carpeting, beige and puce colors are preferred. Such calm surroundings typically are encased within tall steel-and-glass buildings or within long, low, postmodernist structures carved into hillsides and encircled by expanses of well-manicured lawn.

analysts at midcentury), but the pace slowed considerably in the 1980s—even though certain symbolic-analytic jobs, like law and investment banking, mushroomed. (I will return to this point later.)[7]

3

THESE three functional categories cover more than three out of four American jobs. Among the remainder are farmers, miners, and other extractors of natural resources, who together comprise less than 5 percent of American workers. The rest are mainly government employees (including public school teachers), employees in regulated industries (like utility workers), and government-financed workers (American engineers working on defense weapons systems and physicians working off Medicaid and Medicare), almost all of whom are also sheltered from global competition.

Some traditional job categories—managerial, secretarial, sales, and so on—overlap with more than one of these functional categories. The traditional categories, it should be emphasized, date from an era in which most jobs were as standardized as the products they helped create. Such categories are no longer very helpful for determining what a person actually does on the job and how much that person is likely to earn for doing it. Only some of the people who are classified as "secretaries," for example, perform strictly routine production work, such as entering and retrieving data from computers. Other "secretaries" provide in-person services, like making appointments and fetching coffee. A third group of "secretaries" perform symbolic-analytic work closely allied to what their bosses do. To classify them all as "secretaries" glosses over their very different functions in the economy. Similarly, "sales" jobs can fall within any one of the three functional

---

[7]Sass's definition of "professional worker" overlaps significantly with my definition of symbolic analyst (although, as I will explain, not all symbolic analysts are professionals, and not all professionals are symbolic analysts). Sass finds that by 1988 professional workers comprised 20 percent of the American labor force. See Sass, op. cit.

groups: some salespeople simply fill quotas and orders; others spend much of their time performing in-person services, like maintaining machinery; and some are sophisticated problem-identifiers no different from high-priced management consultants. "Computer programmers" (one of the more recent additions to the standard list of occupations) are as varied: They might be doing routine coding, in-person troubleshooting for particular clients, or translating complex functional specifications into software.

That a job category is officially classified "professional" or "managerial" likewise has little bearing upon the function its occupant actually performs in the world economy. Not all professionals, that is, are symbolic analysts. Some lawyers spend their entire working lives doing things that normal people would find unbearably monotonous—cranking out the same old wills, contracts, and divorces, over and over, with only the names changed. Some accountants do routine audits without the active involvement of their cerebral cortices. Some managers take no more responsibility than noting who shows up for work in the morning, making sure they stay put, and locking the place up at night. (I have even heard tell of university professors who deliver the same lectures for thirty years, long after their brains have atrophied, but I do not believe such stories.) None of these professionals is a symbolic analyst.[8]

Nor are all symbolic analysts professionals. In the older, high-volume economy, a "professional" was one who had mastered a particular domain of knowledge. The knowledge existed in advance, ready to be mastered. It had been recorded in dusty tomes or codified in precise rules and formulae. Once the novitiate had dutifully absorbed the knowledge and had passed an examination attesting to its absorption, professional status was automatically conferred—usually through a ceremony of appropriately medieval pageantry and costume. The professional was then au-

---

[8] In the remainder of this book, when discussing symbolic analysts, I shall, on occasion, illustrate my point by referring to lawyers, management consultants, software engineers, and other professionals, but the reader should understand that this is a shorthand method of describing only the symbolic and analytic work undertaken by such professionals.

thorized to place a few extra letters after his or her name, mount a diploma on the office wall, join the professional association and attend its yearly tax-deductible meeting in Palm Springs, and pursue clients with a minimum of overt avarice.

But in the new economy—replete with unidentified problems, unknown solutions, and untried means of putting them together—mastery of old domains of knowledge isn't nearly enough to guarantee a good income. Nor, importantly, is it even necessary. Symbolic analysts often can draw upon established bodies of knowledge with the flick of a computer key. Facts, codes, formulae, and rules are easily accessible. What is much more valuable is the capacity to effectively and creatively *use* the knowledge. Possessing a professional credential is no guarantee of such capacity. Indeed, a professional education which has emphasized the rote acquisition of such knowledge over original thought may retard such capacity in later life.

4

HOW, THEN, do symbolic analysts describe what they do? With difficulty. Because a symbolic analyst's status, influence, and income have little to do with formal rank or title, the job may seem mysterious to people working outside the enterprise web, who are unfamiliar with the symbolic analyst's actual function within it. And because symbolic analysis involves processes of thought and communication, rather than tangible production, the content of the job may be difficult to convey simply. In answering the question "What did you do today, Mommy (or Daddy)?" it is not always instructive, or particularly edifying, to say that one spent three hours on the telephone, four hours in meetings, and the remainder of the time gazing at a computer screen trying to work out a puzzle.

Some symbolic analysts have taken refuge in job titles that communicate no more clearly than this, but at least sound as if they confer independent authority nonetheless. The old hierarchies are breaking down, but new linguistic idioms have arisen to perpetuate the time-honored custom of title-as-status.

Herewith a sample. Add any term from the first column to any from the second, and then add both terms to any from the third column, and you will have a job that is likely (but not necessarily) to be inhabited by a symbolic analyst.

Communications	Management	Engineer
Systems	Planning	Director
Financial	Process	Designer
Creative	Development	Coordinator
Project	Strategy	Consultant
Business	Policy	Manager
Resource	Applications	Adviser
Product	Research	Planner

The "flat" organization of high-value enterprise notwithstanding, there are subtle distinctions of symbolic-analytic rank. Real status is inversely related to length of job title. Two terms signify a degree of authority. (The first or second column's appellation is dropped, leaving a simpler and more elegant combination, such as "Project Engineer" or "Creative Director.") Upon the most valued of symbolic analysts, who have moved beyond mere technical proficiency to exert substantial influence on their peers within the web, is bestowed the highest honor—a title comprising a term from the last column preceded by a dignified adjective like Senior, Managing, Chief, or Principal. One becomes a "Senior Producer" or a "Principal Designer" not because of time loyally served or routines impeccably followed, but because of special deftness in solving, identifying, or brokering new problems.

Years ago, fortunate and ambitious young people ascended career ladders with comfortable predictability. If they entered a core corporation, they began as, say, a second assistant vice president for marketing. After five years or so they rose to the rank of first assistant vice president, and thence onward and upward. Had they joined a law firm, consulting group, or investment bank, they would have started as an associate, after five to eight years ascended to junior partner, and thence to senior partner, managing partner, and finally heaven.

None of these predictable steps necessitated original thought. Indeed, a particularly creative or critical imagination might even be hazardous to career development, especially if it elicited questions of a subversive sort, like "Aren't we working on the wrong problem?" or "Why are we doing this?" or, most dangerous of all, "Why does this organization exist?" The safest career path was the surest career path, and the surest path was sufficiently well worn by previous travelers so that it could not be missed.

Of course, there still exist organizational backwaters in which career advancement is sequential and predictable. But fewer fortunate and ambitious young people dive into them, or even enter upon careers marked by well-worn paths. They dare not. In the emerging global economy, even the most impressive of positions in the most prestigious of organizations is vulnerable to worldwide competition if it entails easily replicated routines. The only true competitive advantage lies in skill in solving, identifying, and brokering new problems.

15

A Digression
on Symbolic Analysis
and Market Incentive

ONE FINAL point about symbolic analysts bears mention, although the reader eager for the plot to thicken may skip to the next chapter without peril. Here I pause to examine the public benefits of symbolic analysis, and how the considerable skills and insights of symbolic analysts can be harnessed for the public good.

Problem-solving, -identifying, and brokering can create substantial value for individual consumers, but these services do not necessarily improve society. Sometimes, of course, there is a convergence between what customers want and what the public needs: Dread diseases are diagnosed and new cures are discovered; musical scores are written, performed, and marketed to millions of appreciative listeners; automobiles become cheaper, faster, safer, and more convenient. At other times, however, symbolic analysts simply enhance some people's wealth while diminishing other people's to an equal extent; or their net effect may be to reduce almost everyone's well-being. A symbolic analyst who discovers yet another extravagant use for fossil fuel or nonbiodegradable plastic, for example, may be richly rewarded but may be helping to deprive future generations of the clean environment enjoyed by their predecessors.

Even in the older, high-volume economy, innovations often had consequences for people not immediately party to them, of course. Some consequences were beneficial: Locomotives transported grain thousands of miles to customers who would not otherwise have had such inexpensive sources of supply. Some side effects were less beneficial: The locomotives also ignited prairie fires. As high-value enterprise supplants high volume, there are ever greater possibilities for innovations that improve the lot of mankind, but there is an equal potential for innovations that reduce the quality of life overall. As the world shrinks and the pace of economic change quickens, such beneficial or harmful side effects loom larger. A new vaccine can protect millions of children; a meltdown at a nuclear power plant can poison the air for just as many.

How do we ensure that symbolic analysts apply their creative energies in the right direction? The mythic contest between the free market and government intervention forces us either to ignore the looming side effects of their activities or to rely on countless government directives to promote the beneficial ones and prevent the harmful ones. Each of these alternatives—exclusive reliance on markets or on government directives—invites abuse and inefficiency. The proper response is to organize the market in ways that motivate symbolic analysts to discover means of helping mankind while inflicting the least amount of harm.

2

THE IDEA of a "free market" apart from the laws and political decisions that create it is pure fantasy anyway. The market was not created by God on any of the first six days (at least, not directly), nor is it maintained by divine will. It is a human artifact, the shifting sum of a set of judgments about individual rights and responsibilities. What is mine? What is yours? What is ours? And how do we define and deal with actions that threaten these borders —theft, force, fraud, extortion, or carelessness? What should we trade, and what should we not? (Drugs? Sex? Votes? Babies?) How should we enforce these decisions, and what penalties should apply to transgressions? As a nation formulates and accumulates answers to these questions, it creates its version of the market.

Answers to these sorts of questions are not found in logic or analysis alone. Different nations, at different times, have answered them in different ways. The answers depend on the values a society professes, the weight it places on solidarity, prosperity, tradition, piety, and so on. In modern nations, government is the principal agency by which the society deliberates, defines, and enforces the norms that organize the market. Judges and legislators, as well as government executives and administrators, endlessly alter and adapt the rules of the game—usually tacitly, often unintentionally, always under the watchful eye and sometimes under the guiding hand of interests with clear stakes in the outcomes of particular decisions. To the extent that rhetoric frames the issue as one grand choice between government and market, it befogs our view of the series of smaller choices about an endless set of alternative ways to structure the rules of ownership and exchange.

"Deregulation," a term which had its heyday in the late 1970s and 1980s, was broadly seen as a manifestation of a decisive swing toward the free market, away from government intervention. In fact, deregulation should only represent a shift in the nature of government action, from commanding specific outcomes to creating and maintaining new markets. By 1980, for example, the airline industry in the United States was deregulated in the sense that the Civil Aeronautics Board no longer passed judgment on air fares or routes. Carriers could now compete on prices and services, to the delight of both passengers and symbolic analysts employed by the airlines to take advantage of new opportunities for creating new products.

This reform did not eliminate the government's responsibility for the air-travel business, however; it merely shifted the responsibilities. Government was now charged with organizing a new market, whose development called for all sorts of decisions: Under what conditions should mergers and acquisitions among airlines be barred because they might stifle competition? How should airport landing slots be apportioned among competing airlines? On what terms should airlines gain access to their competitors' computerized reservation systems? How best to manage the increasingly crowded airspace?

But the ideological fixation on *deregulating* the airlines—on the mythic choice between government control and market freedom—led policy makers to ignore their responsibilities for creating and maintaining this new market. The result: The airline industry became concentrated in the hands of a relatively few large carriers, and competition declined through major hubs. Passenger fares rose. Further, with so many more flights and more passengers, there was a greater risk of accident. The government now had to invest in new systems for controlling airspace, expand safety inspections, and restructure industry incentives to guarantee the proper degree of care. All of this prompted some people to talk about the necessity of "reregulating" the airlines. But that option was irrelevant to the issue at hand. Symbolic analysts in the newly deregulated airline industry took advantage of whatever opportunity they could find to enhance profits. Their efforts can improve public welfare, however, only if the market is properly organized.

The control of air pollution offers another example. After the passage of the Clean Air Act in 1970, the U.S. government issued mountains of regulations—specifying the maximum allowable concentrations of air pollution throughout the nation, and how much airborne toxic matter could be emitted by each of tens of thousands of industrial facilities. Enormous amounts of data were accumulated and analyzed, and even then government could only issue uniform and inflexible rules for whole industries and regions. The uniform rules were perhaps appropriate to high-volume, standardized production, but they took no account of special needs or deviations pursued by high-value enterprise. Nor did they give symbolic analysts any incentive to discover new ways of reducing pollution at lower cost.

Free-marketers (including not a few trade associations and large businesses) repeatedly argued that because the costs of enforcing the Clean Air Act far exceeded its benefits, the regulations should be scaled back. Environmentalists (and, if polls were to be believed, a majority of the American public) disagreed. The debate centered on the value of clean air versus the costs and inefficiencies of regulations to achieve it. Posed in this way, however, the debate ruled out a far more useful line of inquiry: How could government better organize the market to encourage high-value production and motivate symbolic analysts to discover ways of achieving the cleanest possible air at the lowest social cost? This way of framing the debate would have invited consideration of a system of transferable pollution permits. Such permits—issued in numbers equal to the maximum amount of pollution allowed in a particular region—could be bought and sold by polluters, thus allowing each polluter to decide which was cheaper, in light of its own special circumstances: cutting pollution or buying permits. Such a system would preserve clean air but place most of the cost of cleaning it on firms that could control their pollution most cheaply. In addition, it would motivate symbolic analysts to develop more efficient methods of doing the cleaning.[1]

Government abdication of its market-creating responsibilities can have expensive consequences. In the early 1980s, free-marketers assumed that the best way to help the nation's savings and loan banks compete with other lending institutions was to allow them to invest their depositors' savings however they wished. But in the scramble to *deregulate*, policy makers saw only one aspect of the market. Since the government also insured the bank depositors against loss, the symbolic analysts who headed the savings and loans had everything to gain and nothing to lose from speculating wildly. The predictable result was a cost to American taxpayers which, at this writing, is likely to exceed $300 billion.

Here again, the real choice was not between market freedom and centralized control. Policy makers actually faced a decision about how best to protect depositors while allowing savings and loan banks to make a profit. Viewed in this way, a number of reasonable choices might have been made. One would have been to allow the banks greater latitude to invest deposits, but simultaneously to reduce government deposit insurance and require that the banks fully advise depositors of the risk to which their money would now be exposed.

3

NOWHERE is the mythic force of the free market felt more strongly, and defended with more conviction, than on Wall Street, and within the myriad financial and legal institutions connected with it. Here symbolic analysts have been least constrained. Brokerage fees were deregulated in the mid-1970s; many core American corporations could conceal dispiriting declines behind masks of financial manipulation. The rapid and uninhibited movement of money, moreover, has created vast new opportunities for further financial and legal innovation. The Securities and Exchange

---

[1] In 1990, Congress and the Bush administration launched a similar effort, although, at this writing, opposition to it was sufficiently intense so that the project's overall future remained in doubt.

Commission and other pertinent regulators have barely kept up with the pace of symbolic innovation.

Lawyers, investment bankers, arbitrageurs, and futures traders, it should be noted, play a potentially valuable role in an advanced economy by ensuring that assets are applied to their highest and most productive uses. They can be, in this sense, the air-traffic controllers of modern capitalism—guiding the flight patterns of money as it glides around the world and helping it land safely and smoothly where it is most needed. But unless the considerable energies of these symbolic analysts are appropriately channeled toward this useful function, they can cause a great deal of mischief. Unconstrained, there is infinite opportunity for short-term, speculative games of a sort that mathematicians term "zero-sum"—in which one party's gain is another's loss. Like the designers of complex military weapons systems who earn princely sums trying to outfox the designers of other complex military weapons systems, symbolic analysts who sell financial and legal services can accumulate great fortunes by rapidly outmaneuvering one another.

Options for bringing order to this chaos abound. There are many ways to organize financial markets so as to limit the profitability of such games while preserving the benefits of financial intermediation. Capital-gains taxes, for example, could be substantially increased on short-term stockholdings and reduced on longer-term holdings, thus awarding patient investors. In addition, a small transfer tax could be imposed on the sale of each share of stock, making speculative ploys somewhat less remunerative. A third possibility: Eliminate interest deductions on loans used for the purchase of shares of stock; transactions generating real efficiencies should be sufficiently attractive to survive without this extra tax sweetener. Lawyers similarly could be constrained from speculative excess by placing limits on the contingency fees they could collect from litigation over these sorts of financial transactions. But none of these steps, nor any other, has been taken. The predictable result has been large private gains accompanied by the degeneration of legal and financial institutions.

The lucrative thrust and parry is easily observed. Every clever legal argument is met by a more clever one on the other side, every financial innovation by a more innovative one, every step toward more current market information matched by an even faster means of acquiring it. The escalation is boundless: Legal briefs grow heavier; the number of filings, depositions, and interrogatories, larger still. Financial ploys become more complex; the computers and software in trading rooms, more powerful and expensive. Clients, meanwhile, feel compelled to spend ever more in order to gain a bit of ground, or at least avoid costly defeat. From the standpoint of society as a whole, such expenditures represent wasted assets. We would be better off were the contest canceled and truce declared, thus freeing the considerable talents of these symbolic analysts to enhance society's wealth rather than moving it from one set of pockets to another.

Those who facilitate these transactions defy the law of supply and demand: The greater their supply, the greater the demand for their services. Like ballistic missiles toting hydrogen bombs, their mere availability suggests that they might be used, thus compelling everyone else to buy them as well. Only slightly exaggerated is the story of the starving solitary lawyer in a small Kentucky town whose strategy of attracting another lawyer to town eventually brings them both vast riches.

There is a second reason why the supply of these symbolic-analytic services generates its own demand. Lawyers, investment bankers, and financial advisers are among a select group of service providers (whose members also include auto mechanics and physicians) who both tell clients what they need and then, once the decision is reached, fulfill the need. This combination creates obvious opportunities for providing services in excess of what an unsuspecting client might otherwise have found necessary. And because lawyers get paid by the size of the job, and financiers according to the size of the transaction, there is a not inconsiderable incentive to advocate bigness. Codes of professional ethics guard against the more blatant forms of seduction, of course. But in the heat of prospective battle, it is not unusual for legal or financial advisers to sternly warn clients against undue timidity.

As the American economy has merged with the world economy, moreover, the opportunities for legal and financial manipulation have been enhanced. With every uptick or downtick in interest rates or currency values, huge amounts of money now move across national borders in search of better returns, hurtling stock and bond prices upward or plunging them downward with dizzying speed. Such volatility is a speculator's dream. Thousands

of symbolic analysts, eyes glued to computer terminals, seek to out-
wit one another by gaining a split second's advantage in discovering the global money's destination and then moving their own (or
their client's) money there before most of the rest of it arrives. Platoons of lawyers stand ready to help refinance, restructure, and re-
organize financial entities that have moved too slowly, or to contest
claims by someone else who has moved faster, or to litigate over
how the windfall gains or breathtaking losses are to be divvied up.[2]

4

LEGAL and financial symbolic analysis has thus become a major
source of income for a growing number of Americans, as well as
a national pastime for many others. In 1971, approximately
343,000 Americans offered legal services; by 1989, their number
had grown to just under one million—a threefold increase. During
the same interval, the American population grew by just 20 percent. As might be expected with this many lawyers plying their
trade, the number of lawsuits also rose faster than the population,
and the number of threats to litigate skyrocketed, with out-of-
court settlements becoming almost as common as divorces. By
1990, American law firms earned $73 billion, and their earnings
were growing more than 10 percent a year,[3] placing law among
the nation's most buoyant and lucrative industries. A similar surge
occurred in the numbers of investment bankers, financial advisers,
arbitrageurs, and traders—although the stock market setbacks of
1987 and 1989 stunted the growth somewhat. Between 1979 and
1987, employment on Wall Street doubled, from 182,000 to
364,000. Even after the market tumbled—scaring off thousands
of small investors and forcing securities firms to cut their staffs
—Wall Street still employed more Americans than were involved
in the production of steel.

---

[2] For a thoughtful analysis of the excessive costs of financial transactions, see
L. and V. Summers, "When Financial Markets Work Too Well: A Cautious
Case for a Securities Transactions Tax," National Bureau of Economic Re-
search, February 28, 1989.
[3] Annual surveys of law firms and compensation levels are published in *The
American Lawyer*.

The movement of financial assets has, of course, kept pace with the numbers of lawyers and bankers involved in moving them. In the entire year of 1960, a total of 776 million shares of stock were traded on the New York Stock Exchange—about 12 percent of the outstanding shares—and each of those shares had been held, on average, about eight years. By 1987, at the height of the boom, 900 million shares were exchanging hands each *week*, with the result that 97 percent of the outstanding shares were traded during the year. This figure did not include new speculative instruments like index options and futures, which turned over five times faster than stocks, and were held, on average, for a few days or hours. Only a tiny portion of these transactions represented new capital. Almost all shares and instruments merely recirculated, faster and faster.

Salaries, not surprisingly, have grown in tandem. In 1990, major law firms in New York, Washington, Atlanta, Chicago, and San Francisco paid each of their partners between $300,000 and $1 million. Smaller firms in smaller cities offered humbler sums, though still comfortably in six figures. Partners in major securities firms, meanwhile, had to make do with end-of-the-year bonuses that were scandalously modest in comparison with the heady days before 1987, but nonetheless pleasantly in the half-million-dollar range. In 1987, commissions and other trading expenses came to $25 billion—more than one-sixth of all corporate earnings that year.[4] Even within the cloistered walls of academe, where professors never deign to discuss one another's salaries, eyebrows were raised by the revelation that colleagues who taught finance received salaries approximately four times higher than what was paid to ordinary award-winning Renaissance scholars.

Should the financial market suffer a more serious collapse, there is little cause for worry among those who inhabit it. By the 1990s, lawyers, financiers, and speculators stood ready to earn even larger sums undoing the damage they had wrought during the 1980s. Few activities are more rewarding than helping others when they are down, especially if profits await when the market turns up again. When they were not engaged in "financial restructurings," "workouts," and other euphemistically titled operations

---

[4]Securities Industry Association, 1989.

for helping firms skirt bankruptcy, the denizens of Wall Street were solemnly amassing funds for "deleveraged buyouts," intended to reverse what had been done during the boom—this time, reduce the debt load and increase the number of shares of stock. It was anticipated that the bonds of newly bankrupt companies could be purchased for a small fraction of their face value, and new shares issued to the remaining creditors. The newly restructured firms could then be sold for a not inconsiderable profit. In 1990, RJR Nabisco budgeted $250 million for expected fees to investment banks, financial advisers, and lawyers who would help the firm refinance its gigantic debt. Meanwhile, the fastest-growing area of corporate legal practice was bankruptcy. The managing partner of the firm advising Drexel Burnham Lambert in its massive bankruptcy proceedings in 1990 put the matter in practical terms: "From the standpoint of the investment bankers and [lawyers] who created the deals . . . they don't have that work anymore. So now they find it on the reverse of the slope, on restructuring the debt that can't be paid. It's a way of utilizing personnel."[5]

The social cost of this exuberance has extended well beyond the fees directly paid for such services. First is the loss of talent: The symbolic-analytic skills of lawyers and financiers are diverted from other, presumably more productive uses to which they might else be dedicated. Second is the distrust which these activities promote among people whose cooperation is essential to high-value production. Distrust cannot readily be quantified, of course, but there are hints of its magnitude. The high-yield, high-risk "junk" bonds that financed RJR Nabisco's notorious $25 billion leveraged buyout in the fall of 1988, for example, reduced the value of the bonds held by RJR's ordinary creditors by making the whole company more vulnerable to bankruptcy. Because RJR's regular bondholders had not bargained for this added risk, they lost approximately $1 billion. Such loss was of no particular concern to the symbolic analysts who had engineered the deal; what they did was thoroughly profitable in the short run, and entirely legal (there was no law to prevent this sort of thing because no one had ever imagined it might be done). But—and here is the

---

[5] Quoted in Robert J. McCartney, "Wall St. Restructuring Lemons into Lemonade," *Washington Post Weekly Edition*, March 26–April 1, 1990, p. 20.

point—all *future* creditors of American corporations will be far more careful. Henceforth, corporate bonds will automatically include an insurance policy protecting the purchaser from such a ploy. The future cost of such insurance—and of the lawyers and financiers who devised it, and the managers and staff who administered it—will dwarf what RJR Nabisco gained from having manipulated their regular bondholders in the first place.[6]

Anyone who believes that the American economy, or American society generally, has nevertheless on balance benefited from the surging number of lawyers and financiers that now engulf us must be either a lawyer or a financier. The rest of us have cause for doubt. Thousands of new lawyers have not brought us more justice; the legions of financiers have not given us a more productive economy. Western Europeans and East Asians, whose productivity has risen noticeably faster than America's in recent decades, have eschewed litigation and financial manipulation without any apparent diminution in their quality of life.

By the start of the 1990s, Americans who analyzed and manipulated legal and financial symbols were busily extending their services abroad. The Japanese, West Germans, and British (who had long offered the world their own rather buttoned-down financial advice) have been especially eager to accept these services and learn the fancy symbolic-analytic techniques on which they are based. Perhaps they have failed to notice the fallout from these services in America. Or they have fallen prey to a devious plot concocted by politicians in Washington to improve the relative competitiveness of Americans by clogging the veins of European and Asian commerce with the same legal and financial arteriosclerosis that has burdened the United States. More likely, they are victims of a seduction similar to that carried out by weapons merchants around the world. If others are willing to pay for such costly ammunition, it must be worth the price. And in a world so armed, defending yourself requires that you follow suit.

---

[6]As of this writing, lawyers representing the RJR bondholders are devising yet another novel legal theory to support claims against those who sold their shares in the transaction. Called "fraudulent conveyance," the theory has never been properly tested in court in this type of transaction, and it probably never will. Its use is purely strategic—to elicit from the defendants a generous sum of money.

16

American Incomes

A SUMMARY is in order. My argument thus far is that the economic well-being of Americans (or, for that matter, of any other group of people sharing a common political identity) no longer depends on the profitability of the corporations they own, or on the prowess of their industries, but on the value they add to the global economy through their skills and insights. Increasingly, it is the jobs that Americans do, rather than the success of abstract entities like corporations, industries, or national economies, that determine their standard of living.

I have further suggested that American jobs can be grouped into three broad categories for assessing what is added to the global economy. These are routine production services, in-person services, and symbolic-analytic services. People within each category have a distinct competitive position in the world economy. Finally, I have noted that the economic fates of Americans are beginning to diverge. Some Americans are doing well in the global economy; some, far less well. I now want to examine that divergence.

2

DATA on the distribution of American incomes are not free from controversy. Like any data, they can be interpreted in slightly different ways, depending on the weights accorded a host of other changes that have occurred simultaneously, and also depending on which years are selected for measurement and how the measurements are done. But nearly everyone agrees that the trend, at least since the mid-1970s, has been toward inequality.[1]

Controlling for family size, geography, and other changes, the best estimate—which I cited earlier—is that between 1977 and 1990 the average income of the poorest fifth of Americans declined by about 5 percent, while the richest fifth became about 9 percent wealthier. During these years, the average incomes of the poorest fifth of American *families* declined by about 7 percent, while the average income of the richest fifth of American families increased about 15 percent. That left the poorest fifth of Americans by 1990 with 3.7 percent of the nation's total income, down from 5.5 percent twenty years before—the lowest portion they have received since 1954. And it left the richest fifth with a bit over half of the nation's income—the highest portion ever recorded by the top 20 percent. The top 5 percent commanded 26 percent of the nation's total income, another record.[2]

Picture a symmetrical wave that's highest in the middle and then gradually slopes down and out on both ends until merging with the horizon. Through the 1950s and 1960s, the distribution of income in the United States was coming to resemble just this sort of a wave. Most Americans were bunching up in the middle

---

[1] Among the first researchers to plot the trend were Bennett Harrison and Barry Bluestone. For a summary of their analysis, see their *The Great U-Turn* (New York: Basic Books, 1988).

[2] Projections through 1990 are based on the Current Population Survey conducted by the U.S. Bureau of the Census each month, the annual Statistics of Income sample of tax returns, and the Consumer Expenditure Survey carried out quarterly by the Bureau of Labor Statistics. See Congressional Budget Office, "The Changing Distribution of Federal Taxes, 1977–1990," U.S. House of Representatives, Ways and Means Committee, February 1987; also "Tax Progressivity and Income Distribution," U.S. House of Representatives, Ways and Means Committee, March 26, 1990.

Among blacks, whose earnings at all levels continued to trail whites, the gap is wider still. Between 1978 and 1988, the average income of the lowest fifth of black families declined by 24 percent, while that of the top 5 percent increased by almost as much. By the end of the 1980s, the top 5 percent of black families received 47 percent of total black income, compared with 42.9 percent of total white income received by the top 5 percent of white families. "Still Far from the Dream: Recent Developments in Black Income, Employment, and Poverty," Center on Budget Priorities, October 1988.

of the wave, enjoying medium incomes. Fewer Americans were on the sides, either very poor or very rich. Only a tiny minority were at the outermost edges, extremely poor or extremely rich. But beginning in the mid-1970s, and accelerating sharply in the 1980s, the crest of the wave began to move toward the poorer end. More Americans were poor. The middle began to sag, as the portion of middle-income Americans dropped. And the end representing the richest Americans began to elongate, as the rich became much, much richer.

The trend should not be overstated. Some researchers, selecting different years and using different measurements, have found the divergence to be somewhat less pronounced. But overall, the trend is unmistakable. There is good reason to suspect that it is not a temporary aberration, and that the gap will, if anything, grow wider.

3

MANY reasons have been offered to explain the trend toward income inequality. Some people blame the tax system. During the 1980s, Social Security payroll taxes, state and local sales taxes, and so-called user fees such as highway tolls and water charges all increased. These types of taxes inevitably claim a higher portion of the earnings of the poor than of the rich.[3] The Social Security

---

[3] In 1979, state and local sales taxes claimed 6.1 percent of the incomes of the poorest fifth of Americans, and 7.8 percent of the incomes of the wealthiest fifth. By 1990, the burden had shifted: the poorest fifth were paying 7.1 percent of their incomes in state and local sales taxes, and the wealthiest fifth only 2.5 percent. Projected through 1990 from an Urban Institute model on the incidence of state and local sales taxes between 1979 and 1984. Urban Institute, Washington, D.C., 1986.

Mention should also be made of government-sponsored lotteries, from which tax-starved states are gleaning ever more of their revenues. Here, too, the distributional impact is disturbing. A number of studies have shown that lottery ticket sales are highest in low-income areas. Per capita sales in inner-city Detroit, for example, are three times higher than sales in the Detroit suburbs. Lottery sales decline in areas where educational levels are higher. Notably, the revenues so raised rarely find their way back to poor areas. Lottery purchases by Detroit residents contributed $104 million to Michi-

payroll tax, it should be remembered, works exactly like the income tax but in reverse. Rather than exempt low incomes, it exempts high incomes. The tax must be paid even on the first dollar earned, but only up to a certain ceiling ($51,300 as of January 1990). Above the ceiling, no more payments need be made for the year. (Michael Milken, the investment banker noted both for having invented the "junk bond" and for earning $550 million in 1987, fulfilled his 1987 Social Security payment obligations at approximately 12:42 a.m. on January 1.) Social Security also exempts investment income, like interest and capital gains. Between 1978 and 1990, the Social Security payroll tax increased 30 percent. As it did so, the portion of federal revenues derived from Social Security steadily rose, from 21 percent at the start of the decade to 27 percent at the end.[4]

Meanwhile, wealthy Americans—armed with the cleverest symbolic-analytic tax specialists that money could buy—discovered ever more decorous ways of sheltering their incomes. The exploitation of tax loopholes, as well as the loopholes themselves, steadily grew through the 1970s. In 1981, Ronald Reagan cooperated in their efforts by reducing income-tax rates and lowering the rate on capital gains. (Additional legislation in 1986, which reduced the top income-tax rate from 50 to 33 percent in exchange for closing loopholes and increasing the capital-gains rate, marked a small step back toward progressivity, but hardly enough to offset 1981; the budget compromise of 1990, another tiny step.)

The result: In 1980, the bottom fifth of taxpayers paid an average 8.4 percent of their income in federal taxes; by 1990, they were paying 9.7 percent—an increase of one-sixth. The average tax burden on the top fifth of taxpayers, by contrast, dropped from 27.3 percent to 25.8 percent (down one-twentieth).[5] The

---

gan's school aid fund in 1988, while Detroit public schools received back only $80 million in lottery-generated school aid revenue. About $24 million from Detroit lottery sales was given to wealthier school districts. Figures from Charles Clotfelter and Philip Cook, *Selling Hope: State Lotteries in America* (Cambridge: Harvard University Press, 1989).

[4] "Tax Progressivity and Income Distribution."
[5] Ibid. See also Richard A. Musgrave, *Strengthening the Progressive Income Tax* (Washington, D.C.: Economic Policy Institute, 1989). The issue of tax equity has sparked an intense, although not terribly illuminating, debate among

drop was even more precipitous for the very rich: By the end of the 1980s, the top 1 percent of American earners were paying a combined federal-state-local tax rate of only 26.8 percent, compared with 29 percent in 1975 and 39.6 percent in 1966.[6]

The regressive shift in the tax burden surely did not narrow the widening gap between the nation's rich and poor. But, importantly, neither did it cause the divergence. The figures cited at the start of this chapter on the divergence in incomes are *before* the payment of any taxes.

The parsimonious social policies of the Reagan years are another oft-cited villain. During this laissez-faire interval, food-stamp benefits dropped about 13 percent (adjusted for inflation), and many states failed to raise benefits for the poor and unemployed to keep up with inflation. But not even the administration's stinginess explains the growing inequality, which began *before* the Reagan years. Nor does it account for the slide of poor working Americans, virtually none of whom received welfare assistance. Like the changes in the tax code, the tightfisted social policies of Ronald Reagan and his kinder, gentler successor failed to compensate for powerful forces already in motion, but they did not cause them.

Another explanation is the growth in single-parent, lower-income families, which has, undoubtedly, been significant. In 1960, 91 percent of white children and 67 percent of black children in the United States lived with two parents. By 1988, only

---

political partisans, as is to be expected. Apologists argue that, the above-mentioned percentages notwithstanding, the share of *total* federal taxes paid by the top fifth rose during the 1980s from 55.7 percent, to 58.1 percent, while the share paid by the top 5 percent of taxpayers rose from 27.6 percent to 30.4 percent; meanwhile, the share paid by the bottom fifth remained about the same as in 1980. See, for example, Lawrence Lindsey, *The Growth Experiment: How the New Tax Policy Is Transforming the United States Economy* (New York: Basic Books, 1990). This argument is correct so far as it goes, but it does not mean that the system became fairer. All it suggests is that the richest's share of total taxes went up *less* than their share of total income—with the result that their individual tax burdens declined. The poorest's share of the national income dropped while their share of taxes remained the same, so *their* tax burden went up.
[6]See Joseph Pechman, "The Future of the Income Tax," *The American Economic Review*, Vol. 80, No. 1 (March 1990), p. 1. See also "Tax Progressivity and Income Distribution."

79 percent of white children and 39 percent of black children did so. And the connection between single-parent families and poverty is indisputable—particularly for children. Yet even as the numbers of these mostly female-headed families have grown dramatically, their percentage of the poor has risen only modestly. From 1979 to 1987, fully half of the overall increase in poverty in the United States occurred among two-parent families.[7] Poverty rates for two-parent families in which the husband was under twenty-five jumped from 10.5 percent in 1979 to 21.5 percent in 1986.[8] In fact, the increase in the number of single-parent families actually slowed after the late 1970s, just as the gap between the rich and the poor began to widen precipitously.[9]

A final theory attributes the gap to all the young, unskilled, and inexperienced baby-boomers, and women, who surged into the job market in the 1970s and 1980s—and who, quite naturally, would be paid less than more skilled and experienced workers (even if there were no wage discrimination against women). But this explanation also fails to shed much light. The wage gap widened most in the 1980s, after the great surge of baby-boomers and women had come to an end. In addition, the widening gap characterizes every age group. Even among young workers, the richest have become much richer and the poorest, much poorer. Finally, since the relative wages of more educated, older, and female workers increased in the 1980s, by this theory the overall labor force should have become less educated, younger, and more male. In fact, the opposite occurred: The work force overall became slightly more educated, older, and more female.[10]

---

[7] See Mary Jo Bane and David Ellwood, "One Fifth of the Nation's Children: Why Are They Poor?" *Science*, September 1989, pp. 1047–48.

[8] Ibid.

[9] The University of Michigan Panel Study of Income Dynamics, which has been following a representative sample of 5,000 families since 1968, found that only one-seventh of childhood transitions into long-term poverty were associated with family dissolution, while more than half were linked to changes in labor market participation and wages. See also Bane and Ellwood, op. cit.; Center on Budget and Policy Priorities, October 29, 1989.

[10] On this point, see J. Bound and G. Johnson, "Changes in the Structure of Wages During the 1980s: An Evaluation of Alternative Explanations," National Bureau of Economic Research, Working Paper No. 2983, May 1989.

Even taken together, the conventional explanations for the widening gap between rich and poor account for only part of the answer. Interestingly, several other advanced economies—with different tax and welfare policies than the United States, and different demographic swings—have experienced a similar shift toward inequality. That the gap widened noticeably in Margaret Thatcher's Britain is perhaps no surprise, but even the benevolent social-democratic Netherlands has not been immune to the trend.[11] A wide divergence between the incomes of a few at the top and almost everyone else has long been a seemingly immutable feature of life in many underdeveloped economies, of course, but the trend there has a new feature: Today's Third World elites are less likely to be descended from generations of wealthy landholders, more likely to have gained their wealth from the jobs they do. After the land redistribution of the 1950s, for example, Taiwan became one of the world's most egalitarian societies. But, while income is still more evenly distributed there than in most developing nations, the gap between rich and poor widened considerably during the 1980s. The streets of Taipei are now clogged with Mercedes-Benzes, Volvos, and Jaguars, as well as rickety bicycles.[12]

4

ONE IMPORTANT clue: The growth in inequality within the United States (as well as in many other nations) has been dramatic even

---

[11] See Thomas Stark, "The Changing Distribution of Income Under Mrs. Thatcher," in Francis Green (ed.), *The Restructuring of the U.K. Economy* (London: Harvester, 1989); T. Elfring and R. Kloosterman, "The Dutch Job Machine: The Fast Growth of Low-Wage Jobs in Services, 1979–1986," Rotterdam School of Management, Erasmus University, 1989. For data on the divergence of incomes in Canada, see J. Myles, G. Picot, and T. Wannell, "Wages and Jobs in the 1980s: Changing Youth Wages and the Declining Middle," Social and Economic Studies Division, Statistics Canada, Research Paper Series No. 17, 1988. For Europe in general, see *OECD Employment Outlook* (Paris: OECD, September 1985 and subsequent issues).

[12] Nicholas Kristof, "Taiwan Embraces Trappings of New Wealth," *The New York Times*, December 5, 1989, p. A9.

among people who already hold jobs. Recall that through most of the postwar era, at least until the mid-1970s, the wages of Americans at different income levels rose at about the same pace—roughly 2.5 to 3 percent a year. Meanwhile, the wage gap between workers at the top and those at the bottom steadily narrowed—in part, because of the benign influence of America's core corporations and labor unions in raising the bottom and constraining the top.

In those days, poverty was a consequence of not having a job. The major postwar economic challenge was to create enough jobs for all Americans able to work. Full employment was the battle cry of American liberals, arrayed against conservatives who worried about the inflationary tendencies of a full-employment economy.

Unemployment is now less of a problem, however. In the 1970s and 1980s, over 25 million new jobs were created in the United States, 18.2 million of them in the 1980s alone. There is often a mismatch between where the jobs are and where the people are, of course. Many suburban fast-food jobs go unfilled while inner-city kids cannot easily commute to them. And the Federal Reserve Board periodically cools the economy in an effort to fight inflation, thus drafting into the inflation fight many thousands of those Americans who can least afford it. But these impediments notwithstanding, the truth is that by the last decade of the twentieth century, almost all Americans who wanted to work could find a job. And because population growth has been slowing (more on this later), the demand for people to fill jobs is likely to be higher still in years to come. State governors and city mayors continue to worry every time a factory closes and to congratulate themselves every time they lure new jobs to their jurisdictions. Yet the more important issue over the longer term is the *quality* of jobs, not the number.

By the 1990s, many jobs failed to provide a living wage. More than half of the 32.5 million Americans whose incomes fell under the official poverty line—and nearly two-thirds of all poor children—lived in households with at least one worker. This is a much higher rate of working poor than at any other time in the postwar era. The number of impoverished working Americans climbed by nearly 2 million, or 23 percent, between 1978 and

1987 (years at similar points in the business cycle).[13] Among full-time, year-round workers, the number who were poor climbed even more sharply—by 43 percent. In fact, two-parent families with a full-time worker fell further below the poverty line, on average, than any other type of family, including single parents on welfare.[14]

The wage gap has been widening even within the core American corporation (or, more precisely, that portion of the global web that is formally owned and managed by Americans).[15] By 1990, the average hourly earnings of American non-supervisory workers within American-owned corporations, adjusted for inflation, were lower than in any year since 1965. Middle-level managers fared somewhat better, although their median earnings (adjusted for inflation) were only slightly above the levels of the 1970s.

But between 1977 and 1990, top executives of American-owned corporations reaped a bonanza. Their average remuneration rose by 220 percent, or about 12 percent a year, compounded. (This is aside from the standard perquisites of company car, company plane, country club membership, estate planning, physical examinations, and so forth.)[16]

To put this into perspective, consider that in 1960, as pointed out earlier, the typical executive officer of the core American corporation earned about $190,000. This sum was approximately 40 times the wages of the company's average American factory

---

[13] Two-thirds of this widening gap among workers can be attributed to a growing dispersion in wages; the other third, to an increasing divergence in the number of hours actually worked—with many people in part-time jobs who would rather be employed full-time.

[14] Data for 1984. D. Ellwood, *Poor Support: Poverty in the American Family* (New York: Basic Books, 1988), p. 99, Table 4-3.

[15] Data from B. Harrison and B. Bluestone, "Wage Polarization in the United States and the 'Flexibility' Debate," School of Urban and Public Affairs, Carnegie-Mellon University, Working Paper, Fall 1989.

[16] Surveys of executive compensation are made annually by consultants specializing in the field and reported in most major business publications. Few news items attract as much annual attention from corporate executives. See, for example, "Pay Stubs of the Rich and Corporate," *Business Week*, May 7, 1990, p. 56; "Executive Pay," *The Wall Street Journal*, supplement, April 18, 1990; A. Bennett, "A Great Leap Forward for Executive Pay," *The Wall Street Journal*, April 24, 1989, p. B1.

worker. Of course, in 1960, when the maximum tax rate was 90 percent, the CEO's actual take-home pay was considerably less than this, making him (it was always a him) only about 12 times richer than the worker on the line. But by 1988, the chief executive officer of one of America's hundred largest corporations received, on average, $2,025,000. This was 93 times the wages paid to the average American production worker for these corporations. And, given that the top tax rate was only 28 percent, the CEO took home about 70 times more than the worker on the line.[17]

Executives just below the top typically earn a less princely, but no less comfortable, sum—suitable, say, for a duke. When American Express's chief executive, James Robinson, pocketed $2.7 million in 1988, his second-in-command, Louis Gerstner, received an appropriately more modest $2.4 million. According to Graef S. Crystal, an expert on corporate compensation, "[t]here's a suck-up effect, like a vacuum cleaner."[18]

5

A SECOND important clue: The widening income gap is closely related to the level of education. Assume you are a male with a high school diploma but no college education. You also hold a steady job. By 1987 that job was paying you (on average) $27,733. Fourteen years earlier, in 1973, someone with your education would have earned $31,677 on the job (in 1987 dollars). In other

---

[17]An international comparison is illuminating. According to a survey by the compensation specialists Towers, Perrin, Forster, & Crosby, in 1990 the typical U.S. chief executive officer of a company with annual sales of $250 million earned $543,000 in salaries, bonuses, and perquisites. That was over 50 percent more than the $352,000 earned by a similarly situated Japanese executive, 90 percent more than the total compensation (about $287,000) of German and British CEOs, and 400 percent more than the compensation of a typical Korean top executive. The American CEO's money also goes further: The typical CEO can buy three times as much in America with the same dollar as a similar Japanese executive can in Japan, and about twice as much as a German. *Report on International Compensation*, January 1990, pp. 8–14.

[18]Quoted in Patricia O'Toole, "Silk Purse Chronicles," *Lears Magazine*, April 1990, p. 23.

words, with no more than a high school education, your real earnings (adjusted for inflation) actually declined by 12 percent. (If you were black and without a college education, your average earnings declined during the same period by 44 percent.) Assume now that you dropped out of high school. Your steady job in 1987 now earns you (on average) only $16,094. Fourteen years earlier, someone with your education would have earned $19,562. This means that your inflation-adjusted earnings have plunged even further—by 18 percent.[19]

If you are a male graduate of a four-year college, on the other hand, you would be ahead of the game—though only slightly. Your 1987 earnings would be $50,115, as compared with the average income of someone with a four-year college degree in 1973, which was $49,531. The wage gap thus appears to be directly related to education. While a college degree does not guarantee you a much higher income than it did years ago, *without* a college degree you are not even in the running. In 1980, our typical male college graduate earned about 80 percent more than his high school counterpart; by 1990, the gap had nearly doubled.[20]

Other nations have experienced a similar divergence between the earnings of their high school and college graduates (or their equivalents). Even Swedish wage differentials have stopped narrowing.[21] Japan, interestingly, is something of an exception to this rule. There, high school graduates are still keeping pace with college graduates. Between 1979 and 1987, while the earnings of high school graduates plummeted in the United States, Japanese high schoolers increased their earnings by 13 percent. Japanese college graduates, by contrast, did no better than their American counterparts. Apparently social norms operate in

[19]William T. Grant Foundation Commission on Work, Family, and Citizenship, "The Forgotten Half: Non-College Youth in America," January 1988, pp. 18–27.

[20]See M. Blackburn, D. Bloom, and R. Freeman, "Why Has the Economic Position of Less-Skilled Male Workers Deteriorated in the United States?," Brookings Discussion Paper, March 1989. See also C. Juhn, K. Murphy, and B. Pierce, "Wage Inequality and the Rise in Returns to Skill," unpub., November 1989.

[21]G. Standing, *Unemployment and Labour Market Flexibility: Sweden* (Geneva: International Labour Office, 1988).

Japan to raise the salaries and benefits of those on the bottom half of the educational ladder.[22]

One final clue: During the 1980s, the so-called gender gap between the earnings of males and females closed by about a third. Even between relatively uneducated men and women, wages and benefits converged.[23]

In sum, the widening gap between rich and poor seems to be related to a growing divergence in how much money people receive for the work they do. And that divergence, in turn, appears to have something to do with their level of education. If you graduated from college, your earnings improved; if you did not, and especially if you were male, you got poorer. Further, the trend is not limited to the United States; it is occurring in many other places around the globe. To understand its basic cause, it is necessary to return to the global economy, and the different functions that people are coming to perform within it.

---

[22] L. Katz and A. Revenga, "Changes in the Structure of Wages: United States vs. Japan," National Bureau of Economic Research, September 1989.
[23] Data from Bound and Johnson, op. cit.

17

Why the Rich Are Getting Richer and the Poor, Poorer

[T]he division of labour is limited by the extent of the market.

ADAM SMITH, *An Inquiry into the Nature
and Causes of the Wealth of Nations* (1776)

REGARDLESS of how your job is officially classified (manufacturing, service, managerial, technical, secretarial, and so on), or the industry in which you work (automotive, steel, computer, advertising, finance, food processing), your real competitive position in the world economy is coming to depend on the function you perform in it. Herein lies the basic reason why incomes are diverging. The fortunes of routine producers are declining. In-person servers are also becoming poorer, although their fates are less clear-cut. But symbolic analysts—who solve, identify, and broker new problems—are, by and large, succeeding in the world economy.

All Americans used to be in roughly the same economic boat. Most rose or fell together, as the corporations in which they were employed, the industries comprising such corporations, and the national economy as a whole became more productive—or languished. But national borders no longer define our economic fates. We are now in different boats, one sinking rapidly, one sinking more slowly, and the third rising steadily.

2

THE BOAT containing routine producers is sinking rapidly. Recall that by midcentury routine production workers in the United States were paid relatively well. The giant pyramidlike organizations at the core of each major industry coordinated their prices and investments—avoiding the harsh winds of competition and thus maintaining healthy earnings. Some of these earnings, in turn, were reinvested in new plant and equipment (yielding ever-larger-scale economies); another portion went to top managers and investors. But a large and increasing portion went to middle managers and production workers. Work stoppages posed such a threat to high-volume production that organized labor was able to exact an ever-larger premium for its cooperation. And the pattern of wages established within the core corporations influenced the pattern throughout the national economy. Thus the growth of a relatively affluent middle class, able to purchase all the wondrous things produced in high volume by the core corporations.

But, as has been observed, the core is rapidly breaking down into global webs which earn their largest profits from clever problem-solving, -identifying, and brokering. As the costs of transporting standard things and of communicating information about them continue to drop, profit margins on high-volume, standardized production are thinning, because there are few barriers to entry. Modern factories and state-of-the-art machinery can be installed almost anywhere on the globe. Routine producers in the United States, then, are in direct competition with millions of routine producers in other nations. Twelve thousand people are added to the world's population every hour, most of whom, eventually, will happily work for a small fraction of the wages of routine producers in America.[1]

---

[1] The reader should note, of course, that lower wages in other areas of the world are of no particular attraction to global capital unless workers there are sufficiently productive to make the labor cost of producing *each unit* lower there than in higher-wage regions. Productivity in many low-wage areas of the world has improved due to the ease with which state-of-the-art factories and equipment can be installed there.

The consequence is clearest in older, heavy industries, where high-volume, standardized production continues its ineluctable move to where labor is cheapest and most accessible around the world. Thus, for example, the Maquiladora factories cluttered along the Mexican side of the U.S. border in the sprawling shanty towns of Tijuana, Mexicali, Nogales, Agua Prieta, and Ciudad Juárez—factories owned mostly by Americans, but increasingly by Japanese—in which more than a half million routine producers assemble parts into finished goods to be shipped into the United States.

The same story is unfolding worldwide. Until the late 1970s, AT&T had depended on routine producers in Shreveport, Louisiana, to assemble standard telephones. It then discovered that routine producers in Singapore would perform the same tasks at a far lower cost. Facing intense competition from other global webs, AT&T's strategic brokers felt compelled to switch. So in the early 1980s they stopped hiring routine producers in Shreveport and began hiring cheaper routine producers in Singapore. But under this kind of pressure for ever lower high-volume production costs, today's Singaporean can easily end up as yesterday's Louisianan. By the late 1980s, AT&T's strategic brokers found that routine producers in Thailand were eager to assemble telephones for a small fraction of the wages of routine producers in Singapore. Thus, in 1989, AT&T stopped hiring Singaporeans to make telephones and began hiring even cheaper routine producers in Thailand.

The search for ever lower wages has not been confined to heavy industry. Routine data processing is equally footloose. Keypunch operators located anywhere around the world can enter data into computers, linked by satellite or transoceanic fiber-optic cable, and take it out again. As the rates charged by satellite networks continue to drop, and as more satellites and fiber-optic cables become available (reducing communication costs still further), routine data processors in the United States find themselves in ever more direct competition with their counterparts abroad, who are often eager to work for far less.

By 1990, keypunch operators in the United States were earning, at most, $6.50 per hour. But keypunch operators throughout the rest of the world were willing to work for a fraction of this. Thus, many potential American data-processing jobs were disappearing, and the wages and benefits of the remaining ones were in decline. Typical was Saztec International, a $20-million-a-year data-processing firm headquartered in Kansas City, whose American strategic brokers contracted with routine data processors in Manila and with American-owned firms that needed such data-processing services. Compared with the average Philippine income of $1,700 per year, data-entry operators working for Saztec earn the princely sum of $2,650. The remainder of Saztec's employees were American problem-solvers and -identifiers, searching for ways to improve the worldwide system and find new uses to which it could be put.[2]

By 1990, American Airlines was employing over 1,000 data processors in Barbados and the Dominican Republic to enter names and flight numbers from used airline tickets (flown daily to Barbados from airports around the United States) into a giant computer bank located in Dallas. Chicago publisher R. R. Donnelley was sending entire manuscripts to Barbados for entry into computers in preparation for printing. The New York Life Insurance Company was dispatching insurance claims to Castleisland, Ireland, where routine producers, guided by simple directions, entered the claims and determined the amounts due, then instantly transmitted the computations back to the United States. (When the firm advertised in Ireland for twenty-five data-processing jobs, it received six hundred applications.) And McGraw-Hill was processing subscription renewal and marketing information for its magazines in nearby Galway. Indeed, literally millions of routine workers around the world were receiving information, converting it into computer-readable form, and then sending it back—at the speed of electronic impulses—whence it came.

The simple coding of computer software has also entered into world commerce. India, with a large English-speaking population of technicians happy to do routine programming cheaply, is proving to be particularly attractive to global webs in need of this service. By 1990, Texas Instruments maintained a software development facility in Bangalore, linking fifty Indian programmers by satellite to TI's Dallas headquarters. Spurred by this and similar

---

[2] John Maxwell Hamilton, "A Bit Player Buys Into the Computer Age," *The New York Times Business World*, December 3, 1989, p. 14.

ventures, the Indian government was building a teleport in Poona, intended to make it easier and less expensive for many other firms to send their routine software design specifications for coding.[3]

3

THIS shift of routine production jobs from advanced to developing nations is a great boon to many workers in such nations who otherwise would be jobless or working for much lower wages. These workers, in turn, now have more money with which to purchase symbolic-analytic services from advanced nations (often embedded within all sorts of complex products). The trend is also beneficial to everyone around the world who can now obtain high-volume, standardized products (including information and software) more cheaply than before.

But these benefits do not come without certain costs. In particular the burden is borne by those who no longer have good-paying routine production jobs within advanced economies like the United States. Many of these people used to belong to unions or at least benefited from prevailing wage rates established in collective bargaining agreements. But as the old corporate bureaucracies have flattened into global webs, bargaining leverage has been lost. Indeed, the tacit national bargain is no more.

Despite the growth in the number of new jobs in the United States, union membership has withered. In 1960, 35 percent of all nonagricultural workers in America belonged to a union. But by 1980 that portion had fallen to just under a quarter, and by 1989 to about 17 percent. Excluding government employees, union membership was down to 13.4 percent.[4] This was a smaller proportion even than in the early 1930s, before the National Labor Relations Act created a legally protected right to labor representation. The drop in membership has been accompanied by a growing number of collective bargaining agreements to freeze wages at current levels, reduce wage levels of entering workers,

---

[3] Udayan Gupta, "U.S.-India Satellite Link Stands to Cut Software Costs," *The Wall Street Journal*, March 6, 1989, p. B2.
[4] *Statistical Abstract of the United States* (Washington, D.C.: U.S. Government Printing Office, 1989), p. 416, Table 684.

or reduce wages overall. This is an important reason why the long economic recovery that began in 1982 produced a smaller rise in unit labor costs than any of the eight recoveries since World War II—the low rate of unemployment during its course notwithstanding.

Routine production jobs have vanished fastest in traditional unionized industries (autos, steel, and rubber, for example), where average wages have kept up with inflation. This is because the jobs of older workers in such industries are protected by seniority; the youngest workers are the first to be laid off. Faced with a choice of cutting wages or cutting the number of jobs, a majority of union members (secure in the knowledge that there are many who are junior to them who will be laid off first) often have voted for the latter.

Thus the decline in union membership has been most striking among young men entering the work force without a college education. In the early 1950s, more than 40 percent of this group joined unions; by the late 1980s, less than 20 percent (if public employees are excluded, less than 10 percent).[5] In steelmaking, for example, although many older workers remained employed, almost half of all routine steelmaking jobs in America vanished between 1974 and 1988 (from 480,000 to 260,000). Similarly with automobiles: During the 1980s, the United Auto Workers lost 500,000 members—one-third of their total at the start of the decade. General Motors alone cut 150,000 American production jobs during the 1980s (even as it added employment abroad). Another consequence of the same phenomenon: The gap between the average wages of unionized and nonunionized workers widened dramatically—from 14.6 percent in 1973 to 20.4 percent by end of the 1980s.[6] The lesson is clear. If you drop out of high school or have no more than a high school diploma, do not expect a good routine production job to be awaiting you.

Also vanishing are lower- and middle-level management jobs involving routine production. Between 1981 and 1986, more than

---

[5] Calculations from Current Population Surveys by L. Katz and A. Revenga, "Changes in the Structure of Wages: U.S. and Japan," National Bureau of Economic Research, September 1989.

[6] U.S. Department of Commerce, Bureau of Labor Statistics, "Wages of Unionized and Non-Unionized Workers," various issues.

780,000 foremen, supervisors, and section chiefs lost their jobs through plant closings and layoffs.[7] Large numbers of assistant division heads, assistant directors, assistant managers, and vice presidents also found themselves jobless. GM shed more than 40,000 white-collar employees and planned to eliminate another 25,000 by the mid-1990s.[8] As America's core pyramids metamorphosed into global webs, many middle-level routine producers were as obsolete as routine workers on the line.

As has been noted, foreign-owned webs are hiring some Americans to do routine production in the United States. Philips, Sony, and Toyota factories are popping up all over—to the self-congratulatory applause of the nation's governors and mayors, who have lured them with promises of tax abatements and new sewers, among other amenities. But as these ebullient politicians will soon discover, the foreign-owned factories are highly automated and will become far more so in years to come. Routine production jobs account for a small fraction of the cost of producing most items in the United States and other advanced nations, and this fraction will continue to decline sharply as computer-integrated robots take over. In 1977 it took routine producers thirty-five hours to assemble an automobile in the United States; it is estimated that by the mid-1990s, Japanese-owned factories in America will be producing finished automobiles using only eight hours of a routine producer's time.[9]

The productivity and resulting wages of American workers who run such robotic machinery may be relatively high, but there may not be many such jobs to go around. A case in point: In the late 1980s, Nippon Steel joined with America's ailing Inland Steel to build a new $400 million cold-rolling mill fifty miles west of Gary, Indiana. The mill was celebrated for its state-of-the-art technology, which cut the time to produce a coil of steel from twelve days to about one hour. In fact, the entire plant could be run by a small team of technicians, which became clear when Inland

[7]U.S. Department of Labor, Bureau of Labor Statistics, "Reemployment Increases Among Displaced Workers," BLS News, USDL 86-414, October 14, 1986, Table 6.

[8]The Wall Street Journal, February 16, 1990, p. A5.

[9]Figures from the International Motor Vehicles Program, Massachusetts Institute of Technology, 1989.

subsequently closed two of its old cold-rolling mills, laying off hundreds of routine workers. Governors and mayors take note: Your much-ballyhooed foreign factories may end up employing distressingly few of your constituents.

Overall, the decline in routine jobs has hurt men more than women. This is because the routine production jobs held by men in high-volume metal-bending manufacturing industries had paid higher wages than the routine production jobs held by women in textiles and data processing. As both sets of jobs have been lost, American women in routine production have gained more equal footing with American men—equally poor footing, that is. This is a major reason why the gender gap between male and female wages began to close during the 1980s.

4

THE SECOND of the three boats, carrying in-person servers, is sinking as well, but somewhat more slowly and unevenly. Most in-person servers are paid at or just slightly above the minimum wage and many work only part-time, with the result that their take-home pay is modest, to say the least. Nor do they typically receive all the benefits (health care, life insurance, disability, and so forth) garnered by routine producers in large manufacturing corporations or by symbolic analysts affiliated with the more affluent threads of global webs.[10] In-person servers are sheltered from the direct effects of global competition and, like everyone else, benefit from access to lower-cost products from around the world. But they are not immune to its indirect effects.

For one thing, in-person servers increasingly compete with former routine production workers, who, no longer able to find well-paying routine production jobs, have few alternatives but to seek in-person service jobs. The Bureau of Labor Statistics estimates that of the 2.8 million manufacturing workers who lost their jobs during the early 1980s, fully one-third were rehired in service

---

[10]The growing portion of the American labor force engaged in in-person services, relative to routine production, thus helps explain why the number of Americans lacking health insurance increased by at least 6 million during the 1980s.

jobs paying at least 20 percent less.[11] In-person servers must also compete with high school graduates and dropouts who years before had moved easily into routine production jobs but no longer can. And if demographic predictions about the American work force in the first decades of the twenty-first century are correct (and they are likely to be, since most of the people who will comprise the work force are already identifiable), most new entrants into the job market will be black or Hispanic men, or women—groups that in years past have possessed relatively weak technical skills. This will result in an even larger number of people crowding into in-person services. Finally, in-person servers will be competing with growing numbers of immigrants, both legal and illegal, for whom in-person services will comprise the most accessible jobs. (It is estimated that between the mid-1980s and the end of the century, about a quarter of all workers entering the American labor force will be immigrants.[12])

Perhaps the fiercest competition that in-person servers face comes from labor-saving machinery (much of it invented, designed, fabricated, or assembled in other nations, of course). Automated tellers, computerized cashiers, automatic car washes, robotized vending machines, self-service gasoline pumps, and all similar gadgets substitute for the human beings that customers once encountered. Even telephone operators are fast disappearing, as electronic sensors and voice simulators become capable of carrying on conversations that are reasonably intelligent, and always polite. Retail sales workers—among the largest groups of in-person servers—are similarly imperiled. Through personal computers linked to television screens, tomorrow's consumers will be able to buy furniture, appliances, and all sorts of electronic toys from their living rooms—examining the merchandise from all angles, selecting whatever color, size, special features, and price seem most appealing, and then transmitting the order instantly to warehouses from which the selections will be shipped directly to their homes. So, too, with financial transactions, airline and hotel reservations, rental car agreements, and similar contracts,

---

[11]U.S. Department of Labor, Bureau of Labor Statistics, "Reemployment Increases Among Displaced Workers," October 14, 1986.
[12]Federal Immigration and Naturalization Service, *Statistical Yearbook* (Washington, D.C.: U.S. Government Printing Office, 1986, 1987).

which will be executed between consumers in their homes and computer banks somewhere else on the globe.[13]

Advanced economies like the United States will continue to generate sizable numbers of new in-person service jobs, of course, the automation of older ones notwithstanding. For every bank teller who loses her job to an automated teller, three new jobs open for aerobics instructors. Human beings, it seems, have an almost insatiable desire for personal attention. But the intense competition nevertheless ensures that the wages of in-person servers will remain relatively low. In-person servers—working on their own, or else dispersed widely amid many small establishments, filling all sorts of personal-care niches—cannot readily organize themselves into labor unions or create powerful lobbies to limit the impact of such competition.

In two respects, demographics will work in favor of in-person servers, buoying their collective boat slightly. First, as has been noted, the rate of growth of the American work force is slowing. In particular, the number of younger workers is shrinking. Between 1985 and 1995, the number of eighteen- to twenty-four-year-olds will have declined by 17.5 percent. Thus, employers will have more incentive to hire and train in-person servers whom they might previously have avoided. But this demographic relief from the competitive pressures will be only temporary. The cumulative procreative energies of the postwar baby-boomers (born between 1946 and 1964) will result in a new surge of workers by 2010 or thereabouts.[14] And immigration—both legal and illegal —shows every sign of increasing in years to come.

Next, by the second decade of the twenty-first century, the number of Americans aged sixty-five and over will be rising precipitously, as the baby-boomers reach retirement age and live longer. Their life expectancies will lengthen not just because fewer of them will have smoked their way to their graves and more will have eaten better than their parents, but also because they will receive all sorts of expensive drugs and therapies designed to keep

---

[13]See Claudia H. Deutsch, "The Powerful Push for Self-Service," *The New York Times*, April 9, 1989, section 3, p. 1.

[14]U.S. Bureau of the Census, Current Population Reports, Series P-23, No. 138, Tables 2-1, 4-6. See W. Johnson, A. Packer, et al., *Workforce 2000: Work and Workers for the 21st Century* (Indianapolis: Hudson Institute, 1987).

them alive—barely. By 2035, twice as many Americans will be elderly as in 1988, and the number of octogenarians is expected to triple. As these decaying baby-boomers ingest all the chemicals and receive all the treatments, they will need a great deal of personal attention. Millions of deteriorating bodies will require nurses, nursing-home operators, hospital administrators, orderlies, home-care providers, hospice aides, and technicians to operate and maintain all the expensive machinery that will monitor and temporarily stave off final disintegration. There might even be a booming market for euthanasia specialists. In-person servers catering to the old and ailing will be in strong demand.[15]

One small problem: The decaying baby-boomers will not have enough money to pay for these services. They will have used up their personal savings years before. Their Social Security payments will, of course, have been used by the government to pay for the previous generation's retirement and to finance much of the budget deficits of the 1980s. Moreover, with relatively fewer young Americans in the population, the supply of housing will likely exceed the demand, with the result that the boomers' major investments—their homes—will be worth less (in inflation-adjusted dollars) when they retire than they planned for. In consequence, the huge cost of caring for the graying boomers will fall on many of the same people who will be paid to care for them. It will be like a great sump pump: In-person servers of the twenty-first century will have an abundance of health-care jobs, but a large portion of their earnings will be devoted to Social Security payments and income taxes, which will in turn be used to pay their salaries. The net result: no real improvement in their standard of living.

The standard of living of in-person servers also depends, indirectly, on the standard of living of the Americans they serve who are engaged in world commerce. To the extent that *these* Americans are richly rewarded by the rest of the world for what they contribute, they will have more money to lavish upon in-person services. Here we find the only form of "trickle-down" economics that has a basis in reality. A waitress in a town whose

---

[15]The Census Bureau estimates that by the year 2000, at least 12 million Americans will work in health services—well over 6 percent of the total work force.

major factory has just been closed is unlikely to earn a high wage or enjoy much job security; in a swank resort populated by film producers and banking moguls, she is apt to do reasonably well. So, too, with nations. In-person servers in Bangladesh may spend their days performing roughly the same tasks as in-person servers in the United States, but have a far lower standard of living for their efforts. The difference comes in the value that their customers add to the world economy. I shall return to this issue in a later chapter.

5

UNLIKE the boats of routine producers and in-person servers, however, the vessel containing America's symbolic analysts is rising. Worldwide demand for their insights is growing as the ease and speed of communicating them steadily increases. Not every symbolic analyst is rising as quickly or as dramatically as every other, of course; symbolic analysts at the low end are barely holding their own in the world economy. But symbolic analysts at the top are in such great demand worldwide that they have difficulty keeping track of all their earnings. Never before in history has opulence on such a scale been gained by people who have earned it, and done so legally.

Among symbolic analysts in the middle range are American scientists and researchers who are busily selling their discoveries to global enterprise webs. They are not limited to American customers. If the strategic brokers in General Motors' headquarters refuse to pay a high price for a new means of making high-strength ceramic engines dreamed up by a team of engineers affiliated with Carnegie-Mellon University in Pittsburgh, the strategic brokers of Honda or Mercedes-Benz are likely to be more than willing.

So, too, with the insights of America's ubiquitous management consultants, which are being sold for large sums to eager entrepreneurs in Europe and Latin America. Also, the insights of America's energy consultants, sold for even larger sums to Arab sheikhs. American design engineers are providing insights to Olivetti, Mazda, Siemens, and other global webs; American marketers, techniques for learning what worldwide consumers will buy; American advertisers, ploys for ensuring that they actually do. American architects are issuing designs and blueprints for opera houses, art galleries, museums, luxury hotels, and residential complexes in the world's major cities; American commercial property developers, marketing these properties to worldwide investors and purchasers.

Americans who specialize in the gentle art of public relations are in demand by corporations, governments, and politicians in virtually every nation. So, too, are American political consultants, some of whom, at this writing, are advising the Hungarian Socialist Party, the remnant of Hungary's ruling Communists, on how to salvage a few parliamentary seats in the nation's first free election in more than forty years. Also at this writing, a team of American agricultural consultants are advising the managers of a Soviet farm collective employing 1,700 Russians eighty miles outside Moscow. As noted, American investment bankers and lawyers specializing in financial circumnavigations are selling their insights to Asians and Europeans who are eager to discover how to make large amounts of money by moving large amounts of money.

Developing nations, meanwhile, are hiring American civil engineers to advise on building roads and dams. The present thaw in the Cold War will no doubt expand these opportunities. American engineers from Bechtel (a global firm notable for having employed both Caspar Weinberger and George Shultz for much larger sums than either earned in the Reagan administration) have begun helping the Soviets design and install a new generation of nuclear reactors. Nations also are hiring American bankers and lawyers to help them renegotiate the terms of their loans with global banks, and Washington lobbyists to help them with Congress, the Treasury, the World Bank, the IMF, and other politically sensitive institutions. In fits of obvious desperation, several nations emerging from communism have even hired American economists to teach them about capitalism.

Almost everyone around the world is buying the skills and insights of Americans who manipulate oral and visual symbols— musicians, sound engineers, film producers, makeup artists, directors, cinematographers, actors and actresses, boxers, scriptwriters, songwriters, and set designers. Among the wealthiest of symbolic analysts are Steven Spielberg, Bill Cosby, Charles Schulz, Eddie Murphy, Sylvester Stallone, Madonna, and other star directors and performers—who are almost as well known on the streets of Dresden and Tokyo as in the Back Bay of Boston. Less well rewarded but no less renowned are the unctuous anchors on Turner Broadcasting's Cable News, who appear daily, via satellite, in places ranging from Vietnam to Nigeria. Vanna White is the world's most watched game-show hostess. Behind each of these familiar faces is a collection of American problem-solvers, -identifiers, and brokers who train, coach, advise, promote, amplify, direct, groom, represent, and otherwise add value to their talents.[16]

There are also the insights of senior American executives who occupy the world headquarters of global "American" corporations and the national or regional headquarters of global "foreign" corporations. Their insights are duly exported to the rest of the world through the webs of global enterprise. IBM does not export many machines from the United States, for example. Big Blue makes machines all over the globe and services them on the spot. Its prime American exports are symbolic and analytic. From IBM's world headquarters in Armonk, New York, emanate strategic brokerage and related management services bound for the rest of the world. In return, IBM's top executives are generously rewarded.

6

THE MOST important reason for this expanding world market and increasing global demand for the symbolic and analytic insights of Americans has been the dramatic improvement in worldwide communication and transportation technologies. Designs, instructions, advice, and visual and audio symbols can be communicated more and more rapidly around the globe, with evergreater precision and at ever-lower cost. Madonna's voice can be transported to billions of listeners, with perfect clarity, on digital compact disks. A new invention emanating from engineers in

---

[16] In 1989, the entertainment business summoned to the United States $5.5 billion in foreign earnings—making it among the nation's largest export industries, just behind aerospace. U.S. Department of Commerce, International Trade Commission, "Composition of U.S. Exports," various issues.

Battelle's laboratory in Columbus, Ohio, can be sent almost anywhere via modem, in a form that will allow others to examine it in three dimensions through enhanced computer graphics. When face-to-face meetings are still required—and videoconferencing will not suffice—it is relatively easy for designers, consultants, advisers, artists, and executives to board supersonic jets and, in a matter of hours, meet directly with their worldwide clients, customers, audiences, and employees.

With rising demand comes rising compensation. Whether in the form of licensing fees, fees for service, salaries, or shares in final profits, the economic result is much the same. There are also nonpecuniary rewards. One of the best-kept secrets among symbolic analysts is that so many of them enjoy their work. In fact, much of it does not count as work at all, in the traditional sense. The work of routine producers and in-person servers is typically monotonous; it causes muscles to tire or weaken and involves little independence or discretion. The "work" of symbolic analysts, by contrast, often involves puzzles, experiments, games, a significant amount of chatter, and substantial discretion over what to do next. Few routine producers or in-person servers would "work" if they did not need to earn the money. Many symbolic analysts would "work" even if money were no object.

7

AT MIDCENTURY, when America was a national market dominated by core pyramid-shaped corporations, there were constraints on the earnings of people at the highest rungs. First and most obviously, the market for their services was largely limited to the borders of the nation. In addition, whatever conceptual value they might contribute was small relative to the value gleaned from large scale—and it was dependent on large scale for whatever income it was to summon. Most of the problems to be identified and solved had to do with enhancing the efficiency of production and improving the flow of materials, parts, assembly, and distribution. Inventors searched for the rare breakthrough revealing an entirely new product to be made in high volume; management consultants, executives, and engineers thereafter tried to speed and synchronize its manufacture, to better achieve scale efficiencies; advertisers and marketers sought then to whet the public's appetite for the standard item that emerged. Since white-collar earnings increased with larger scale, there was considerable incentive to expand the firm; indeed, many of America's core corporations grew far larger than scale economies would appear to have justified.

By the 1990s, in contrast, the earnings of symbolic analysts were limited neither by the size of the national market nor by the volume of production of the firms with which they were affiliated. The marketplace was worldwide, and conceptual value was high relative to value added from scale efficiencies.

There had been another constraint on high earnings, which also gave way by the 1990s. At midcentury, the compensation awarded to top executives and advisers of the largest of America's core corporations could not be grossly out of proportion to that of low-level production workers. It would be unseemly for executives who engaged in highly visible rounds of bargaining with labor unions, and who routinely responded to government requests to moderate prices, to take home wages and benefits wildly in excess of what other Americans earned. Unless white-collar executives restrained themselves, moreover, blue-collar production workers could not be expected to restrain their own demands for higher wages. Unless both groups exercised restraint, the government could not be expected to forbear from imposing direct controls and regulations.

At the same time, the wages of production workers could not be allowed to sink too low, lest there be insufficient purchasing power in the economy. After all, who would buy all the goods flowing out of American factories if not American workers? This, too, was part of the tacit bargain struck between American managers and their workers.

Recall the oft-repeated corporate platitude of the era about the chief executive's responsibility to carefully weigh and balance the interests of the corporation's disparate stakeholders. Under the stewardship of the corporate statesman, no set of stakeholders—least of all white-collar executives—was to gain a disproportionately large share of the benefits of corporate activity; nor was any stakeholder—especially the average worker—to be left with a share that was disproportionately small. Banal though it was, this idea helped to maintain the legitimacy of the core

American corporation in the eyes of most Americans, and to ensure continued economic growth.

But by the 1990s, these informal norms were evaporating, just as (and largely because) the core American corporation was vanishing. The links between top executives and the American production worker were fading: An ever-increasing number of subordinates and contractees were foreign, and a steadily growing number of American routine producers were working for foreign-owned firms. An entire cohort of middle-level managers, who had once been deemed "white collar," had disappeared; and, increasingly, American executives were exporting their insights to global enterprise webs.

As the American corporation itself became a global web almost indistinguishable from any other, its stakeholders were turning into a large and diffuse group, spread over the world. Such global stakeholders were less visible, and far less noisy, than national stakeholders. And as the American corporation sold its goods and services all over the world, the purchasing power of American workers became far less relevant to its economic survival.

Thus have the inhibitions been removed. The salaries and benefits of America's top executives, and many of their advisers and consultants, have soared to what years before would have been unimaginable heights, even as those of other Americans have declined.

18

The Education of
the Symbolic Analyst (I)

I have never seen anybody improve on the art and technique of inquiry by any means other than engaging in inquiry.

JEROME BRUNER, *On Knowing* (1962)

AS THE value placed on new designs and concepts continues to
grow relative to the value placed on standard products, the demand for symbolic analysis will continue to surge. This burgeoning demand should assure symbolic analysts ever higher incomes
in the years ahead.

Of course, the worldwide supply of symbolic analysts is growing
as well. Millions of people across the globe are trying to learn
symbolic-analytic skills, and many are succeeding. Researchers
and engineers in East Asia and Western Europe are gathering
valuable insights into microelectronics, microbiotics, and new materials, and translating these insights into new products. Young
people in many developing nations are swarming into universities
to learn the symbolic and analytic secrets of design engineering,
computer engineering, marketing, and management. By 1990,
for example, more than one-third of all nineteen-year-old Ar-
gentines, Singaporeans, and South Koreans were pursuing college
degrees.

But even with a larger supply, it is likely that Americans will
continue to excel at symbolic analysis. For two reasons: First, no
nation educates its most fortunate and talented children—its future symbolic analysts—as well as does America. Second, no nation

possesses the same agglomerations of symbolic analysts already in place and able to learn continuously and informally from one another. While these two advantages may not last forever, American symbolic analysts will continue to enjoy a head start for the foreseeable future at least.

2

AMERICANS love to get worked up over American education. Everyone has views on education because it is one of the few fields in which everyone can claim to have had some direct experience. Those with the strongest views tend to be those on whom the experience has had the least lasting effect. The truly educated person understands how multifaceted are the goals of education in a free society, and how complex are the means.

Recall that America's educational system at midcentury fit nicely into the prevailing structure of high-volume production within which its young products were to be employed. American schools mirrored the national economy, with a standard assembly-line curriculum divided neatly into subjects, taught in predictable units of time, arranged sequentially by grade, and controlled by standardized tests intended to weed out defective units and return them for reworking.

By the last decade of the twentieth century, although the economy had changed dramatically, the form and function of the American educational system remained roughly the same. But now a palpable sense of crisis surrounded the nation's schools, featuring daily lamentations in the media about how terrible they had become. The fact, however, was that most schools had not changed for the worse; they simply had not changed for the better. Early in his presidential campaign, George Bush bestowed upon himself the anticipatory title of "Education President." But, although he continued to so style himself after his election, the title's meaning remained elusive, since Bush did not want to spend any more federal money on education and urged instead that the nation's schools fix themselves. Some people who called themselves educational "reformers" suggested that the standard curriculum should become even more uniform across the nation and that standardized tests should be still more determinative of what was poured into young heads as they moved along the school conveyor belt. (Of course, standardized tests remained, as before, a highly accurate method for measuring little more than the ability of children to take standardized tests.) Popular books contained lists of facts that every educated person should know. Remarkably often in American life, when the need for change is most urgent, the demands grow most insistent that we go "back to basics."

The truth is that while the vast majority of American children are still subjected to a standardized education designed for a standardized economy, a small fraction are not. By the 1990s, the *average* American child was ill equipped to compete in the high-value global economy, but within that average was a wide variation. American children as a whole are behind their counterparts in Canada, Japan, Sweden, and Britain in mathematical proficiency, science, and geography.[1] Fully 17 percent of American seventeen-year-olds are functionally illiterate.[2] Some American children receive almost no education, and many more get a poor one. But some American children—no more than 15 to 20 percent—are being perfectly prepared for a lifetime of symbolic-analytic work.

The formal education of the budding symbolic analyst follows a common pattern. Some of these young people attend elite private schools, followed by the most selective universities and prestigious graduate schools; a majority spend childhood within high-quality suburban public schools where they are tracked through advanced courses in the company of other similarly fortunate symbolic-analytic offspring,[3] and thence to good four-year colleges. But their experiences are similar: Their parents are interested and involved in their education. Their teachers and professors are attentive to their academic needs. They have access to state-of-the-art science laboratories, interactive computers and video systems in the classroom, language laboratories, and high-tech school libraries. Their classes are relatively small; their peers are intellectually stimulating. Their parents take them to museums

---

[1] A dismally large number of surveys have charted the relative backwardness of the average American student. For a sample, see "U.S. Students Near the Foot of the Class," *Science*, March 1988, p. 1237.

[2] *National Assessment of Educational Progress*, various issues.

[3] On the tracking system, see Jeanne Oakes, *Keeping Track: How Schools Structure Inequality* (New Haven: Yale University Press, 1985).

and cultural events, expose them to foreign travel, and give them music lessons. At home are educational books, educational toys, educational videotapes, microscopes, telescopes, and personal computers replete with the latest educational software. Should the children fall behind in their studies, they are delivered to private tutors. Should they develop a physical ailment that impedes their learning, they immediately receive good medical care.

The argument here is not that America's formal system for training its future symbolic analysts is flawless. There is room for improvement. European and Japanese secondary students routinely outperform even top American students in mathematics and science. Overall, however, no other society prepares its most fortunate young people as well for lifetimes of creative problem-solving, -identifying, and brokering. America's best four-year colleges and universities are the best in the world (as evidenced by the number of foreign students who flock to them);[4] the college-track programs of the secondary schools that prepare students for them are equally exceptional. In Japan, it has been the other way around: The shortcomings of Japanese universities and the uninspiring fare offered by Japanese secondary schools have been widely noted. Japan's greatest educational success has been to ensure that even its slowest learners achieve a relatively high level of proficiency.[5]

3

THE UNDERLYING content of America's symbolic-analytic curriculum is not generally addressed openly in suburban PTA meet-

---

[4] In fact, university education is one of the few remaining industries in which the United States retains a consistently positive trade balance. As a university teacher, I continuously "export" my lectures and seminars to the rest of the world by virtue of the fact that over a third of my graduate students are foreign nationals.

[5] See Merry White, *The Japanese Educational Challenge* (New York: Free Press, 1987); Thomas Rohlen, *Japan's High Schools* (Berkeley: University of California Press, 1983); W. Jacobson et al., *Analyses and Comparisons of Science Curricula in Japan and the United States* (New York: Teachers College of Columbia University, International Association for the Evaluation of Educational Achievement, 1986).

ings, nor disclosed in college catalogues. Yet its characteristics and purposes are understood implicitly by teachers, professors, and symbolic-analytic parents.

Budding symbolic analysts learn to read, write, and do calculations, of course, but such basic skills are developed and focused in particular ways. They often accumulate a large number of facts along the way, yet these facts are not central to their education; they will live their adult lives in a world in which most facts learned years before (even including some historical ones) will have changed or have been reinterpreted. In any event, whatever data they need will be available to them at the touch of a computer key.

More important, these fortunate children learn how to conceptualize problems and solutions. The formal education of an incipient symbolic analyst thus entails refining four basic skills: *abstraction, system thinking, experimentation*, and *collaboration*.[6]

Consider, first, the capacity for abstraction. The real world is nothing but a vast jumble of noises, shapes, colors, smells, and textures—essentially meaningless until the human mind imposes some order upon them. The capacity for abstraction—for discovering patterns and meanings—is, of course, the very essence of symbolic analysis, in which reality must be simplified so that it can be understood and manipulated in new ways. The symbolic analyst wields equations, formulae, analogies, models, constructs, categories, and metaphors in order to create possibilities for reinterpreting, and then rearranging, the chaos of data that are already swirling around us. Huge gobs of disorganized information can thus be integrated and assimilated to reveal new solutions, problems, and choices. Every innovative scientist, lawyer, engineer, designer, management consultant, screenwriter, or advertiser is continuously searching for new ways to represent reality which will be more compelling or revealing than the old. Their tools may vary, but the abstract processes of shaping raw data into workable, often original patterns are much the same.

For most children in the United States and around the world, formal education entails just the opposite kind of learning. Rather

---

[6]Suggestions for further reading about these skills, and how formal education can enhance them, can be found at the end of this book in "A Note on Additional Sources."

than construct meanings for themselves, meanings are imposed upon them. What is to be learned is prepackaged into lesson plans, lectures, and textbooks. Reality has already been simplified; the obedient student has only to commit it to memory. An efficient educational process, it is assumed, imparts knowledge much as an efficient factory installs parts on an assembly line. Regardless of what is conveyed, the underlying lesson is that it is someone else's responsibility to interpret and give meaning to the swirl of data, events, and sensations that surround us. This lesson can only retard students' ability to thrive in a world brimming with possibilities for discovery.

America's most fortunate students escape such spoon-feeding, however. On the advanced tracks of the nation's best primary and secondary schools, and in the seminar rooms and laboratories of America's best universities, the curriculum is fluid and interactive. Instead of emphasizing the transmission of information, the focus is on judgment and interpretation. The student is taught to get *behind* the data—to ask why certain facts have been selected, why they are assumed to be important, how they were deduced, and how they might be contradicted. The student learns to examine reality from many angles, in different lights, and thus to visualize new possibilities and choices. The symbolic-analytic mind is trained to be skeptical, curious, and creative.

4

SYSTEM thinking carries abstraction a step further. Seeing reality as a system of causes and consequences comes naturally to a small baby who learns that a glass of milk hurled onto a hardwood floor will shatter, its contents splashing over anyone in the vicinity, and that such an event—though momentarily quite amusing—is sure to incur a strong reaction from the adult in charge. More refined forms of system thinking come less naturally. Our tendency in later life is often to view reality as a series of static snapshots— here a market, there a technology, here an environmental hazard, there a political movement. Relationships among such phenomena are left unprobed. Most formal education perpetuates this compartmental fallacy, offering up facts and figures in bite-sized units of "history," "geography," "mathematics," and "biology," as if each were distinct and unrelated to the others. This may be an efficient system for conveying bits of data, but not for instilling wisdom. What the student really learns is that the world is made up of discrete components, each capable of being substantially understood in isolation.

To discover new opportunities, however, one must be capable of seeing the whole, and of understanding the processes by which parts of reality are linked together. In the real world, issues rarely emerge predefined and neatly separable. The symbolic analyst must constantly try to discern larger causes, consequences, and relationships. What looks like a simple problem susceptible to a standard solution may turn out to be a symptom of a more fundamental problem, sure to pop up elsewhere in a different form. By solving the basic problem, the symbolic analyst can add substantial value. The invention of a quickly biodegradable plastic eliminates many of the problems of designing safe landfills; a computerized workstation for the home solves the myriad problems of rush-hour traffic.

The education of the symbolic analyst emphasizes system thinking. Rather than teach students how to solve a problem that is presented to them, they are taught to examine why the problem arises and how it is connected to other problems. Learning how to travel from one place to another by following a prescribed route is one thing; learning the entire terrain so that you can find shortcuts to wherever you may want to go is quite another. Instead of assuming that problems and their solutions are generated by others (as they were under high-volume, standardized production), students are taught that problems can usually be redefined according to where you look in a broad system of forces, variables, and outcomes, and that unexpected relationships and potential solutions can be discovered by examining this larger terrain.

5

IN ORDER to learn the higher forms of abstraction and system thinking, one must learn to experiment. Small children spend most of their waking hours experimenting. Their tests are random and repetitive, but through trial and error they increase their capacity to create order out of a bewildering collage of sensations and to comprehend causes and consequences. More advanced forms of experimentation also entail many false starts, often resulting in frustration, disappointment, and even fear. Exploring a city on your own rather than following a prescribed tour may take you far afield—you may even get lost, for a time. But there is no better way to learn the layout or to see the city from many different points of view. Thus are symbolic analysts continuously experimenting. The cinematographer tries out a new technique for shooting scenes; the design engineer tries out a new material for fabricating engine parts. The habits and methods of experimentation are critical in the new economy, where technologies, tastes, and markets are in constant flux.

But most formal schooling (both in the United States and elsewhere) has little to do with experimentation. The tour through history or geography or science typically has a fixed route, beginning at the start of the textbook or the series of lectures and ending at its conclusion. Students have almost no opportunity to explore the terrain for themselves. Self-guided exploration is, after all, an inefficient means of covering ground that "must" be covered.

And yet in the best classes of the nation's best schools and universities, the emphasis is quite different. Rather than being led along a prescribed path, students are equipped with a set of tools for finding their own way. The focus is on experimental techniques: holding certain parts of reality constant while varying others in order to better understand causes and consequences; systematically exploring a range of possibilities and outcomes and noting relevant similarities and differences; making thoughtful guesses and intuitive leaps and then testing them against previous assumptions. Most important, students are taught to accept responsibility for their own continuing learning. (Japan's schools, it should be noted, are weakest in this dimension.)

6

FINALLY, there is the capacity to collaborate. As has been noted, symbolic analysts typically work in teams—sharing problems and solutions in a somewhat more sophisticated version of a child's play group. The play of symbolic analysts may appear undirected, but it is often the only way to discover problems and solutions that are not known to be discoverable in advance. Symbolic analysts also spend much of their time communicating concepts—through oral presentations, reports, designs, memoranda, layouts, scripts, and projections—and then seeking a consensus to go forward with the plan.

Learning to collaborate, communicate abstract concepts, and achieve a consensus are not usually emphasized within formal education, however. To the contrary, within most classrooms in the United States and in other nations, the overriding objective is to achieve quiet and solitary performance of specialized tasks. No talking! No passing of notes! No giving one another help! Here again, the rationale is efficiency and the presumed importance of evaluating individual performance. Group tasks are not as easily monitored or controlled as is individual work. It is thus harder to determine whether a particular student has mastered the specified material.

Yet in America's best classrooms, again, the emphasis has shifted. Instead of individual achievement and competition, the focus is on group learning. Students learn to articulate, clarify, and then restate for one another how they identify and find answers. They learn how to seek and accept criticism from peers, solicit help, and give credit to others. They also learn to negotiate—to explain their own needs, to discern what others need and view things from others' perspectives, and to discover mutually beneficial resolutions. This is an ideal preparation for lifetimes of symbolic-analytic teamwork.

Again, the claim here is not that America's schools and colleges are doing their jobs adequately. The argument is narrower: That our best schools and universities are providing a small subset of America's young with excellent basic training in the techniques essential to symbolic analysis. When supplemented by interested and engaged parents, good health care, visits to museums and symphonies, occasional foreign travel, home computers, books, and all the other cultural and educational paraphernalia that symbolic-analytic parents are delighted to shower on their progeny, the education of this fortunate minority is an exceptionally good preparation for the world that awaits.

19

The Education of
the Symbolic Analyst (II)

THE EDUCATION of the symbolic analyst does not end with graduation. As the data on American incomes reveal, a college education is usually necessary but far from sufficient for symbolic-analytic success. Learning continues on the job.

Herewith the second reason why America's symbolic analysts will continue to excel in global markets: In the United States as in no other nation, symbolic analysts are concentrated in specialized geographic pockets where they live, work, and learn with other symbolic analysts devoted to a common kind of problem-solving, -identifying, and brokering. The cities and regions around which they have clustered, and the specialties with which these places are identified, are valued around the world: Los Angeles in music and film; the San Francisco Bay area and greater Boston in science and engineering; New York and Chicago in global finance; Washington, D.C., in international affairs, government relations, and the worldwide marketing of weapons; New York for law, advertising, and publishing. Within these areas, and in many others, exist more specific zones of super-specialized symbolic analysis, also sold directly to world markets: just north and west of Boston, software engineers who have particular experience in computer graphics; between Little Rock and Fayetteville, Arkansas, scientists specializing in molecular biology and biotechnology; along New York's Park Avenue, between Forty-second and Fifty-ninth streets, bankers with expertise in the Korean financial market; near Minneapolis, researchers specializing in medical devices and instruments; south of Portland, Oregon, specialists in advanced semiconductors; in Irvine and Pasadena, California, industrial designers specializing in automobiles and consumer electronic products; and around every major American university, teams of professors, graduate students, and recent graduates selling world-class expertise in particular technologies, markets, or management practices.

Such symbolic-analytic zones cannot easily be duplicated elsewhere on the globe. While specific inventions and insights emanating from them traverse the globe in seconds, the cumulative, shared learning on which such ideas are based is far less portable. Other nations may try, with varying degrees of success, to create a Hollywood, a Wall Street, or a Silicon Valley. But to do so requires more than money. Each of these symbolic-analytic zones represents a complex of institutions and skills which has evolved over time. To contrive exactly the right balance is no easy task.[1]

These zones serve as design centers, development laboratories, and strategic-brokering hubs for worldwide operations. The plans, designs, images, formulae, and strategies that spring from them enter global webs, where they are added to other high-value concepts issuing from other symbolic-analytic zones and to high-volume objects fabricated and assembled around the world. While it is of course possible to solve, identify, and broker new problems without living in one of these pockets, proximity helps. The budding movie director can gain significant insight into the making of a successful motion picture without setting foot in Hollywood. The point is that one can learn so much, so easily, by being there.

Recall the importance of on-the-job learning to symbolic analysis. The fortunate student gains from formal education the techniques and habits of abstraction, system thinking, experimentation, and collaboration—all of which are prerequisites for a lifetime of creative problem solving, identifying, and brokering. From then on, learning comes from doing. The struggle over complex problems yields new insights and approaches relevant to even more complex problems, and so on, as learning builds on itself.

---

[1] Among the seminal studies of the development of regional agglomerations are R. Vernon, *Metropolis 1985* (Cambridge: Harvard University Press, 1960), and M. Hall, *Made in New York* (Cambridge: Harvard University Press, 1959). For a list of more recent studies, see "A Note on Additional Sources" at the end of the text.

Abstraction becomes more sophisticated; system thinking expands and deepens; the repertoire of experimental techniques widens; collaborative skills improve.

Recall also the importance of rapid, informal communications among participants. Since complex problems usually cannot be structured in advance, continuous and even haphazard sharing of puzzles and solutions reveals new possibilities that no person would have uncovered alone. Within the symbolic-analytic zone, insights and experiences are widely shared. The sharing extends beyond the immediate working team to include friends, former associates, informal acquaintances. It occurs spontaneously over lunches, at dinner parties, over drinks, at the gym. Such sharing is a feature of daily gossip—the continuous chatter about who's doing what, who's discovering what, where the action is. Software engineers specializing in computer graphics, who work and live in the same Boston "technoburb," informally pick up new tricks from one another as they trade war stories. So, too, with scriptwriters working in and around Hollywood, advertising executives on Madison Avenue, Washington lobbyists, Chicago futures traders, New York editors and publishers, and so on—informally, at all hours. When one's job is to think about and communicate abstract ideas, "work" occurs wherever and whenever ideas are communicated. Thus the creative benefits of proximity.

2

THERE are other benefits. The local gossip serves as a highly efficient and highly specialized job grapevine. It alerts everyone in the area to who is good at doing what and where skills can be best utilized. In this way strategic brokers can readily locate the exact talents and skills needed to identify and solve specific problems—the record producer who took a similarly weak backing band and coaxed a hard-edged performance out of them, the lawyer who structured a similar kind of contract and devised a novel arbitration clause, the software engineer who figured out a simple way to program a complex graphic-user interface. And problem-solvers and -identifiers like these can likewise discover more opportunities to apply, and thus refine, what they know.

Here, the young symbolic analyst finds opportunity. The rumor mill reveals who has solved or identified what problem for which strategic broker and, more revealingly, whose star is ascending and whose is descending. The budding scriptwriter goes to Hollywood not because of the air quality but because of the opportunities available there for learning the craft and making the right connections. Contemporary speech identifies the phenomenon, widespread within symbolic-analytic zones, of "networking"—the studied process of knowing what is happening and simultaneously making oneself known.

Within the zone, the symbolic analyst moves from project to project, adding experience and skill—from one software problem to another, to another movie script, another advertising campaign, another financial restructuring. Sometimes the next project is undertaken with the same team that worked together on the preceding project under the auspices of the same firm. The symbolic analyst may remain for years with this organization, working with teams drawn from the same pool of partners or employees. Often, however, the tenure will be shorter. At the extreme, the symbolic analyst will free-lance—jumping from firm to firm, and team to team, as different projects beckon. But even under these more fluid arrangements, team members are likely to have worked with one another before on different projects, for different firms. The engineers and marketers who join together to create a new computer graphic software under the auspices of a start-up firm may include many of the same engineers and marketers who tackled another software project three years before for another start-up.

In sum, the symbolic-analytic zone functions as a kind of large, informal organization all its own, whose members' skills are combined in certain ways for particular projects and subsequently recombined in different ways for others. Information travels quickly within this fluid geographic organization. The computer graphics specialists informally stay in touch even when they are not working together—sharing judgments about which firms and projects seem most promising and which are likely to fold. They get word the moment a strategic broker has financing for a new project and when a star software engineer is signed up to work on it. They quickly gauge their chances of joining the new team and whether they should try. In this highly efficient but informal system, talents and abilities continuously shift to wherever they can add the most value.

3

THERE is yet another advantage stemming from the concentration of symbolic analysts within such zones. Their numbers and proximity create a local market for all kinds of specialized in-person services and facilities needed at hand. It is no accident that Hollywood is home to a conspicuously large number of voice coaches, fencing trainers, dancing instructors, performers' agents, and suppliers of photographic, acoustic, and lighting equipment. Also found in close proximity are restaurants with precisely the ambiance favored by producers wooing directors and directors wooing screenwriters, and everyone else in Hollywood wooing everyone else. There are sound stages for state-of-the-art recording, delivery services experienced in moving large and delicate props, and car rental agencies specializing in classic and antique cars as well as conspicuous limousines. Services like these cannot be found in Des Moines; there is not sufficient demand for them. Yet the supply of them in Hollywood creates further demand for them there. Hollywood becomes even more attractive to symbolic analysts specializing in activities that require such services.

Also relevant are public amenities found in or near symbolic-analytic zones, like convention centers, research parks, world-class universities, international airports, and convenient transport to mountain or seashore. The convention center allows symbolic analysts to meet and congregate in large numbers for presentations, exhibits, and intense rounds of networking. The research park, made conveniently accessible through the state's power of eminent domain, gives symbolic analysts adequate and sometimes low-cost working space in proximity to one another. The university offers a steady supply of bright and eager graduates delighted to labor at low initial wages for the opportunity to gain experience in the hope of greater rewards later on. The international airport provides direct access to the rest of the world. The mountains or seashores offer easy access to recreation.

So important are these public amenities, in particular the university and the airport, that their presence would stimulate some collective symbolic-analytic effort even on parched desert or frozen tundra. A world-class university and an international airport combine the basic rudiments of global symbolic analysis—brains, and quick access to the rest of the world.[2]

4

SYMBOLIC-ANALYTIC zones evolve. The initial spur may be the presence of some such set of public amenities coupled with a few inventive geniuses. This promising setting attracts some symbolic analysts, whose presence attracts others. As the group gains experience solving and identifying problems, they begin to add value to global enterprise webs. Some of them break off to start their own firms or otherwise recombine their skills to tackle new projects. Strategic brokers, attracted by this growing concentration of specialized skills, bring even more complex problems, which, in turn, enhance the skills of those who work on them. As even more value is added to global enterprise webs, the area begins to gain a worldwide reputation for the unique skills and insights of the symbolic analysts working there, which attracts additional talent from around the nation (and even the world). Meanwhile, specialized services become available, making the area even more attractive. This pattern, or one like it, has marked the evolution of America's international centers of software engineering, finance, publishing, music and film, broadcasting, advertising, management consulting, and automotive design, among many others.

Such an evolutionary pattern is not inevitable, of course. Many budding symbolic-analytic zones have failed to blossom into world centers. The point is that when it does succeed the process is likely to be gradual, complex, and dependent on many public and private interactions. Hence the difficulty of attempting to replicate such symbolic-analytic nodes from scratch in other places around the globe.

---

[2] For two excellent discussions about the relationship between universities and regional economic development, see Adam Jaffe, "Universities and Regional Patterns of Commercial Innovation," *REI Review*, Case Western Reserve University, September 1989; and Stuart W. Leslie, "From Backwater to Powerhouse: Stanford Engineering and Silicon Valley," *Stanford*, March 1990.

Even if a zone does emerge as a worldwide center, there are no guarantees it will remain one. Success may, in fact, contribute to subsequent decline. The zone may become too congested, polluted, or expensive to attract the young, talented symbolic analysts it once did. On such grounds have perennial predictions of the imminent demise of Hollywood, Silicon Valley, and midtown Manhattan been based. Or the very intensity and speed of communications within the zone may jeopardize it. Energies of symbolic analysts may be diverted too readily from sustained innovation to prevailing fashion; gossip may serve less as a source of useful data than of gamesmanship. It is not unheard of, within such tightly knit communities, that trade secrets are disclosed, insider stock tips are exchanged, or trusted employees defect to competitors, carrying away customers and clients. Such escapades generate lawsuits, and worse. Symbolic-analytic centers are not infrequently the scenes of furious claims and counterclaims, recriminations, and seemingly endless grudges and disputes. These, in turn, may serve to further enliven the local scuttlebutt, but they do not foster a climate of trusting relationships.

Such regressive tendencies notwithstanding, America's symbolic-analytic zones remain, for the most part, wondrously resilient. Within them, America's symbolic analysts continue to improve their abilities to solve, identify, and broker ever more challenging conceptual problems. Competition from foreign symbolic analysts is intensifying, of course. But without direct access to such large, dynamic learning communities, non-Americans begin at a substantial disadvantage.

Part Four
The Meaning of Nation

20
The Problem Restated

IN THE life of a nation, few ideas are more dangerous than good solutions to the wrong problems. Proposals for improving the profitability of American corporations are now legion, as are more general panaceas for what ails American industry. Politicians and pundits talk loosely of "restoring" or "restarting" American business, as if it were a stalled, broken-down jalopy in need of a thorough tune-up. Others offer plans for regaining America's competitive edge and revitalizing the American economy. Many of these ideas are sound. Some are silly. But all suffer from vestigial thinking about exactly what it is that must be restored, restarted, regained, or revitalized. They assume as their subject an American economy centered upon core American corporations and comprising major American industries—in other words, the American economy at midcentury, which easily dominated what limited world commerce there was. But as we have seen, this image bears only the faintest resemblance to the global economy at the end of the century, in which money and information move almost effortlessly through global webs of enterprise. There is coming to be no such thing as an American corporation or an American industry. The American economy is but a region of the global economy—albeit still a relatively wealthy region. In this light, then, it becomes apparent that all of the entities one might wish to revitalize are quickly ceasing to exist.

This new reality has already dawned upon officials charged with managing the fiscal and monetary policies of nations from such outposts as Washington, Tokyo, and Bonn. They have learned that macroeconomic policy cannot be invoked unilaterally without taking account of the savings that will slosh in or out of the nation as a result. Cooperative management is essential simply because there are no longer separate economies to be managed. If interest rates rise in Germany, money will flow there from America and Japan—unless, of course, the latter raise their interest rates as well. Latin American officials likewise have learned that money can flee instantly to more stable regions of the globe, where returns are higher and more predictable, thus confounding any effort to pay down a national debt. And leaders of Eastern Europe, China, and Arkansas, among many other places, are adapting to the ineluctable fact that capitalists will come to their jurisdictions not on an eleemosynary impulse but only out of greed; thus are officials in all such locations seeking to make their environs as hospitably remunerative as possible.

Less well understood have been the consequences of this transformation for the work that people do, and for what they earn for their labors. Regardless of the profitability or market share of a nation's corporations, the economic success of a nation (or, more accurately, the region of the global economy denominated by the nation's political borders) must be judged ultimately by how well its citizens are able to live and whether these standards of living can be sustained and improved upon in the future.

Living standards include more than the level of material comfort available for purchase, of course. Clean air and water, personal safety, and pleasant vistas are aspects of life on which most sentient individuals place considerable value, although some people, and some cultures, may be more willing than others to sacrifice such intangibles for material gain. This is particularly true if the alternative is starvation. Thus, more often than not, the two realms of well-being go together. The world's poorest, lacking the barest necessities, also often endure squalid and unsafe surroundings; the world's rich, possessing a surfeit of tangible playthings, also enjoy some of the most pleasant and secure environments.

Increasingly, one's capacity to command both tangible and intangible wealth is determined by the value that the global economy places on one's skills and insights. The ubiquitous and irrepressible law of supply and demand no longer respects national borders. In this new world economy, symbolic analysts hold a dominant position. American symbolic analysts are especially advantaged. The quality of the nation's universities is unsurpassed; its best primary and secondary schools are among the finest in the world; no other country provides the same quality of on-the-job training within entire regions specializing in one or another kind of symbolic analysis. In this Americans can take pride.

For the two other major categories of worker, however, the law of supply and demand does not bode well. Routine producers, confronted with an immense and rapidly growing pool of unskilled and semiskilled laborers worldwide, find their incomes slipping and their jobs disappearing. In-person servers, while largely sheltered from such direct competition, suffer the indirect effects and find themselves in an increasingly precarious position. A shrinking labor pool within America's borders may ease their plight somewhat in the future, but competition from workers who otherwise would have entered into routine production, from immigrants, and from labor-saving machinery may offset much of the gain. Primarily as a result of these trends, the earnings of Americans (as well as those of citizens of many other nations) have begun to diverge. Hence the challenge: to improve the living standards of the majority of Americans now occupying the two latter categories, who are losing ground in the global economy.

2

THE PROBLEM is far from insoluble. In fact, the range of potential solutions is well understood. Finding the political will to implement them poses a considerably greater challenge.

One response is to offset the polarizing tendencies of the new global economy through a truly progressive income tax, coupled with the closure of gaping tax loopholes. (One hole, large enough to drive a family dynasty through, is the failure of current law to tax unrealized capital gains at death, thus allowing children to inherit assets whose value may have ballooned during their parents' lifetimes, without ever having to pay taxes on the gain. Another hole: mortgage interest deductions sufficiently large to finance the most palatial of estates. A third: low and easily circumvented estate and gift taxes.)

There have been times in our nation's history when the idea of a progressive income tax was not considered especially radical.

In 1917, on the eve of World War I, Woodrow Wilson proposed and Congress enacted a steeply progressive tax code with a top rate on individual incomes of 83 percent. The top rate declined sharply during the 1920s, but by 1935 it was back up to 79 percent, now coupled with a tax on inherited wealth. There were loopholes even then, of course, but the effective rate on America's wealthiest taxpayers was still in the range of 50 percent. When Franklin D. Roosevelt said that no American should be able to keep more than $25,000 of what he earned (the equivalent of about $200,000 in 1990 dollars), no one accused him of losing his mind or of abdicating his political future. Gradually, however, tax progressivity was eroded by additional loopholes and special exemptions and by inflation-induced "bracket creep" (which slowly pushed lower-income workers into higher tax brackets), finally dissolving almost entirely with the tax "reforms" of the late 1970s and 1980s. Meanwhile, Social Security payroll taxes inched upward, as did state and local sales taxes, property taxes, user fees, and government reliance on lotteries—all taking larger bites out of the paychecks of the poor than out of the income of the rich.

Today, the ideal of tax progressivity seems faintly quaint in the United States, although several other industrialized nations continue to regard it as a viable means for moderating income inequities. By 1990, America's income-tax rate on its wealthiest citizens was the lowest of any industrialized nation.[1] A more progressive income tax is no panacea for widening income disparities rooted in the emerging worldwide division of labor, of course, but it would at least ameliorate the trend. The contrary strategy —featuring a low marginal tax on the highest incomes and a growing reliance on Social Security payroll taxes, sales taxes, user fees, property taxes, and lotteries—moves us in exactly the opposite direction.

A second response to the widening gap is to guard against class rigidities by ensuring that any reasonably talented American child can become a symbolic analyst—regardless of family income or

---

[1] Data through 1990 compiled by Citizens for Tax Justice, Washington, D.C., February 1990. It should be noted that other nations employ sales taxes and property taxes as well, so that it is not unambiguously the case that America's total tax system is the most regressive of the lot.

race. Here we see the upside of the globalized economy. Unlike America's old hierarchical and somewhat isolated economy, whose white-collar jobs were necessarily limited in proportion to the number of blue-collar jobs beneath them, the global economy imposes no particular limit upon the number of Americans who can sell symbolic-analytic services worldwide. In principle, all of America's routine production workers could become symbolic analysts and let their old jobs drift overseas to developing nations. The worldwide demand for symbolic analysis is growing so briskly that even under these circumstances real wages would still move steadily upward.

In practice, of course, the task of transforming a majority of the American work force into symbolic analysts would be daunting. It would require early intervention to ensure the nutrition and health of small children and to enroll them in stimulating preschool programs. And not even the most gifted of such children could aspire to such jobs unless the nation provided excellent public schools in every city and region and ample financial help to young people who wanted to attend college. Further, a large pool of symbolic analysts within the nation would require substantial additional investments in universities, research parks, airports, and other facilities conducive to symbolic-analytic work. Finally, to ensure that American symbolic analysts received sufficient on-the-job training, government would have to induce global enterprises (of whatever putative nationality) to contract with Americans for complex problem-solving and -identifying. As implausibly ambitious as these initiatives may seem, many other societies are pursuing them: Japan, South Korea, Singapore, and several Western European nations have embarked upon vigorous programs of education, research, infrastructure, and on-the-job training, all designed to enlarge their pools of symbolic analysts.

3

EVEN under these most optimistic circumstances it is doubtful that there would be radical growth in the number of Americans who became research scientists, design engineers, management consultants, advertising and marketing specialists, film producers, directors, editors and publishers, software engineers, writers, architects, or—even if the world really needed them—investment bankers and lawyers. So other responses are also needed. One is to increase the number of Americans who could apply symbolic analysis to production and in-person services. There is ample evidence, for example, that access to computerized information can enrich production jobs by enabling workers to alter the flow of materials and components in ways that generate new efficiencies. Production workers empowered by computers thus have broader responsibilities and more control over how production is organized. They cease to be "routine" workers—becoming, in effect, symbolic analysts at a level very close to the production process.[2]

Of course, since millions of other production workers around the world are seeking to learn these same advanced production techniques, America's production workers would still face formidable competition from foreigners willing to labor for a fraction of even the minimum American wage. Extra training may retard the loss of these production jobs or the decline in their real wages, but it is far from a solution to the problems faced by unskilled and semiskilled American workers competing worldwide.

A similar transformation in in-person service jobs could have a more lasting effect, however. Consider, for example, the checkout clerk whose computer enables her to control inventory and decide when to reorder items from the factory. Instead of replacing her, the computer empowers her to assume more responsibility and thus add greater value to the enterprise. The number of such technologically empowered jobs is limited only by the ability of in-person servers to learn on the job. This means that a far greater number of Americans would need a solid grounding in mathematics, basic science, and reading and communication skills. So once again, comfortably integrating the American work force into the new world economy turns out to

---

[2] A work force so trained "can exercise critical judgment as it manages the surrounding machine systems. Work becomes more abstract as it depends upon understanding and manipulating information. . . . A new array of work tasks offer unprecedented opportunities for a wide range of employees to add value to products and services." Shoshana Zuboff, *In the Age of the Smart Machine* (New York: Basic Books, 1987), p. 6.

rest heavily on education and training, as well as nutrition and health care sufficient to allow such learning to occur.[3]

Finally, but by no means the least, are the problems of the long-term poor, who lack many of the prerequisites for becoming independent and productive members of society. Their predicament defies easy remedy, but at least four hopeful conclusions can be drawn from the welter of studies that have been done to date. First, most job-training programs directed at this group are effective, in the limited sense that people who finish them are more likely to be employed than welfare recipients who have not. Second, poor, single mothers are much more likely to finish a training program and obtain an adequately paying job if they have access to free day care for their children while they train. Third, before they can get a good job, most long-term poor need remedial courses in reading, writing, and mathematics. Finally, poor children do much better in school, and are more likely to get a job later on, if they are enrolled in an intensive preschool program before they enter kindergarten.[4] It is not beyond their, or our, capacities for many of these least fortunate members of society to lead full and productive lives.

4

THIS abbreviated catalogue of ways to improve the plight of America's globally vulnerable citizens is not intended as a definitive guide, but rather to suggest the realms of policy in which such solutions are apt to be found. I do not want to minimize the difficulty of designing and executing such remedies effectively, but only to show that they are neither mysterious nor beyond our grasp. The fundamental difficulty is not in imagining or imple-

---

[3] A number of studies have been undertaken on the types of training likely to be most useful. For a particularly promising example, see R. Lerman and H. Pouncy, "Why America Should Develop a Youth Apprenticeship System," Progressive Policy Institute, Policy Report No. 5, March 1990.

[4] For a summary of the studies on which these conclusions are based, see P. Cottingham and D. Ellwood (eds.), *Welfare Policies for the 1990s* (Cambridge: Harvard University Press, 1989).

menting solutions. The greatest challenge comes in summoning the political determination to embark upon them. Good education, training, health care, and public infrastructure—available to all Americans—will be costly.

The reader may appropriately object that "more money" is no solution. Clearly it is not the whole solution. *Methods* of educating, training, providing health care, and building and maintaining infrastructure can surely be improved upon. But while money may not be sufficient, it is certainly a necessary prerequisite, and the facile assumption that money already has been dedicated generously to these ends is false, as I will show in more detail in the next chapter.

If there are to be additional expenditures, who is to pay? Most working Americans, already under a heavy tax load, cannot afford to shoulder the added financial burden of higher levels of public spending. It would have to be borne instead by the one group of Americans whose earnings have been increasing—our symbolic analysts. Of course, symbolic analysts would also bear the cost of any changes in the tax code designed to redistribute income and thus to reduce the polarizing domestic effects of a globalized economy.

Thus a central question concerns the extent to which America's fortunate citizens—especially symbolic analysts, who, with about half the nation's income, constitute the greatest part of the most fortunate fifth of the population—are willing to bear these burdens. But herein lies a paradox: As the economic fates of Americans diverge, the top may be losing the long-held sense of connectedness with the bottom fifth, or even the bottom four-fifths, that would motivate such generosity.

Ironically, as the rest of the nation grows more economically dependent than ever on the fortunate fifth, the fortunate fifth is becoming less and less dependent on them. The economic interdependence that Tocqueville observed in nineteenth-century America is slipping away. Increasingly, the fortunate fifth are selling their expertise on the global market and are able to maintain and enhance their standard of living and that of their children even as that of other Americans declines. No longer does their well-being depend exclusively or primarily on the productivity, purchasing power, or wage restraint exercised by the other four-fifths of the population. The American executive software engineer, linked to his worldwide web by computer, modem, and facsimile machine, is apt to be more dependent on design engineers in Kuala Lumpur, fabricators in Taiwan, bankers in Tokyo and Bonn, and sales and marketing specialists in Paris and Milan than on routine production workers in a factory on the other side of town.

Yet without the support of the fortunate fifth, it will be almost impossible to muster the resources, and the political will, necessary for change. To this issue I now turn.

21

The Decline
of Public Investment

HISTORY is replete with examples of people wishing to secede
from alliances with certain other people. In the nineteenth century, the Southern states tried to secede from the Union. Centuries
before, Martin Luther led a secession from the Holy See. At this
writing, Poles, Hungarians, East Germans, and Lithuanians are
attempting much the same from the Soviet empire. Staten Island
would like to secede from New York City. Secession is also common to high-tech engineers, investment bankers, and lawyers, who
defect from their business associates to form their own firms.
Many working women these days are financially able to secede
from unhappy or unrewarding marriages. While the reasons for
such withdrawals vary, where an economic motive exists it is usually because the defectors conclude that they will do better on
their own. The union is unnecessarily costly or constraining, and
the defectors no longer wish to subsidize partners who fail to pull
their own weight.

Secession need not be explicit. It does not require a declaration
of war, or even a formal revocation of contract. It can happen
quietly, almost imperceptibly, as in a marriage whose partners
slowly drift apart. One day, the players awaken to a new reality.
They discover they are no longer part of the same team.

Something of this sort has been occurring in the United States.
America's symbolic analysts have been seceding from the rest of
the nation. The secession has taken many forms, but it is grounded
in the same emerging economic reality. This group of Americans

no longer depends, as it once did, on the economic performance of other Americans. Symbolic analysts are linked instead to global webs of enterprise, to which they add value directly.

The secession is occurring gradually, without fanfare. For many symbolic analysts (including me and, perhaps, you), it has been taking place without explicit knowledge or intent. While symbolic analysts pledge national allegiance with as much sincerity and resolve as ever, the new global sources of their economic well-being have subtly altered how they understand their economic roles and responsibilities in society.

2

ONE FORM of secession has been noted: the decreasing tax burden on symbolic analysts and the increasing tax burden (including Social Security payroll taxes, sales taxes, user fees, property taxes, and lotteries) on lower-income Americans. Concomitant with this shift in the tax burden has been a withdrawal of government funding from programs that would make the less fortunate four-fifths of the population more productive by improving their skills and helping them transport themselves and their products to market.

The two phenomena—the shift of the tax burden from wealthier to poorer Americans, and the withdrawal of public funding—are, of course, related, since poorer Americans cannot afford to pay more taxes to support public programs even if the programs would improve their earnings over the long term. Tax revolts by middle- and lower-income Americans whose real earnings have slowly declined are only to be expected when tax burdens shift further in their direction.

In the early postwar years, government expenditures on education, training, highways, and other "public improvements" were justified to the more fortunate by pointing to their salutary effects on the nation as a whole. Tocqueville's logic of "self-interest properly understood" lay behind many of the initiatives of the era. But in more recent years, as symbolic analysts have come to depend less on other Americans, the traditional justification has apparently lost some of its potency.

Consider infrastructure. Many of America's symbolic analysts transmit their concepts through the air via private telecommunications systems and transport their bodies through the air via private airlines. Most other workers rely primarily on public highways, bridges, ports, trains, buses, and subways in order to add economic value. Yet in the United States spending to maintain and upgrade these latter sorts of facilities has declined steadily. In the 1950s, the nation committed itself to building a modern transportation system. Infrastructure then absorbed over 6 percent of the nation's nonmilitary federal budget each year, or just under 4 percent of gross national product, where it remained through most of the 1960s. Public spending on the nation's transportation system declined in the 1970s, and declined even more sharply in the 1980s, to the point where the nation was spending only 1.2 percent of its nonmilitary budget (about 3 percent of GNP) on building and maintaining infrastructure. Hence the specter of collapsing bridges and crumbling highways. In 1989, the U.S. Department of Transportation estimated that simply to repair the nation's 240,000 bridges would require an expenditure of $50 billion; to repair the nation's highways, $315 billion. Spending on *new* infrastructure has fallen even more dramatically, from 2.3 percent of GNP in 1963 to only 1 percent in 1989.[1]

The *federal* government's withdrawal has been especially precipitous. By the end of the 1980s, Washington was annually investing about the same amount of money in infrastructure (in constant dollars) as it invested thirty years before, although the gross national product had grown 144 percent in the interim. Physical capital investment dropped from over 24 percent of total federal outlays in 1960 to less than 11 percent in 1991.[2] And much of what the federal government *has* underwritten in recent years has been dedicated to downtown convention centers, office parks,

---

[1] Data from the U.S. Department of Commerce. See also calculations by Brian Cromwell, "Capital Subsidies and the Infrastructure Crisis," *Economic Review*, Federal Reserve Bank of Cleveland, 1989.

[2] Figures from David Aschauer, "Is Public Expenditure Productive?" *Journal of Monetary Economics*, March 1989, pp. 177–200, and from Alicia Munnell, "Productivity and Public Investment," *New England Economic Review*, January–February 1990, pp. 3–22.

research parks, and other amenities utilized mostly by symbolic analysts.

Expenditure on public elementary and secondary education has shown a similar pattern. Many politicians and business leaders (and many average citizens) are quick to claim that the crisis in public education is unrelated to a lack of public funding. A premise of their argument—that there are many means of improving American schools that do not require large public outlays—is surely correct. Pushing responsibility for what is taught and how it is taught down to teachers and parents, and away from educational bureaucracies, is one such step (analogous to the shift in responsibility within the corporation from high-volume hierarchies to high-value webs). Giving parents some choice over which school their child attends is another (so long as the poorest children, whose parents are least likely to be able or willing to shop, do not get left behind in the worst schools). But to claim that these types of reforms will be sufficient is being less than ingenuous. In order to have smaller classes and attract better-qualified teachers, more money is also necessary.[3]

Controlled for inflation, public spending on primary and secondary education, per student, has increased since the mid-1970s, but not appreciably faster than it did during the previous fifteen-year period. Between 1959 and the early 1970s, annual spending per student grew at a brisk 4.7 percent in real terms—more than a full percentage point above the increase in the gross national product per person; since 1975, annual spending per pupil has continued to rise about 1 percent faster than the rate of growth of GNP per person. But there are several reasons for believing the more recent increases to be inadequate. First is the comparative measure of what other nations are spending. By the late

---

[3] That smaller classes and better-qualified teachers result in a better education is one of the few propositions on which most educational researchers agree. See, for example, David Cord and Alan Krueger, "Does School Quality Matter? Returns to Education and the Characteristics of Public Schools in the U.S.," National Bureau of Economic Research, Working Paper No. 3358, May 1990. See also R. Eberts, E. Schwartz, and J. Stone, "School Reform, School Size, and Student Achievement," *Economic Review*, Federal Reserve Bank of Cleveland, vol. 26, No. 2, June 1990.

1980s, America's per-pupil expenditures (converted to dollars using 1988 exchange rates) were below per-pupil expenditures in eight other nations, including Sweden, Norway, Japan, Denmark, Austria, West Germany, Canada, and Switzerland.[4]

Comparisons aside, the demands on public education in the United States have significantly increased during the past fifteen years owing to growing numbers of broken homes, single parent families, immigrants (both legal and illegal), and poor children. There is also the undeniable fact that talented individuals are no longer drawn to teaching as readily as they were two decades ago: Previous generations of American schoolchildren benefited from the limited career options available to talented women, other than teaching. By the late 1980s, that constraint had been removed. Talented women (and men) were in demand in a wide range of occupations. The law of supply and demand is not repealed at the schoolhouse door: If talented people are to be drawn to teaching, teachers must be paid enough to attract such individuals. Yet average teacher salaries in 1990 (adjusted for inflation) were only 4 percent higher than in 1970, when career choices were far more limited.

Finally, the average figures on per-pupil expenditure in the United States disguise growing disparities among states and among school districts. During the 1980s, federal support for elementary and secondary education dropped by a third. States and localities picked up the bill, but for some of them the burden has been especially heavy. Although per-pupil expenditures in-

---

[4]International comparisons are hazardous, not only because of differences in the measurements used by different countries, but also because different societies may have different objectives for their educational systems. There is also the question of how the measurements are to be done, given different exchange rates. Using a 1985 exchange rate, when the dollar was at its height in comparison with the currencies of other industrialized nations, puts the United States in fourth place, but this comparison obviously is skewed by the abnormally high dollar at the time. For these and related calculations, see *Digest of Educational Statistics* (U.S. Department of Education, National Center for Education Statistics, Washington, D.C. 1988). See also M. E. Rasell and L. Mishel, "Shortchanging Education: How U.S. Spending on Grades K–12 Lags Behind Other Industrialized Nations," Economic Policy Institute, January 1990.

creased in wealthier states and school districts, many poorer states and districts—already coping with the most intractable social problems—have barely been able to fund even a minimum-quality public education. This is an important point, to which I will return in a later chapter.

Meanwhile, even as tax-free day care for children of symbolic analysts has become a de rigueur provision of law firms, management consulting companies, and investment banks, public funding for preschool education for poor children has appreciably dwindled. In 1989, fewer than a fifth of poor three- and four-year-olds were able to participate in Head Start—a preschool program costing approximately $4,000 per child, whose graduates are more likely to gain a high school diploma, attend college, and find employment than comparable children not enrolled in the program.[5] By contrast, nearly two out of three four-year-olds whose families have incomes over $35,000 a year attended preschool in 1989.[6] (At this writing, the Bush administration has proposed increased funding to permit most poor four-year-olds to participate in Head Start. This is a welcome initiative, but even with this boost the program still will serve fewer than a third of all eligible children.[7])

Also because of government cutbacks, many capable young people in the United States no longer receive the federal dollars that were their only hope of affording a college education. Tuition at public and private universities rose during the 1980s by 26 percent on average (adjusted for inflation) while the incomes of

---

[5] For an assessment of the Head Start program, see R. Darlington and I. Lazar, "The Lasting Effects After Preschool," U.S. Department of Health and Human Services (Washington, D.C.: U.S. Government Printing Office, 1979).

[6] Figures from the Children's Defense Fund, Washington, D.C.

[7] See "Competitive Assessment of the President's Fiscal Year 1991 Budget," Council on Competitiveness, Washington, D.C., May 1990, pp. 6–7. Where preschool programs for poor children have had more teachers and social workers than in the typical Head Start program, children have shown even larger gains. See Jean Layzer, "Evaulation of New York City Project Giant Step," Apt Associates, Cambridge, Mass., April 1990. See also Amy Stuart Wells, "Preschool Program in New York City Is Reported to Surpass Head Start," *The New York Times*, May 16, 1990, p. B7.

families in the middle and lower ranks of American households declined. Instead of filling the growing gap, however, the government helped widen it. During the 1980s, guaranteed student loans fell by 13 percent—marking yet another previous commitment reneged on.

In 1965, the nation decided that all students qualified to attend college should have access to higher education. The resulting Higher Education Act established a system of grants and loan guarantees for low-income students, thus increasing from 22 to 26 percent the portion of university students from families with incomes at or below the median. But by 1988, with grants and loan guarantees drying up, the proportion of low-income university students fell back below 20 percent.[8] For the first time in the nation's history, the proportion of the population attending college has begun to decline; younger men, aged twenty-five to thirty-four are now less likely to have completed four years of college than were the baby-boomers just ahead of them. The high costs of education have helped push them out.[9]

Public funding to train and retrain workers, meanwhile, dropped by more than 50 percent during the 1980s, from $13.2 billion to $5.6 billion.[10] Private training, the costs of which corporations deduct from their taxable income, has hardly made up the difference. American corporations claim to spend some $30 billion a year training their employees, but most of these funds have been used on what is termed, euphemistically, "executive

---

[8] Data from the American Higher Education Research Program, American Council on Education, 1989. See also Barbara Vobejda, "Class, Color, and College: Higher Education's Role in Reinforcing the Social Hierarchy," Washington *Post Weekly Edition*, May 15–21, 1989, p. 6.

[9] Until the 1990s, each generation of Americans had been better educated than the generation preceding it. In 1980, 25 percent of men aged thirty-five to forty-four had completed four years of college; by 1990, 31 percent of men within this age group had done so. But by 1990, *younger* men were less educated than the generation before them: 25 percent of them had completed four years of college, compared with 27 percent of the same age group in 1980. Younger women were becoming slightly better educated, however: In 1990, 24 percent of women aged 25 to 34 had completed four years of college; 23 percent of women aged 35 to 44 had done so. Ibid.

[10] Figures from "Unprotected: Jobless Workers," Center on Budget and Policy Priorities, Washington, D.C., 1989.

training."[11] Such training is, of course, available only to the most dedicated (and already valuable) employees. College graduates are 50 percent more likely to be trained by their corporations than are high school graduates; within high-tech industries, employees with postgraduate degrees are twice as likely to receive training as mere college graduates.[12] Training, then, is typically provided to those who need it least.

3

THE OFFICIAL reason given for why America cannot invest more money in infrastructure, education, and training is that we cannot afford it. In his inaugural address, George Bush noted regretfully, "We have more will than wallet"—a frequent lamentation. But only excessive politeness should constrain one from inquiring: Whose will? Whose wallet? Even if the necessary funds cannot be reallocated from elsewhere in the federal budget—surely a heroic assumption, given the number of B-1 bombers and other military exotica being created to ward off communists, most of whom no longer exist (as such)—the claim that America cannot afford to spend more on the productivity of all its citizens remains a curious one.

In 1989, Americans had about $3,500 billion to spend, after paying taxes. The lower four-fifths of the population received a little under half of this sum (about $1,745 billion), which did not permit them any more consumption than a decade earlier; their belts were as tight as before.[13] The top fifth of the population,

---

[11]While the precise content of this elusive process is difficult to determine, I have personal experience which may shed some light. On more than one occasion I have been hired to lecture to a group of executives who, after two intellectually strenuous hours with me, proceed through a similarly rigorous daylong schedule: a sumptuous lunch, followed by an afternoon of tennis and golf, culminating with top-shelf cocktails and a five-course dinner.

[12]L. A. Lillard and H. W. Tan, "Private Sector Training: What Are Its Effects?," Report to the Department of Commerce, Rand Corporation, Santa Monica, Calif., 1986.

[13]Contrary to popular wisdom about Americans saving too little and spending too much, actual consumption by the bottom four-fifths of the American

mostly comprising symbolic analysts, received the rest (about $1,755 billion)—more than the other four-fifths of the population combined. Accordingly, symbolic analysts loosened their belts considerably. Recall that their incomes have been increasing, on average, by 2 to 3 percent a year after inflation (and if they are in the most fortunate tenth of earners, faster than this), even as the incomes of other Americans have stagnated or declined.

While average working Americans may justly feel that they have been surrendering a larger percentage of their earnings in taxes (including Social Security payroll taxes, sales taxes, and property taxes), tax burdens on Americans *overall* have not increased since the mid-1960s. Total tax receipts amounted to 31.1 percent of gross national product in 1969, 31.1 percent in 1979, and 32 percent in 1989. It is just that the burden has been shifted from relatively wealthier Americans to relatively poorer Americans.

Were the tax code as progressive as it was even as late as 1977, symbolic analysts would have paid approximately $93 billion more in taxes than they in fact paid in 1989.[14] Between 1990 and 2000, they would be contributing over a trillion dollars more. This tidy sum, when added to money no longer spent on weapons systems and large standing armies,[15] would yield almost $2 trillion—a significant down payment on the productivity of the rest of the population.[16]

As of this writing, I am unaware of a ground swell of support among business leaders or politicians for increasing the taxes on the top fifth of American earners. The budget compromise of

---

population hardly increased at all during the 1980s. Only the fortunate fifth of households experienced rapid growth of real consumption during these years. See Robert R. Blecker, *Are We on a Consumption Binge? The Evidence Reconsidered* (Washington, D.C.: Economic Policy Institute, January 1990).

[14] Almost all of this sum would have been paid by the top 10 percent of income earners. Calculations from *Inequality and the Federal Budget Deficit* (Washington, D.C.: Citizens for Tax Justice, March 1990).

[15] Were military spending steadily reduced through the decade of the 1990s by about 50 percent, the total savings by the year 2000 would come close to $1 trillion.

[16] I have not included the costs of the current savings and loan bailout in my calculations, since the bailout is nothing more than a huge transfer of money from American taxpayers to other Americans. The bailout does not actually use up scarce resources.

1990 did represent a small step back toward progressivity, but not a substantial change in attitude. And in fact, the administration currently in Washington has sought instead to reduce tax rates on appreciating capital assets. The apparent justification for lowering, rather than raising, federal taxes on wealthy investors (who own most of these capital assets) is that such a step would motivate them to invest their savings in new enterprise. Profit-seeking, resolutely self-interested individuals, it is assumed, will spur the American economy forward. Should there come to be substantial fiscal savings owing to the collapse of Soviet communism and the concomitant difficulty of finding dangerous enemies against whom we must arm, the administration (in cooperation with a coterie of economists, business lobbyists, and conservative pundits) has signaled its determination to apply such savings to further tax cuts and reductions in the federal budget deficit rather than to public investments in education, training, and infrastructure. The logic justifying these positions (if "logic" is the appropriate term) deserves further examination.

22

The Uses
of Vestigial Thought

> By force of [a] happy knack of clannish fancy, the common man is enabled to feel that he has some sort of metaphysical share in the gains which accrue to the business men who are citizens of the same "commonwealth."
>
> THORSTEIN VEBLEN,
> *The Theory of Business Enterprise* (1904)

TAXES on the wealthy must be lowered, public spending must be cut, and government budget deficits must be reduced. These propositions, so much in vogue by the last decade of the century that they nearly qualified as articles of faith among many policy makers in the United States and elsewhere, are generally justified by the same vestigial view of the economy we have encountered before. They are premised on the mistaken notion that distinctly national capital is critical to the future wealth of a nation.

In this traditional view, all national economic activity is divided between a public sector and a private sector. The public sector spends money, while the private sector earns and invests it. Private investors finance research and development, factories, and equipment, from which the nation reaps a higher standard of living. All else is assumed to be consumption. From this simplified picture is derived the admonition, delivered with ever greater alarm, that public-sector spending must be constrained lest it "crowd out" private investment, thereby diminishing the nation's capacity to earn what it spends. (The national income accounts, through which such simplified pictures are often perpetuated, classify all public-sector activity as expenditure, not investment.) In turn, private investment is seen primarily as the domain of the wealthy—who, unlike the poor, earn enough to be able to choose investment over, or on top of, consumption. The wealthy must, of course, be properly motivated to make this beneficent choice —thus the notion that their tax load should be lightened.

2

THIS picture was never entirely accurate, of course. Even a century ago in America, government expenditures on highways, canals, railroads, and schools were no less investments in the nation's future than were new factories and equipment. Nevertheless, in past years there was a certain logic to concerns that government spending might "crowd out" private investment. When capital moved less freely across national borders, it was generally true that its cost in any one country depended on the level of national saving. If a nation's citizens failed to save their earnings, or their government taxed away and then spent most of what they earned, only a small pool of national capital would remain for private investment in research, factories, and equipment within the nation. And because the supply of capital was so limited, and the demand for it so great, borrowers would have to pay high interest rates in order to utilize it. As a result, many worthwhile private investments would be deferred. National growth would be stunted.

By the 1990s, however, the savings of many nations were combining into a vast pool which sloshed across national borders in search of the highest returns. As a result, one nation's savings were easily invested in another nation. Not only were foreign savings coming to the United States, but the private savings of Americans were wandering all over the world—sometimes finding their way into the far-flung operations of global American-owned corporations, sometimes into companies in which foreigners owned a majority stake. The savings of wealthier Americans no longer—to use the felicitous phraseology of conservative economists—"trickled down" to American corporations and thence to the rest of the American population. To put it more accurately, these savings "trickled out" to wherever on the globe the best investments happened to be.

The increasingly unimpeded movement of capital worldwide is reducing the connection between the level of national savings and the cost of capital within a nation. In fact, by the 1990s the cost of capital was coming to be about the same in all advanced nations.[1] This means, of course, that reductions in public spending and tax cuts for wealthy American investors are coming to have little direct bearing upon how much private capital is invested in the nation's factories, equipment, and research and development.[2]

There is, however, a growing connection between the amount and kind of investments that the *public* sector undertakes and the capacity of the nation to attract worldwide capital. Herein lies the new logic of economic nationalism: The skills of a nation's work force and the quality of its infrastructure are what makes it unique, and uniquely attractive, in the world economy. Investments in these relatively immobile factors of worldwide production are what chiefly distinguish one nation from another; money, by contrast, moves easily around the world.

A work force that is knowledgeable and skilled at doing complex things, and which can easily transport the fruits of its labors into the global economy, will entice global money to it. The enticement can develop into a virtuous relationship: Well-trained workers and modern infrastructure attract global webs of enterprise, which invest and give workers relatively good jobs; these

---

[1] The question of how closely national savings are connected to the cost of capital was the subject of lively debate during the 1980s. In 1980, Martin Feldstein and C. Horioka claimed that the relationship was direct, and that changes in a nation's savings rate dramatically affected the rate of national investment ("Domestic Saving and International Capital Flows," *Economic Journal*, vol. 90, 1980, pp. 314–29). But as capital controls were eased among nations, and the technologies and infrastructure of worldwide capital mobility were perfected, the costs of capital began to converge among nations. By 1990 there was virtually no difference in interest rates on loans within major industrial countries, as long as the contracts were in a common currency. Of course, contracts in different currencies would continue to reflect their differing risks of inflation and of changes in relative currency values. See J. Frankel, "Quantifying International Capital Mobility in the 1980s," National Bureau of Economic Research, Working Paper No. 2856, February 1989.

[2] Of course, an increase in public expenditure in any nation, or a decrease in savings, reduces the total amount of *worldwide* savings, and thus exerts a slight upward pressure on *global* interest rates.

jobs, in turn, generate additional on-the-job training and experience, thus creating a powerful lure to other global webs. As skills increase and experience accumulates, a nation's citizens add greater and greater value to the world economy—commanding ever-higher compensation and improving their standard of living.

Without adequate skills and infrastructure, however, the relationship is likely to be the reverse—a vicious circle in which global investment can be lured only by relatively low wages and low taxes. These enticements in turn make it more difficult for the nation to finance adequate education and infrastructure in the future; the resulting jobs provide little or no on-the-job training and experience pertinent to more complex jobs in the future, and so on.

3

WHICH is it to be? A virtuous relationship with world capital or a vicious one? Much depends on the implicit social choices buried within political decisions about the strength of the public's will and the thickness of its wallet.

The proper view of a national economy as a region of the global economy draws its most important distinctions between investment and consumption—between what is spent to create future wealth and what is spent to satisfy current needs and wants. This logic suggests why, contrary to the assumptions of so many in government and the public, there is nothing terribly wrong with being indebted to foreigners—so long as the borrowings are invested in factories, schools, roads, and other means of enhancing future production. In fact, taking on debt for these purposes is preferable to maintaining a balanced budget by deferring or cutting back on such investments. Debt is only a problem if the money is squandered on consumption. Any competent businessperson understands the soundness of this principle: If necessary, you borrow in order to invest in the greater future productivity of your enterprise. Once achieved, the new levels of productivity enable you to pay back the debt and enjoy higher returns thereafter. Problems arise, however, if instead of investing the money you have borrowed in productive capacity, you spend it at fancy restaurants and at the racetrack. Regrettably, this is what the fortunate fifth of Americans did on a grand scale for much of the 1980s.

More investment is necessary but not sufficient. A further distinction must be drawn between investments that enhance the value of work performed by a nation's citizens and those that merely create income-producing assets around the globe. Investments in factors of production which are unique to the nation—particularly in the nation's citizens and in all the transportation and communication systems linking them together and to the rest of the world—are critically important to the nation's future. This is both because the return on human capital is rising relative to that on financial capital, and because such public investments uniquely help the nation's citizens add value to the world economy.

In short, the future standard of living of Americans, like that of any other nation's citizens, depends upon their capacity to moderate their overall consumption (both public and private) while simultaneously making investments in their unique resources—people and infrastructure—and thereby attracting global investors to do the same. This logic compels a different strategy than one permitting or encouraging wealthy citizens to keep an ever-larger portion of what they earn, while scaling back public-sector investment. And yet, paradoxically, the latter is exactly the policy that America's leaders have embraced in the last decade of the twentieth century.

Politicians and business leaders are quick to note the central importance of national economic strength, but not to comprehend the basis of that strength. "Increased economic strength is . . . fundamental to success in the global competition with rising economic superpowers," noted the Bush administration in its 1991 budget submission to Congress. "Thus there is a first-order issue for the budget (and the economic policy it represents): How can it best preserve and build upon America's strengths, while advancing the American economy toward even greater capacities for leadership and growth?"[3] Having posed the correct question, Bush's budget wizards then answered it backwards. They advocated public parsimony—or outright cuts—in infrastructure, education, training, and related public endeavors, accompanied by

---

[3] Introduction to budget submission to Congress, February 1, 1990.

reductions in the tax rate on capital gains. "National economic strength" was tacitly equated with the discretionary income of wealthy Americans and the presumed propensity of the wealthy to invest it in ways that would benefit other Americans. Further, the administration signaled that it would use whatever savings resulted from smaller defense outlays to reduce the budget deficit rather than invest more in schools, roads, and other public assets.

There are two possible explanations for this tenacious perversity. The more optimistic, and less cynical, is that otherwise intelligent men and women occupying positions of leadership in American business and government have simply failed to understand the global economic changes that now engulf us. The premises upon which they base their daily decisions, and their prescriptions for the nation, date from a time when America was a relatively closed economy organized around high-volume, standard production. America's leaders are no different from most other Americans: products and purveyors of vestigial thought. This is the optimistic explanation because it holds out the hope that, in time, America's leaders—most of them symbolic analysts—will come to recognize the new reality and will alter their decisions and prescriptions accordingly; it is a less cynical explanation because it assumes they are motivated at least in part by a concern for the future well-being of their less fortunate fellow citizens. It is toward a somewhat less charitable—and less benign—explanation that I now turn.

23
The New Community

Ilium, New York, is divided into three parts. In the north-west are the managers and engineers and civil servants and a few professional people; in the northeast are the machines; and in the south, across the Iroquois River, is the area known locally as the homestead, where almost all of the people live.

KURT VONNEGUT, JR.,
Player Piano (1952)

THE HYPOTHESIS that some degree of rational calculation, rather than simple delusion, underlies the disengagement of symbolic analysts from the broader public is evinced by how the symbolic analyst has chosen to live. In allocating personal income, the symbolic analyst has shown no lack of willingness to engage in collective investment. But increasingly, the public goods that result are shared only with other symbolic analysts. Symbolic analysts take on the responsibilities of citizenship, but the communities they create are composed only of citizens with incomes close to their own. In this way, symbolic analysts are quietly seceding from the large and diverse publics of America into homogeneous enclaves, within which their earnings need not be redistributed to people less fortunate than themselves.

The pattern is familiar. With each sought-after reduction in their taxes, symbolic analysts in effect withdraw their dollars from the support of public spaces shared by all and dedicate the savings to private spaces they share with other symbolic analysts. As public parks and playgrounds deteriorate, there is a proliferation of private health clubs, golf clubs, tennis clubs, skating clubs, and every other type of recreational association in which costs are divided up among members. So also with condominiums, cooperatives, and the omnipresent "residential communities" which dun their members in order to undertake efforts that financially strapped local governments can no longer afford to do well—maintaining private roadways, mending sidewalks, pruning trees, repairing streetlights, cleaning swimming pools and paying for a lifeguard, and—notably—hiring security guards to protect life and property. By 1990, private security guards comprised fully 2.6 percent of the nation's work force, double the percentage in 1970, and outnumbering public police officers in the United States. Taking note of this striking growth, the Bureau of Labor Statistics has accorded the occupation the honor of a separate job category all its own. With revenues of the ten largest guard companies rising 62 percent in the 1980s, in real terms, private security was one of the fastest-growing industries in the United States (even faster than the legal profession).[1]

2

THE SAME pattern of secession has been apparent on a grander scale in America's major cities. By the 1990s, most urban centers had splintered, in effect, into two separate cities—one composed of symbolic analysts whose conceptual services were linked to the world economy; the other, of in-person servers (custodial, secu-

---

[1] See "The Growth of Private Security," in William C. Cunningham and Todd H. Taylor, *Private Security and Police in America* (Portland, Ore.: Chancellor Press, 1985). See also L. Uchitelle, "Sharp Rise of Private Guard Jobs," *The New York Times*, October 14, 1989, p. A16.

One of the fastest-growing job categories among government workers, meanwhile, has been that of prison guard. Between 1960 and 1980, the prison population of the United States doubled; between 1980 and 1990, it doubled again. The American Correctional Association forecasts another doubling by 1995 (American Correctional Association, Report on the State of the Nation's Prisons, January 1990). In 1989, spending on prisons was the fastest-growing category of state budgets. See E. J. Dionne, Jr., "Prison Spending Rises Fastest in State Budgets," *The New York Times*, August 8, 1989, p. A16.

rity, taxi, clerical, parking, retail sales, restaurant) whose jobs were dependent on the symbolic analysts.[2] Few routine producers remained within America's cities. Between 1953 and 1984, for example, New York City lost about 600,000 routine factory jobs; during the same interval, it added about 700,000 symbolic-analytic and in-person service jobs.[3] In Pittsburgh, routine production jobs dropped from almost half the city's employment in 1953 to less than 20 percent by the mid-1980s; the other two categories made up the difference, as the city amassed America's third-largest concentration of corporate headquarters.[4]

The separation of symbolic analysts from in-person servers within cities has been reinforced in several ways. By the 1990s, most large cities possessed two school systems—a private one for the children of symbolic analysts and a public one for the children of in-person servers, the few remaining routine producers, and the unemployed.[5] Symbolic analysts are known to spend considerable time and energy ensuring that their children gain entrance to good private schools, and then small fortunes keeping them there—dollars that under a more progressive tax code could have financed better public education. The separation also has been maintained by residential patterns. Symbolic analysts live in areas of the city that, if not beautiful, are at least aesthetically tolerable and reasonably safe; precincts not meeting these minimum standards of charm and security have been left to those less fortunate.

Here again, symbolic analysts have pooled their resources—to the exclusive benefit of themselves. Public funds have been applied

---

[2] The trend has been confirmed in a number of studies. See, for example, Thierry Noyelle, *Beyond Industrial Dualism* (Boulder, Colo.: Westview Press, 1987); Saskia Sassen, *The Mobility of Labor and Capital* (Cambridge: Cambridge University Press, 1987); John Kasarda, "Dual Cities: The New Structure of Urban Poverty," *New Perspectives Quarterly*, Winter 1987.

[3] These data are from John Kasarda, "Urban Industrial Transition and the Underclass," *Annals of the AAPSS*, January 1989.

[4] B. Frieden and L. Sagalyn, *Downtown, Inc.: How America Rebuilds Cities* (Cambridge: MIT Press, 1989); see also J. Kasarda, "Economic Restructuring and America's Urban Dilemma," in M. Dogan and J. Kasarda (eds.), *Economic Restructuring and America's Urban Dilemma* (Beverly Hills, Calif.: Sage, 1988).

[5] See, for example, Paul Ong et al., "Inequalities in Los Angeles," Graduate School of Architecture and Urban Planning, University of California at Los Angeles, June 1989.

in earnest to downtown "revitalization" projects, entailing the construction of clusters of postmodern office buildings (replete with fiber-optic cables, private branch exchanges, satellite dishes, and other state-of-the-art transmission and receiving equipment), multilevel parking garages, hotels with glass-enclosed atriums rising twenty stories or higher, upscale shopping plazas and gallerias, theaters, convention centers, and luxury condominiums. Ideally, the projects are entirely self-contained, with air-conditioned walkways linking residential, business, and recreation functions. The fortunate symbolic analyst is thankfully able to shop, work, and attend the theater without risking direct contact with the outside world—in particular, the other city.[6]

Elaborating on the same principle, several cities have authorized property owners in certain upscale districts to assess one another a special surtax for amenities unavailable to other residents, like extra garbage collections, street cleaning, and security. One such New York district, situated in the tony area between Thirty-eighth and Forty-eighth streets and Second and Third avenues, raised $4.7 million from its members in 1989, of which $1 million underwrote a private police force of uniformed guards and plainclothes investigators.[7] The new community of like incomes, with the power to tax and the power to enforce the law, is thus becoming a separate city within the city.

3

WHEN not living in urban enclaves, symbolic analysts have congregated in residential suburbs and, increasingly, in what are termed "exurbs" in the surrounding countryside. The most desirable of such locations border symbolic-analytic zones of universities, research parks, or corporate headquarters, in pleasant environs such as Princeton, New Jersey; northern Westchester and Putnam counties, New York; Palo Alto, California; Austin, Texas; Bethesda, Maryland; and Raleigh-Durham, North Caro-

---

[6] See William Schmidt, "Riding a Boom, Downtowns Are No Longer Downtrodden," *The New York Times*, October 11, 1987, p. A28.
[7] "A Private Police Force Patrols Midtown Area," *The New York Times*, August 22, 1989, p. A23.

lina. American engineers and strategists employed by American-owned automobile companies, for example, do not live in Flint or Saginaw, Michigan, where the companies' routine workers reside; they cluster in their own towns of Troy, Warren, and Auburn Hills. The vast majority of the financial specialists, lawyers, and executives working for the insurance companies of Hartford would never consider living there; after all, Hartford is one of the poorest cities in the nation. Instead, they flock to Windsor, Middlebury, and other nearby Connecticut townships, which are, unsurprisingly, among the wealthiest in the nation.

Suburban and exurban townships like these offer another convenient means of secession into communities of comparable income. Property taxes in well-heeled communities serve much the same function as any other method of pooling resources among symbolic analysts while avoiding having to subsidize anyone else. In-person servers who provide symbolic analysts with housecleaning, day-care, retail, restaurant, automotive, and related services tend to reside in poorer townships nearby, and thus do not share directly in local public amenities.

The federal government has cooperated in these efforts by shifting responsibility for many public services to state and local governments. Federal grants comprised almost 27 percent of state and local spending at their peak in 1978. Ten years later, the federal share had dwindled to 17 percent.[8] Grants to local governments were hardest hit. Most vulnerable to budget cuts have been programs of direct aid to localities; many of these programs had been introduced during the Johnson and Nixon administrations.[9] In the 1980s, federal dollars for clean water, job training, low-income housing, job transfer, sewage treatment, and garbage disposal shrank by more than $50 billion a year. The federal share of spending on local transit declined by 50 percent. (At this writing, the Bush administration has proposed that states and localities

---

[8] U.S. Advisory Commission on Intergovernmental Relations, *Significant Features of Fiscal Federalism* (1988 ed.), Vol. 2, p. 115; see also John Shannon, "Federalism's Fiscal Fable," *Intergovernmental Perspective*, Summer 1988, p. 22.

[9] Steven D. Gold, "State Finances in the New Era of Fiscal Federalism," in Thomas Swartz (ed.), *The Changing Face of Fiscal Federalism* (Armonk, N.Y.: M. E. Sharpe, 1990).

take on even more of the costs of building and maintaining roads.) By 1990, New York City received only 9.6 percent of its total revenues from the federal government, as compared with 16 percent in 1981.

Like a hot potato, states have quickly transferred many of these new expenses to cities and towns, with the result that by the start of the 1990s localities were bearing more than half of the costs of water and sewage, roads, parks, welfare, and public schools. In New York State, they were bearing 75 percent of these costs, up from 40 percent in the late 1970s.[10]

Cities and towns with wealthier inhabitants could, of course, bear these burdens relatively easily. Poorer jurisdictions, faced with the twin problems of lower incomes and a greater demand for social services, have had more difficulty. This is precisely the point: As Americans continue to segregate according to what they earn, the shift in financing public services from the federal government to the states, and from the states to cities and towns, has functioned as another means of relieving America's wealthier citizens of the burdens of America's less fortunate.

For most of the nation's history, poorer towns and regions steadily gained ground on wealthier areas, as American industry spread to Southern and Western states in search of cheaper labor. This trend ended sometime in the 1970s, as American industry moved on to Mexico, Southeast Asia, and other places around the world. Since then, most poorer towns and regions in the United States have grown relatively poorer; most wealthier towns and regions, relatively wealthier. American cities and counties with the lowest per-person incomes in 1979 had dropped even further below the nation's average by the late 1980s; cities and counties with the highest incomes headed in the opposite direction. There has been a similar divergence among the states.[11]

---

[10]See, generally, Helen Ladd, "State and Local Governments in the 1980s," unpub. Duke University, December 2, 1989. See also "The State of the States," National Council of State Governments, 1990, and various issues.
[11]*Statistical Abstract of the United States*, "Per Capita Money Income of 50 Largest Cities," Table 732, p. 451; "Per Capita Money Income by State," Table 731, p. 450 (Washington, D.C.: U.S. Government Printing Office, 1989). See also *Sourcebook of Demographics and Buying Power for Every Zip Code in the United States* (New York: CACI, 1989, 1990).

The growing segregation of Americans by income, when coupled with the shift in the burden of financing public services from the federal government to the states and localities, has resulted in growing inequalities of service. Increasingly, where you live determines the quality of public service you receive. While Philadelphia's taxes were triple those of its suburbs, the suburbs enjoyed far better schools, hospitals, recreation, and police protection.[12] In 1985, about $323 was spent per resident of Erie, Pennsylvania, on infrastructure such as roads, bridges, sewage, and water treatment; $872 was spent per resident of San Francisco. It is no coincidence that the average resident of Erie earned $9,520 that year while the average resident of San Francisco pocketed $13,100.[13]

4

NOWHERE has the resulting inequality in government service been more apparent than in the public schools. By 1990, the federal government's share of the costs of primary and secondary education across the nation had dwindled to around 6 percent. The remaining 94 percent was divided about equally between the states and local school districts. States harboring a higher concentration of symbolic analysts could, of course, afford to spend more on their schools than states with a lower proportion. In 1990, the

[12] Michael de Courey Hinds, "After Renaissance of 1970s and 1980s, Philadelphia Is Struggling to Survive," *The New York Times*, June 21, 1990, p. A16.

[13] For more detailed comparisons among many American cities, see Randall W. Eberts, "Public Infrastructure and Regional Economic Development," *Economic Review*, Federal Reserve Bank of Cleveland, Vol. 26, No. 1 (January–April 1990), p. 15. A number of studies have shown public capital stock to be positively and significantly correlated with per capita personal income in the locale. See K. Duffy-Deno and R. Eberts, "Public Infrastructure and Regional Economic Development: A Simultaneous Equations Approach," Working Paper No. 8909, Federal Reserve Bank of Cleveland, August 1989; C. Hutton and R. Schwab, "Regional Productivity Growth in U.S. Manufacturing: 1951–1978," *American Economic Review*, Vol. 74, No. 1 (March 1984), pp. 152–62.

average public school teacher in Arkansas received $20,300; in Connecticut, $33,500.[14]

Even between adjoining towns within the same state, the differences could be quite large. By way of illustration, consider three Boston-area communities located within minutes of each other. All three are predominantly white, and most residents within each earn roughly the same as their neighbors. But the disparity of incomes *between* towns is substantial. Northwest of Boston lies the town of Belmont, inhabited mainly by symbolic analysts and their families. In 1988, the average teacher in the Belmont public schools earned $36,100. Only 4 percent of Belmont's eighteen-year-olds dropped out of high school before graduating, and more than 80 percent of Belmont's graduating seniors chose to continue their education after high school in a four-year college. Next to Belmont, just north of Boston, is the town of Somerville, most of whose residents are in-person servers or routine workers. In 1988, the average Somerville teacher earned just $29,400. A third of Somerville's eighteen-year-olds did not finish high school, and fewer than a third planned to attend college. To the east, on the other side of the Mystic River, lies Chelsea, whose inhabitants are the poorest of the three towns. Most are in-person servers and routine workers, but many are unemployed or employed only part-time. The average teacher in Chelsea, facing what is surely a more daunting educational challenge than in Belmont, earned $26,200 in 1988, almost a third less than the average teacher in Belmont. More than half of Chelsea's eighteen-year-olds did not graduate from high school, and only 10 percent planned to attend college.[15]

Similar disparities could be found all over the nation. New Trier High School, in one of Chicago's most affluent suburbs, paid its teachers 50 percent more than the highest-paid teacher in Du Sable, Illinois, one of the poorest. Public schools in White Plains and Great Neck, two of the richest suburbs of New York, spent twice as much per pupil as schools in the Bronx. Starting pay for teachers in suburban Milwaukee was double that of rural Wisconsin. Students at Highland Park High School, in a wealthy

---

[14] *Statistical Abstract of the United States*, Table 223, p. 137.
[15] Data from *Boston* magazine, September 1989, p. 144.

suburb of Dallas, enjoyed a campus replete with a planetarium, indoor swimming pool, closed-circuit television studio, and state-of-the-art science laboratory. Highland Park spent about $6,000 a year to educate each of its students. This was almost twice that spent per pupil by the towns of Wilmer and Hutchins in southern Dallas County, whose no-frills high school lacked even adequate classroom space.[16]

The courts have become involved, but it is not an issue open to easy judicial remedy. Among the four-fifths of Americans left in the wake of the symbolic analysts' secession are many poor blacks, but racial exclusion is not the primary motive for the separation, nor is it a necessary consequence. Lower-income whites are similarly excluded; high-income black symbolic analysts, often welcomed. The segregation is economic rather than racial (although, in America, economically motivated segregation often results in de facto racial segregation). Where courts have found a pattern of racially motivated segregation, it usually has involved lower-income white communities bordering on lower-income black neighborhoods. Where courts have ordered states to better equalize state spending across school districts, vast differences in local property values—and thus local tax revenues—still have resulted in substantial inequalities. Where courts or state governments have tried to impose limits on what affluent communities can pay their teachers, as in California, not a few parents in upscale communities have simply removed their children from the public schools and applied the money they might otherwise have been willing to pay in higher local school taxes toward private school tuition instead. And, of course, even if statewide expenditures were better equalized, poorer states would continue to be at a substantial disadvantage relative to wealthier ones.

5

THE IDEA of "community" has always held a special attraction for Americans. The notion is equally appealing to politicians on the

---

[16]Dallas *Times Herald*, February 26, 1990, p. 5.

right and the left of the ideological spectrum. Ronald Reagan celebrated America's "bedrock, its communities where neighbors help one another, where families bring up kids together, where American values are born."[17] Mario Cuomo, of a different political leaning, has been almost as lyrical. "Community . . . is the reality on which our national life has been founded."[18] There is only one problem with Reagan's and Cuomo's campaigns for community. In real life, most Americans no longer live in traditional communities. The majority live in suburban subdivisions bordered by highways and punctuated by shopping malls, or in tony condominiums and residential communities, or in ramshackle apartment buildings and housing projects. Most commute to work and socialize on some basis other than geographic proximity to where they sleep. And most pick up and move every five years or so to a different neighborhood.[19]

There is only one thing Americans increasingly have in common with their neighbors, and this commonality lies at the heart of the new American "community." It is their income levels. You can bet without much risk that you earn about the same amount as the folks down the street. Your educational backgrounds are similar, you pay roughly the same amount in taxes, and you indulge the same consumer impulses. The best definition of "community" is now the zip code used by direct-mail marketers to target likely customers. "Tell me someone's zip code and I can predict what they eat, drink, and drive—even think," enthuses the founder of one zip-code marketing firm.[20] It is known, for example, that the residents of Chelsea, Massachusetts, read the *National Enquirer*, watch Roller Derby, use curling irons and hair lotions, and eat white bread and snack cakes. Belmont's inhabitants play racquetball and golf, use electric toothbrushes, depilatories, and personal computers, and eat wheat bread and oat-bran muf-

---

[17] Address to the Annual Concretes and Aggregates Convention, January 31, 1984.
[18] The Newsday Education Symposium, March 4, 1987.
[19] On Americans' propensity to move, see U.S. Bureau of the Census, *Current Population Survey*, various issues. See also Michael Weiss, *The Clustering of America* (New York: Harper & Row, 1988), p. 30.
[20] Weiss, op. cit., p. 1.

fins. Incomes, and the tastes that go with them, increasingly define the new American community.

Americans who own their homes do, however, share with their neighbors a common political cause. They have a near-obsessive concern over maintaining or upgrading property values. And this shared interest is responsible for much of what has brought neighbors together in recent years. People who are complete strangers to one another, although they may live on the same street or within the same condominium complex, suddenly feel intense solidarity when it is rumored that low-income housing will be constructed in their midst or that a poorer school district will be consolidated with their own.

The renewed emphasis on "community" in American life has justified and legitimized these economic enclaves. If generosity and solidarity end at the borders of our common property values, then symbolic analysts can be virtuous citizens at little cost. Since almost everyone in their "community" is by definition as well off as they are, there is no cause for a stricken conscience. If inhabitants of another neighborhood are poorer, let them look to one another. Why should *we* pay for *their* schools? So the argument goes, without acknowledging that the critical assumption has already been made: "we" and "they" belong to fundamentally different communities. Through such reasoning it has become possible to maintain a preferred self-image of generosity toward, and solidarity with, one's "community" without owing any responsibility to "them," in another "community." Symbolic analysts—firmly connected to the global economy—thus are made to feel increasingly justified in withdrawing into enclaves bounded by other symbolic analysts, paying only what is necessary to ensure that everyone within the enclave is sufficiently well educated and has access to the infrastructure he or she needs in order to succeed in the global economy.

6

THE READER may object by noting that symbolic analysts are in fact devoting substantial resources and energies to helping the rest of society, but they have chosen to do so voluntarily, instead of through their tax payments. "It's time to reject the notion that advocating government programs is a form of personal charity," said Ronald Reagan. "Generosity is a reflection of what one does with his or her resources—and not what he or she advocates the government do with everyone's money."[21] The argument is fair enough. Government is not the only device for redistributing wealth. Perhaps symbolic analysts have not seceded at all; maybe their formal withdrawal from the rest of the population has been more than compensated for by their private generosity. George Bush noted that the real magnanimity of America was to be found in a "brilliant diversity" of private charities, "spread like stars, like a thousand points of light in a broad and peaceful sky."[22]

No nation congratulates itself more enthusiastically on its charitable acts than America; none engages in a greater number of charity balls, bake sales, benefit auctions, and border-to-border hand-holdings for good causes. Most of this is sincerely motivated; much of it is admirable. But close examination reveals that these and other forms of benevolence rarely in fact help the poor. Particularly suspect is the one-third to one-half of all private giving that derives from Americans in the top income-tax bracket. Studies have revealed that such donations do not flow mainly to social services for society's less fortunate citizens–to better schools, community health clinics, or recreational facilities for impoverished families. Instead, most of the contributions of America's wealthy go to the places where wealthy people are entertained, inspired, cured, or educated—to art museums, opera houses, theaters, symphony orchestras, ballets, private hospitals (nearly all of whose patients have health insurance), and elite universities. The contributions of less wealthy symbolic analysts are correspondingly lower, but they tend in the same general direction.[23]

In other words, when symbolic analysts voluntarily share their wealth, they do so according to the same principle by which they pool it for their other purposes: to enhance the quality of life for themselves and other symbolic analysts. The only difference between charitable giving and the other ways in which symbolic analysts pool their resources is that the former induces other tax-

[21] Reagan, op. cit.
[22] Acceptance speech before the Republican National Convention, 1988.
[23] Data from T. Odendahl, *Charity Begins at Home: Generosity and Self-Interest Among the Philanthropic Elite* (New York: Basic Books, 1990), pp. 12–27.

payers to put up 28 cents (under the current tax law) of every dollar so dedicated. Charitable agencies display a similar tendency. In one study, political scientist Lester Salamon and his colleagues found that fewer than one-third of charitable agencies in the United States focused on a poor clientele.[24]

The same holds true for corporate philanthropy. In recent years, America's largest corporations have been sounding the alarm about the nation's fast-deteriorating primary and secondary schools. Few are more eloquently impassioned about the need for better schools than American corporate executives. "How well we educate all of our children will determine our competitiveness globally, and our economic health domestically, and our communities' character and vitality," noted the Business Round Table, a Washington-based association of the chief executives of the largest American-owned corporations.[25] Accordingly, there are now numerous "partnerships" between corporations and public schools, corporate-funded scholarships for poor children qualified to attend college, and programs through which corporations "adopt" local schools by making conspicuous donations of computers, books, the time of senior employees, and even, occasionally, money. That such eleemosynary activities are loudly touted by corporate public relations staffs should not detract from their worthy effects.

But despite the hoopla, corporate donations to education actually tapered off markedly in the 1980s. While in the 1970s corporate giving to education jumped an average of 15 percent a year, by the late 1980s it was climbing at a snail's pace—in 1987, only 5.1 percent over 1986; in 1988, only 2.4 percent over 1987. And, notably, most of it was allocated to colleges and universities—in particular, to the alma maters of symbolic analysts, where their children and grandchildren would likely follow

---

[24]L. M. Salamon, J. C. Musselwhite, Jr., and C. J. De Vita, "Partners in the Public Service: Government and the Nonprofit Sector in the Welfare State," *Working Papers* (Washington, D.C.: Independent Sector and the United Way Institute, 1986), pp. 3–38.
[25]"The Role of Business and Education: Blueprint for Action," Business Round Table, Washington, D.C., September 1988. See also "Business Means Business About Education: A Synopsis of the Business Round Table's Company Educational Partnerships," Business Round Table, Washington, D.C., June 1989.

in their footsteps. Only 1.5 percent of corporate giving in 1989 was directed toward primary and secondary schools.[26]

This tiny sum was, notably, smaller than the amounts received by corporations from states and locales in the form of subsidies and tax breaks quietly procured under threat that the corporation otherwise would move to a more congenial tax base. The ironic result is that states and localities have been left with less corporate revenue with which to spend on schools and other community needs. The executives of General Motors, for example, who have been among the loudest to proclaim the need for better schools, have also been among the most relentless pursuers of local tax abatements. As one writer to *The New York Times* explained, GM's successful efforts to eliminate its taxes in Tarrytown, New York, where the corporation has had a factory since 1914, reduced local revenues by $2.81 million in 1990, thus forcing the town to lay off scores of teachers.[27] All told, the corporate share of local property tax revenues dropped from 45 percent in 1957 to around 16 percent in 1987. The newfound generosity of American-owned corporations toward America's less fortunate communities has been no match for the dramatic withdrawal of corporate tax revenues from the same localities.[28]

---

[26]Council of Economic Priorities, "Corporate America in the Classroom," January 1990. See also "Giving in the U.S.A.," American Association of Fund Raising Council, 1989.

[27]Carin Rubenstein, "The Deadbeat of America," *The New York Times*, March 17, 1990, p. A22.

[28]"Significant Features of Fiscal Federalism," Advisory Commission on Intergovernmental Relations, Washington, D.C., various issues.

24
The Politics
of Secession

DESIRE to end the relationship is rarely sufficient to accomplish the feat of secession. Secessionists must also undo the political and legal ties that bind them to their undesired compatriots. The latter can be expected to resist such efforts, especially if they have benefited from the compact. The politics of secession are thus rarely cordial.

Yet the secession of symbolic analysts from the rest of America has proceeded calmly and quietly. The four-fifths of the population whose economic future is growing more precarious has not vociferously contested the disengagement of the one-fifth whose economic future is becoming ever brighter. The widening divergence in their incomes, the growing difference in their working conditions, the regressive shift of the tax burden, the difference in the quality of primary and secondary education available to their children, the growing disparity in their access to higher education, the increasing difference in recreational facilities, roads, security, and other local amenities available to them—no part of this broad trend toward inequality has generated overt resentment from the majority of citizens. There has been no significant demand that the nation return to a more progressive system of taxation; no organized insistence that large sums of money, so raised, be dedicated to the education, training, transport, and general well-being of the rest of the population; and no noticeable withdrawal of support for either of the major parties, under whose policies these disparities have grown. This acquiescence deserves explanation.

2

FOR A time it appeared as if America's routine producers would have sufficient political potency to impose tariffs, quotas, and other, less visible forms of trade protection upon the American market, thus forcing America's symbolic analysts and all other Americans to pay higher prices by contracting with them instead of with lower-paid routine producers abroad. This was a regular occurrence in the 1970s and 1980s. Not a few politicians were elected and reelected on the strength of their avowed conviction that America should be protected from unscrupulous foreigners.

Eventually, however, protectionism lost its political allure. Politicians who were among the most outspoken proponents of protection fared poorly in both the 1984 and 1988 presidential elections. By the last decade of the century, politicians of every hue denied adamantly that they were "protectionists." The only halfway respectable rationale for closing the American market was as a means of forcing another nation to open its market, and even this tactical justification was regarded as somewhat dubious. In future years, the demand that American industry be protected from low-wage foreign competitors can be expected to disappear. There are several reasons why.

First is the change in strategy of the core American corporation and of the symbolic analysts who populate its headquarters. American corporations that sided with routine workers in calling for protection during the late 1960s, 1970s, and early 1980s had evolved by the end of the 1980s into global webs that were dependent on the free movement of goods, services, money, and technology across borders. In 1984 Goodyear Tire and Rubber joined with its unionized workers to demand that the U.S. government mercilessly penalize several South Korean firms for "dumping" their tires in America at prices below cost. Five years later, however, Goodyear had become more cosmopolitan in its outlook. When the Bush administration threatened to retaliate against South Korea for allegedly barring American imports, Goodyear's executives were among the first to urge a more conciliatory approach. The change in attitude was not the result of more thoughtful reflection by the firm's top managers about the benefits to the nation of unencumbered international trade. It was, rather, the consequence of a profound change in corporate strategy. In 1989, Goodyear's strategic brokers were in the process of acquiring a large tract of land in South Korea on which they planned to construct a $110 million tire factory—a plant large enough to fabricate 10,000 tires a day. Any move by the Bush administration that might limit the sales of such tires to the United States, or otherwise antagonize the South Korean government, would reduce the value of this significant investment. Without the support of core American corporations like Goodyear and their symbolic analysts, however, organized labor was left on its own to argue for protection. Labor's voice, steadily quieting as the number of routine producers in America dwindled, would be no match for the voices on the other side, growing ever louder and more convincing.

Of the declining number of Americans who have remained in routine production, moreover, a growing portion have become entwined in global webs. Many of them are now employed by, dependent for components and services upon, or suppliers of foreign-owned corporations. For these workers, trade protection hurts more than it helps. It might raise the price of supplies coming from abroad or deter foreign investors and strategic brokers from hiring them in the future. In the late 1980s, American-owned producers of semiconductor chips withdrew their demand that inexpensive chips from Japan be barred from the United States, after their computer customers threatened to move their operations abroad in order to retain access to the prized Japanese chips.[1]

As protectionism wanes, the symbolic analysts associated with American-owned corporations will, of course, continue to press for special subsidies, favorable tax treatment, particular immunities from antitrust law, and other forms of government largesse—even as they vigorously eschew protectionism. They will argue that such benefits are critical to "American competitiveness." While outright protection of the American market would

---

[1] Noticeably absent from the group of American semiconductor manufacturers that originally sought protection in 1985 were Motorola and Texas Instruments, both of which by then were producing large numbers of chips in Japan—some of which they intended to ship back to the United States.

hamper their global strategies, special favors that do not interfere with the free flow of goods and services across the U.S. border can only help the bottom line. In pursuit of such public benevolence, American executives of American global corporations (or, more accurately, the strategic brokers who manage the American-owned portions of global webs) will continue to exercise considerable influence in Washington. Their Washington lobbyists are well connected; their trade associations, large and vocal; their campaign contributions and PACs, larger and still more vocal. Their demands for treatment not available to foreign-owned corporations (that is, to the foreign-owned portions of global webs) will be convincing to many legislators and executive branch officials habituated into believing that these favors will help the corporations that embody American industry, and, thus, the American economy. No foreign-owned global corporation will be able to summon this much influence on the Potomac, not even the free-spending Japanese. As I have noted, however, the American-owned corporation's claim to special privilege is increasingly dubious. All global webs—regardless of the nationality of the majority of shareholders or of top executives—are busily investing money, developing technologies, and contracting with workers all over the world. From the standpoint of the nation's citizens, the crucial issue is which work force adds the most value to these global webs and which is trained to add additional value in the future—not which nation's investors own what part of them.

3

OUTRIGHT protection of routine producers may be declining (as is the number of routine producers themselves) but another conflict is taking its place. The desire among symbolic analysts for unconstrained access to the rest of the world will become a sticking point with in-person servers. Recall that, as their appellation suggests, in-person servers do tasks that must be done *in person*. Symbolic analysts cannot contract with foreigners to undertake in-person services in other nations. Symbolic analysts thus share a portion of their worldwide earnings with in-person servers every time they walk into a retail store or a restaurant; each time they have their houses, cars, bodies, or tools repaired; whenever they take a ride in a cab, or use the services of a secretary, nurse, or security guard. Because of this relationship, the standard of living of in-person servers rises or falls with the global success of their symbolic-analytic customers. A relatively few star software designers, lawyers, product engineers, management consultants, or movie directors can support, indirectly, a much larger number of in-person servers, as the symbolic analysts' global earnings spread throughout the local economy.

Symbolic analysts would, of course, prefer that this constraint be removed, in the sense that they would ideally like to be able to obtain in-person services of the highest quality and lowest price from anywhere on the globe—just as they can obtain routine production and symbolic-analytic services from around the world. For their part, American in-person servers would naturally prefer that the constraint remain, so that symbolic analysts cannot replace them with others from around the world who are willing to work harder for less money.

Symbolic analysts are not without alternatives. They can, for example, encourage the adoption of (and thwart any efforts to block) automated bank tellers, robotized parking-garage attendants, retail sales over the home computer, and similar technologies capable of providing in-person services at lower cost. But such technologies, as has been observed, are apt to supplant only a fraction of in-person servers. Moreover, as American population growth slows, the demand for in-person services is likely to outrun supply, exerting an upward push on wages.

By 1990, concerns already were being expressed about pending labor shortages. Retailers, hospitals, fast-food restaurants, and custodial firms, among others, reported difficulties in finding in-person servers to work for them at or near the minimum wage. Other employers faced shortages of more skilled in-person servers such as executive secretaries, paralegals, nurses, and hospital technicians.

It should be noted that the term "labor shortage" rarely means that workers cannot be found at any price. Its real meaning is that desired workers cannot be found at the price that employers and customers wish to pay. At any given time, many people are working part-time who would prefer to work full-time. There is also a residual work force comprising retirees, high schoolers, and parents (almost always mothers) who would be willing to work part-time if the pay was sufficiently high to lure them away from their other pursuits. Most important, there is a large group of people who are available to work but lack the necessary skills. They know nothing about how to repair a car, lay a brick, or take a blood sample. Or they are functionally illiterate and/or innumerate and are thus unable to read simple directions or provide correct change. Employers would not normally hire these workers, but in a severe "labor shortage," they have no choice. Not only must they hire them, they must also train them. In sum, the most direct means of remedying a "labor shortage" is to offer better wages and training. Such a strategy obviously improves the relative position of those receiving the higher wages and training.

But there is a less costly alternative for symbolic analysts confronting a "labor shortage": Open the nation's borders to immigrants, who are invariably eager to provide in-person services for low wages. If the immigrants are already skilled, so much the better. "Immigration . . . can help provide us with whatever skills we may be lacking [and] diminish labor shortages that may be coming our way," enthused two policy analysts from Washington's conservative American Enterprise Institute at a gathering in late 1989. The potential savings seem obvious: "When they come, they come at little cost to us. Many immigrants have already had their educations completed and paid for elsewhere."[2] Note the logic here. Immigrants can remedy "labor shortages" by alleviating upward pressure on the wages of in-person servers already in the United States and also by reducing the necessity of having to train Americans for such jobs. *The Wall Street Journal*, whose editorials provide a near-perfect barometer of conservative pressure points, was far more explicit: "Our own view remains that the problem is not too many immigrants, but too few. . . . As long as we don't train enough [Americans] ourselves, immigration is a saving grace."[3]

---

[2] Ben Wattenberg and Karl Zinmeister, American Enterprise Institute Policy Conference, December 1989.

[3] Editorial, *The Wall Street Journal*, February 2, 1990, p. A8. The Bush administration offered similar advice: "With projections of a rising demand for skilled workers in coming years, the nation can achieve even greater benefits from immigration." The report recommends "increasing quota lev-

Even as such advice issued forth, the nation had been opening its borders ever wider to immigrants. Some 8 million of them crossed into the United States legally in the 1980s—almost as many as in the first decade of the century. The nation also harbors an estimated 3.4 million illegal immigrants.[4] Congress has been attentive to the needs of employers for yet additional labor. Faced with a "labor shortage" of nurses in the 1980s, American hospitals began recruiting nurses from the Philippines and Ireland to come to the United States on temporary work visas; in 1989, Congress decided that the nursing shortage was sufficiently serious that these temporary nurses—more than 10,000 of them—should be granted permanent American citizenship. Another amendment to the immigration laws, sponsored by congressional Republicans with the explicit backing of American-owned corporations, creates a new category of skilled "independent" immigrants, to whom an extra 54,000 visas will be issued each year. As a result of these and other measures, the portion of the American population born in another nation has begun to rise once again, after a long decline, reaching well above 6 percent by 1990.[5]

Is unrestricted immigration good for the American economy? Is it good for America? It depends, once again, on what is meant by these terms. As I have stressed, the "American economy" is a collection of people living and working within the borders of the United States. Its success is not a function of the profitability of American-owned enterprise, but of the value that these people add to the world economy—which depends, in turn, on their

---

els for potential immigrants with higher levels of basic and specific skills." *Economic Report of the President* (Washington, D.C.: U.S. Government Printing Office, February 1990).

[4] For a means of estimating the number of illegal immigrants, see George J. Borjas, *Friends or Strangers: The Impact of Immigrants on the United States Economy* (New York: Basic Books, 1990), pp. 22–31. Borjas bases his estimate of illegal aliens on the number of Mexican-born people who die in the United States and the number who are apprehended trying to cross the Mexican border into the United States illegally. Note that his estimate is limited to illegal aliens from Mexico; the total number is likely to be much greater than this.

[5] U.S. Department of Justice, U.S. Immigration and Naturalization Services, *Statistical Yearbook of the Immigration and Naturalization Service* (Washington, D.C.: U.S. Government Printing Office, 1990).

training, education, health, and the ease with which they can transport and communicate the products of their efforts.

If you happen to be a symbolic analyst in America, an influx of new immigrants is likely to save you money, particularly if they already have good basic educations and possess useful skills. If you are an in-person server already in the American labor force, however, immigration is a more qualified blessing. You benefit from the new immigrants' education, energy, and eagerness to work for low wages, no less than does every other American. But to the extent that their presence remedies pending "labor shortages," it reduces the pressure on other Americans to pay more for your services. Thus will your wages fail to rise quite as much or as fast as otherwise (although they probably will not fall by any significant amount).[6] More important over the long term, symbolic analysts will have less and less incentive to invest their earnings in your training and education and thereby render you more valuable in the future. When *The Wall Street Journal* opines that educated immigrants are a "saving grace" as long as "we don't train enough" people within the United States to take on in-person service jobs, the "we" refers to the more wealthy among us, who might otherwise feel an enlightened self-interest in devoting a larger portion of their incomes to educating and training the rest.

For these reasons, immigration policy will become a point of growing contention between America's symbolic analysts and in-person servers in coming years. As the debate over how wide to open the American market to foreign goods and services loses much of its force, the debate over how wide to open it to foreign workers can only intensify. Yet, here again, symbolic analysts will most likely prevail.

---

[6] Studies have shown that the average wages of American-born workers are only slightly lower in labor markets where immigrants concentrate (controlled for differences in level of schooling, age, and economic activity). See, for example, Jean B. Grossman, "The Substitutability of Natives and Immigrants in Production," *Review of Economics and Statistics*, Vol. 64 (November 1982), pp. 596–603; George J. Borjas, "The Sensitivity of Labor Demand Functions to Choice of Dependent Variable," *Review of Economics and Statistics*, Vol. 68 (February 1986), pp. 58–66; George J. Borjas, "Immigrants, Minorities, and Labor Market Competition," *Industrial and Labor Relations Review*, Vol. 40 (April 1987), pp. 382–92.

4

TO THE extent that freer movement of goods, services, money, technology, and people across borders further enriches symbolic analysts, there is more wealth to be shared with routine producers and in-person servers—or so, at least, in theory. Symbolic analysts comprise no more than 20 percent of America's voting-age population. The other four-fifths, with a wide majority of the votes, could mandate that a larger proportion of the burgeoning incomes of symbolic analysts be taxed and transferred to them—either directly, as income supplements, or indirectly, in the form of public investments in their education, training, health care, and access to good roads, clean water, and recreation. In practice, the lower four-fifths of Americans is unlikely to impose such demands on the top fifth.

One reason may be a basic lack of understanding. The intricacies of the tax code and the Social Security system, the federal budget, off-budget subsidies and tax breaks, and state and local budgets are difficult even for presumably intelligent and conscientious politicians (and their expert-stuffed staffs) to understand, let alone the average citizen. Taken together with the subtleties of international economics and finance, the overall picture is almost impossible to make sense of. In the small sliver of time between getting home from the job, putting kids to sleep, and falling, exhausted, into bed, there is little temptation to pore through stacks of government statistics. Newspapers and television news are of little help. Disaster, murder, pillage, and war are far more stimulating fare than global direct investment and the taxation of capital gains. The media carefully avoid complex explanations and context for fear that their harried listeners and readers will seek more entertaining diversion.

There is also the continuing dominance of vestigial thought. For most people, the American economy is still composed of American industries, and American industries are made up of American corporations whose continued profitability and global market share depend, in turn, upon American investors who must be motivated to risk their capital. And because, in this picture, American jobs and the wages connected with them depend on the vitality of the American economy, it follows that all Americans must ensure that American investors enjoy returns sufficiently generous to remain highly motivated. Accordingly, it is assumed that the nation cannot afford more money for roads, bridges, clean water, health care for the poor, training, and education. After all, first things first; for the economic health of the nation, private profits are a first priority. The reality, of course, is quite the opposite—as we have seen. But still the old picture lingers. It lingers because it is consistent with the way the economy used to be organized; because this is how most Americans remember it from its buoyant days a generation ago; and because business leaders and the media portray it so. To change a dominant conception of reality requires substantial energy and not inconsiderable initiative. Indeed, this change often does not occur until the gap between what is and what is assumed to be looms so large as to render conventional pronouncements nonsensical. That day will arrive eventually, but it will not arrive any time soon.

Added to the difficulties of understanding and accepting what is occurring is the assumption of just deserts—a notion that lies deep in the American consciousness and has done so since the beginning of the Republic. According to this principle, the wealthy have reached their station because they have earned it. Their wealth is a measure of their worth; their worth, a sign of their worthiness. To separate the wealthy from their wealth would be an unjust confiscation. They should pay taxes like everyone else, of course, and that they pay a larger sum than the rest of the population is only fair, since their resulting sacrifice is no greater in proportion. But they should not be made to bear a proportionally much larger burden. Embedded within this argument is a deeper assumption, also profoundly American, that anyone can make it with enough hard work, guts, and gumption. Someday I, or my children, may be there among the wealthy, and when that pinnacle of success has been attained I do not want *my* (or my child's) fortune to be confiscated. Upward mobility is part of the American creed.

But here again, we encounter the perils of vestigial thought. The withdrawal of symbolic analysts into enclaves of good schools, excellent health care, and first-rate infrastructure—leaving much of the rest of the population behind—reduces the likelihood that routine producers or in-person servers, or their progeny, will ever become symbolic analysts. This reality severs the presumed connection between high incomes and inherent worthiness, of course. High incomes are more attributable to the good fortune of being reared in symbolic-analytic households within symbolic-analytic enclaves than to possessing unique talent or tolerance for hard work. In time, as this reality also becomes more apparent, the principle of just deserts, too, will grow less compelling.

5

STILL another explanation for the docility of the less advantaged four-fifths is their sense that political action would have no effect in any event. They are resigned to what is occurring, because they assume that symbolic analysts hold all the cards; the game is rigged from the start, so why play? In comparison with most other democracies, Americans exercise their right to vote with a remarkable lack of enthusiasm. Voter turnout for national elections has dipped below 50 percent, and among those who do cast their ballots, higher-income Americans predominate.[7] As for the rest: "Many of the young, the wage-earning poor, the unemployed, or dependent poor . . . these are the people who do not vote or who have, more and more, stopped voting."[8]

Anticipated political futility is a self-fulfilling prophecy. Politicians are unlikely to be especially attentive to the needs of "constituents" unwilling to vote, help get out the vote, or contribute to political campaigns. Many in America's lower four-fifths are engaged in a political vicious circle where cynicism about American politics is rewarded by government decisions which confirm their worst suspicions, thus engendering still more cynicism and passivity.

---

[7] See V. R. A. Teixeira, *Why Americans Don't Vote: Turnout Decline in the United States: 1960–1984* (Westport, Conn.: Greenwood Press, 1987); Frances Fox Piven and Richard Cloward, *Why Americans Don't Vote* (New York: Pantheon, 1989), pp. 114–15; William Crotty, *American Parties in Decline* (2nd ed.; Boston: Little, Brown, 1984), Ch. 1; Walter Dean Burnham, *The Current Crisis in American Politics* (New York: Oxford University Press, 1982), pp. 172–73; Thomas Byrne Edsall, *The New Politics of Inequality* (New York: W. W. Norton, 1984), especially Ch. 5.

[8] Richard Valelly, "Vanishing Voters," *The American Prospect*, Vol. 1 (Spring 1990), p. 140.

Even politicians of Democratic persuasion, who in decades past drew much of their strength from the lower four-fifths, have tended to turn their attention away from poorer Americans precisely as these Americans have turned their attention away from politics. When campaign money poured into Republican coffers from wealthy individuals, corporations, and trade associations during the 1980s, many Democratic politicians felt that they had no alternative but to seek money from the same sources. Congressional Democrats had little difficulty convincing American business leaders and Wall Street bankers that it was smarter to back incumbent Democrats than aspiring Republicans. It was an honest sales pitch. Incumbents are much more likely to win, especially with a little help from their friends. It was also, apparently, a convincing pitch. In the 1988 elections, 97 percent of House and 85 percent of Senate incumbents who ran for reelection regained their seats. As a result, money from traditionally Republican sources began to flow toward the Democrats. In 1988, 64 percent of all money raised by political action committees (PACs) went to Democratic incumbents in the House of Representatives and the Senate, while almost none went to their Republican challengers. Most of this windfall ($31.7 million) came from corporate, Wall Street, and trade association PACs, rather than from trade unions (which contributed less than $24 million) or other traditional sources of Democratic funding.[9]

It is, of course, difficult to represent the little fellow when the big fellow picks up the tab. The problem is not one of corruption. The new inhibition working upon many Democratic politicians is more subtle. The anticipated need for additional campaign money in the future tends to constrain bold thinking about the nation's problems and to close off alternatives that would be strongly opposed by those possessing the money, such as a steeply progressive income tax. It tends also to drown out the voices of those less willing or able to provide the funding or otherwise engage in political activity. The Democrats' attentiveness to the interests of symbolic analysts only confirms what the rest of the population assumes about the futility of political action, thus encouraging them to be even more passive.

---

[9] Data from the Federal Election Commission and Common Cause, 1989.

Were the lower four-fifths of the population more politically active, their total campaign contributions and their efforts to get out the vote could overwhelm the pecuniary resources of symbolic analysts, who, though wealthy, are far fewer in number. But there is no easy way to mobilize this great force and snap the vicious circle of political futility. Between the mid-1930s, and the 1960s, organized labor mobilized America's working class in support of education, social services, and a progressive income tax. But the global economy has eroded the strength of organized labor, and the number of American routine producers continues to dwindle. In-person servers, whose numbers are increasing, cannot be organized as readily; they tend to work in small establishments, and are dispersed over wide geographical areas in many different lines of work. While most other Western democracies still feature active labor movements which give political representation to the economic interests of their work forces, America no longer does. The consequences are political lethargy among most American workers and a self-fulfilling prophecy that politicians are working for the guys at the top.

6

EVEN if all these impediments did not exist, the lower four-fifths of the population would still be reluctant to press demands upon the top fifth. The reason is economic. The rest of the population is dependent upon how and where symbolic analysts decide to dedicate their energies and money. The dependence of in-person servers is direct; wealthy symbolic analysts in their midst attract money from the rest of the world and spend a part of it on local services. Routine producers, although not dependent on *American* symbolic analysts exclusively, nonetheless rely on the decisions of strategic brokers of whatever nationality to give them work and, hopefully, to train them to become more valuable and productive.

The dependency is not symmetrical. Symbolic analysts represent the most mobile part of any nation's work force. They do not rely on nearby factories (as do routine producers); nor do they depend on large numbers of customers in close geographic proximity in order to make their sales (as do in-person servers). Symbolic analysts can work almost anywhere there exist a telephone, fax, modem, and airport. While symbolic analysts are likely to draw intellectual sustenance from the presence of other symbolic analysts in the special zone of the city or exurb where they work, they are not bound to work even there; there are other symbolic-analytic centers to which they might relocate. Nor do the weights of tradition and extended family bear heavily on their locational decisions, as they sometimes do on routine producers and in-person servers. With more money to spend on housing and child care, symbolic analysts are less dependent on relatives living nearby. In fact, symbolic analysts spend a great deal of time on the move—at meetings with clients and customers in distant cities, on temporary assignment in a factory or laboratory in another nation, at trade shows and conventions around the world.

This asymmetry puts symbolic analysts in a strong bargaining position. Routine producers and in-person servers are loath to do anything that might deter symbolic analysts from coming to their city or region, or even to their nation; they are equally careful to avoid antagonizing symbolic analysts already in their midst. In fact, the incentives are quite the opposite. The lower, less mobile four-fifths of the population is prepared to provide symbolic analysts with generous inducements to come or to stay.

7

THIS uneven bargaining power is most apparent when routine producers try to convince symbolic analysts to contract with them. Consider, for example, the executives of the Hyster Company, whom we met earlier when they sought to prevent Japanese-owned companies from selling inexpensive forklift trucks in the United States. In September 1982, Hyster's strategic brokers informed public officials in the five states and four nations where routine producers assembled Hyster's forklift trucks that some Hyster plants would have to close. The governments were invited to bid to keep local jobs; operations would be retained wherever they were most generously subsidized. The resulting auction was a great success for Hyster. By February 1983 Hyster had collected $72.5 million in direct aid from various jurisdictions. The United Kingdom offered $20 million as ransom for 1,500 jobs in Irvine, Scotland. Several American towns—including Kewanee, Illinois;

Sulligent, Alabama; and Berea, Kentucky—surrendered a total of $18 million in direct grants and subsidized loans to attract or preserve around 2,000 jobs. Home ties made no difference. In Portland, Oregon, where Hyster's world headquarters was located, a $20 million loan from the state employees' pension fund was insufficient to prevent the local Hyster plant from closing. The biggest winner was Danville, Illinois. This city of 39,000—with an unemployment rate of 16 percent at the time—agreed to provide roughly $10 million in operating subsidies and training grants. The sad irony, of course, was that even the routine production jobs that were preserved remained in jeopardy. The long-term demand for forklift trucks was growing slowly in the United States, and routine producers in Third World nations could assemble them far more cheaply.

Other global webs have sparked similar bidding wars. When Mitsubishi's Diamond-Star Motors announced in 1985 that it would begin assembling automobiles in America, four states (Illinois, Indiana, Michigan, and Ohio) competed for the plant. The winner was Illinois, with a ten-year package of direct aid and incentives worth $276 million—or about $25,000 per year for every new job that Mitsubishi would create in the state. Such incentives are becoming ever more generous: In 1977, the state of Ohio induced Honda to build its auto plant there by promising $22 million in subsidies and tax breaks; by 1986 it took a $100 million package from Kentucky for Toyota to create about the same number of jobs there.[10]

State and local officials have not the slightest qualms about bidding for the business of global webs, even if the webs are nominally owned and controlled by foreigners. This is, of course, in contrast to federal officials, who, as we have seen, draw a sharp distinction between American-owned and foreign-owned corporations. The reason for the difference is political. The strategic brokers who manage American-owned corporations have sufficient influence in Washington to claim federal largesse exclusively

---

[10] See *The Economist*, February 18, 1989, p. 32; see also James K. Jackson, "Japan: Increasing Investment in the United States," Congress Research Service, Report No. 87-747E (Washington, D.C.: U.S. Government Printing Office, 1987).

for themselves. Their influence is magnified through their national trade associations and, often, through their "government affairs staffs" (a Washington euphemism for corporate lobbyists) located within easy reach of both Capitol Hill and pricey Washington restaurants. But they have far less influence in state capitals and city halls, other than those where their headquarters and major plants already are located. Not even the largest American-owned corporation maintains a government affairs office or supports a trade association exerting ongoing influence in Indianapolis or Little Rock. State and local officials are thus left free to bargain with symbolic analysts from around the world. In fact, in a twist of irony, state and local governments often maintain offices in *foreign* cities, seeking out potential deals.

In consequence, states, cities, and even countries have found themselves bidding against one another for the same global jobs. Who successfully lures the jobs becomes a matter of state and local pride, as well as employment; it may also bear significantly upon the future careers of state and local politicians who have pledged to win them. The possibility of a new factory in the region sets off a furious auction; a casual threat to move one already situated initiates equally impassioned rounds of negotiation. The total amount of subsidies and tax breaks thus flowing to global firms of whatever nationality is much higher than it would be without such bidding. Nations whose constituent parts refrain from these internecine battles end up paying far less to lure jobs their way; nations that agree with one another to refrain from bidding altogether come out even further ahead.[11]

Such subsidies and tax breaks obviously reduce the amount of public money available to support primary and secondary schools, local highways and bridges, recreation, waste treatment facilities,

---

[11] An analogous situation suggests the magnitude of the difference. When it came time to bid for rights to televise the 1992 Olympic Games, the European Economic Community bid as a whole. In the United States, by contrast, each television network made its own separate bid. The two markets contain roughly the same number of people and not a great disparity in buying power. Nevertheless, because of the differences in bidding, the EEC got the rights to televise the Olympics in Europe for $70 million. The winning network in the United States paid $700 million to televise the Olympics in America.

and other local amenities. Ironically, as I have stressed, these are just the sorts of public investments that are necessary for building the good jobs of the future. Poorer states and cities, most of them desperate to obtain (or keep) routine production jobs, are thus placed in a bind: Either they provide such subsidies and tax breaks for routine jobs which may not even survive much longer than a decade or so, or they give up the contest and invest their shrinking tax bases in education and infrastructure, whose payoffs are decades away.

8

WHEN it comes to bargaining with symbolic analysts, in-person servers are in no better position than routine producers. The possibility that symbolic analysts might relocate their homes, laboratories, or offices where in-person services are cheaper or where taxes are lower operates as a powerful inhibition.

The lure of cheaper in-person services abroad is rarely sufficient to prompt symbolic analysts to emigrate, but less extreme moves are becoming common. For example, one of the attractions of a vacation on a Caribbean island, the Mexican Gulf coast, or Baja California, by contrast with Miami Beach or San Diego, is that in-person service can be had in the former regions for a fraction of the cost in the latter. So, too, with second homes, conventions, and business meetings. Tourism is fast becoming one of the Third World's major exports, catering to wealthy symbolic analysts from the north.

As transportation and communication costs decline, moreover, symbolic analysts can more efficiently move their work temporarily to regions on the globe where good in-person services can be had cheaply. American and West German investors, for example, are constructing a $100 million state-of-the-art film studio in Baja California, to which American directors, writers, producers, and actors will go when it is time to shoot their films. Studio maintenance and all other in-person services will be provided by Mexicans for a small fraction of the price that Hollywood in-person servers would charge.

Still more common is the lure of other jurisdictions promising lower taxes. Throughout the 1980s, the symbolic-analytic high-technology zone encircling Boston shifted outward to southern New Hampshire and northern Rhode Island, as symbolic analysts chose to live and work where taxes were lower. Researchers have documented a similar movement by skilled immigrants from nations where they are compelled to share a larger portion of their incomes to nations that tax them less. The "brain drain" from equalitarian Europe to less equalitarian America offers some evidence of this phenomenon.[12] Another illustration is found in immigration patterns between the United States and Canada. Most of the Americans who emigrate to Canada have been relatively low-skilled routine producers or in-person servers; most of the Canadians who come to the United States have been high-skilled symbolic analysts. Why? Both nations offer a similar array of job possibilities. But a pertinent difference is that Canada has a more equalitarian distribution of income and offers more generous social insurance than does the United States. Thus do unskilled Americans find in Canada a hospitable environment where they can enjoy greater income security; and thus do skilled Canadians find in the United States a hospitable environment where they can retain more of their earnings for themselves.[13]

In sum, because in-person servers and routine producers need symbolic analysts much more than symbolic analysts need them,

---

[12]Studies include V. B. Agarwal and D. R. Winkler, "Migration of Professional Manpower to the United States," *Southern Economic Journal*, Vol. 50 (January 1984), pp. 814–30; W. Huang, "A Pooled Cross-Section and Time-Series Study of Professional Indirect Immigration to the United States," *Southern Economic Journal*, Vol. 54 (July 1987), pp. 95–109. The economics of the brain drain are addressed in Walter Adams, *The Brain Drain* (New York: Macmillan, 1968), and J. N. Bhagwati and M. Partington, *Taxing the Brain Drain: A Proposal* (Amsterdam: North-Holland, 1976).

[13]Several studies have revealed this pattern. See, for example, George J. Borjas, *International Differences in the Labor Market Preferences of Immigrants* (Kalamazoo, Mich.: W. E. Upjohn Institute for Employment Research, 1988), Ch. 9; D. Bloom and M. K. Gunderson, "An Analysis of the Earnings of Canadian Immigrants," in R. B. Freeman (ed.), *Immigration, Trade, and the Labor Market* (Chicago: University of Chicago Press, 1990); J. Edward Taylor, "Undocumented Mexico-U.S. Migration and the Returns to Households in Rural Mexico," *American Journal of Agricultural Economics*, Vol. 69 (August 1987), pp. 626–38.

the former have little political leverage over the latter. They cannot force symbolic analysts to share their incomes with them or to invest in their futures. The politics of secession are relatively peaceful, in other words, because the other side lacks any political artillery.

25
Who Is "Us"?

It is right to prefer our own country to all others, because
we are children and citizens before we can be travelers
and philosophers.

GEORGE SANTAYANA,
The Life of Reason (1905)

WHAT is the role of a nation within the emerging global economy,
in which borders are ceasing to exist? My answer has, I hope, been
clear. Rather than increase the profitability of corporations flying
its flag, or enlarge the worldwide holdings of its citizens, a nation's
economic role is to improve its citizens' standard of living by enhancing the value of what they contribute to the world economy.
The concern over national "competitiveness" is often misplaced.
It is not what we own that counts; it is what we do.

Viewed in this way, the problem in Britain, as in the United
States, is that while some citizens are adding substantial value,
most are not. In consequence, the gap between those few in the
first group and everyone else is widening. To improve the economic position of the bottom four-fifths will require that the
fortunate fifth share is wealth and invest in the wealth-creating
capacities of other citizens. Yet as the top becomes ever more
tightly linked to the global economy, it has less of a stake in the
performance and potential of its less fortunate compatriots. Thus
the emerging dilemma in many nations.

History rarely proceeds in a direct line, however. Those who
project that today's steady improvement (or deterioration) over
yesterday's will become even more pronounced tomorrow often
end up embarrassed when the future finally arrives. In the inter-
vening moments there will occur an earthquake, a potent idea, a

revolution, a sudden loss of business confidence, a scientific discovery—reversing the seemingly most intransigent of trends and causing people to wonder how they could ever have been deluded into believing that any other outcome was ever remotely possible. The predictable failure of all prediction notwithstanding, the public continues to pay attention to stock analysts, trend spotters, futurologists, weather forecasters, astrologers, and economists. Presumably, such respect is due less to the accuracy of their prophecies than to the certainty with which they are delivered.

The reader of these pages is duly warned. An all-too-simple extrapolation of the past into the future would show a continuing rise in the fortunes of symbolic analysts and a steady decline in the fortunes of almost everyone else. The costs of worldwide transportation and communications will continue to decline—creating an ever larger market, and burgeoning demand, for the services of a nation's problem-solvers, -identifiers and brokers, but simultaneously generating an ever larger supply of unskilled workers. In consequence, symbolic analysts will become even wealthier; routine producers will grow poorer and fewer in number; and, with the enhanced mobility of world labor and the versatility of labor-saving machinery, in-person servers will become less economically secure.

The fortunes of the most well-off and the least will thus continue to diverge. By 2020, the top fifth of the nation's earners will account for more than 60 percent of all the income earned by its citizens; the bottom fifth, for 2 percent. Symbolic analysts will withdraw into ever more isolated enclaves, within which they will pool their resources rather than share them with other citizens or invest them in ways that improve other citizens productivity. An ever smaller proportion of their incomes will be taxed and thence redistributed or invested on behalf of the rest of the public. Government spending on education, training, and infrastructure will continue to decline as a proportion of the nation's total income; any savings attributable to a smaller defense budget will result in further tax reductions and the diminution of the fiscal deficit. Poorer cities, townships, and states will be unable to make up the difference.

Distinguished from the rest of the population by their global linkages, good schools, comfortable lifestyles, excellent health care, and abundance of security guards, symbolic analysts will complete their secession from the union. The townships and urban enclaves where they reside, and the symbolic-analytic zones where they work, will bear no resemblance to the rest of the nation; nor will there be any direct connections between the two. The nation's poorest citizens, meanwhile, will be isolated within their own enclaves of urban and rural desperation; an ever-larger proportion of their young men will fill the nation's prisons. The remainder of the population, growing gradually poorer, will feel powerless to alter any of these trends.

It is not that simple, of course. Other events will likely intervene to deflect this trajectory. Not the least is the inability of symbolic analysts to protect themselves, their families, and their property from the depredations of a larger and ever more desperate population outside. The peace of mind potentially offered by platoons of security guards, state-of-the-art alarm systems, and a multitude of prisons is limited.

There is also the possibility that symbolic analysts will decide that they have a responsibility to improve the well-being of their compatriots, regardless of any personal gain. A new patriotism would thus be born, founded less upon economic self-interest than upon loyalty to the nation.

2

WHAT do we owe one another as members of the same society who no longer inhabit the same economy? The answer will depend on how strongly we feel that we are, in fact, members of the same society.

Loyalty to place—to one's city or region or nation—used to correspond more naturally with economic self-interest. Individual citizens supported education, roads, and other civic improvements, even when the individual was likely to enjoy but a fraction of what was paid out in the short term, because it was assumed that such sacrifices would be amply rewarded eventually. Civic boosterism, public investment, and economic cooperation were consistent with Tocqueville's principle of "self-interest rightly understood." As our fellow citizens grew wealthier and more productive, we benefited by their ability to give us more in exchange for what we offered them. And as we resisted opportunistic behavior, so did they, with the result that we benefited all the more. The resulting networks of economic interdependence induced the habits of citizenship.

Between 1950 and the early 1970s, the American economy as a whole began to exemplify this principle. Labor, business, and the broader public, through its elected representatives, tacitly cooperated to promote high-volume production; the resulting efficiencies of scale generated high profits; some of the profits were reinvested to create even vaster scale, and some were returned to production workers and middle-level managers in the form of higher wages and benefits. As a result, large numbers of Americans entered the middle class, ready to consume the output of this burgeoning system.

But as the borders of cities, states, and even nations no longer come to signify special domains of economic interdependence, Tocqueville's principle of enlightened self-interest is less compelling. Nations are becoming regions of a global economy; their citizens, laborers in a global market. National corporations are turning into global webs whose high-volume, standardized activities are undertaken wherever labor is cheapest worldwide, and whose most profitable activities are carried out wherever skilled and talented people can best conceptualize new problems and solutions. Under such circumstances, economic sacrifice and restraint exercised within a nation's borders is less likely to come full circle than it was in a more closed economy.

The question is whether the habits of citizenship are sufficiently strong to withstand the centrifugal forces of the new global economy. Is there enough of simple loyalty to place—of civic obligation, even when unadorned by enlightened self-interest—to elicit sacrifice nonetheless? We are, after all, citizens as well as economic actors; we may work in markets but we live in societies. How tight is the social and political bond when the economic bond unravels?

The question is relevant to all nations subject to global economic forces—forces which are reducing the interdependence of their citizens and separating them into global winners and losers. In some societies, where national allegiances are stronger than in others, the balance between societal ties and economic ties tilts toward the former. The pull of the global economy notwithstanding, national allegiances are sufficiently potent to motivate the winners to continue helping the losers. The "we're all in it together" nationalism that characterizes such places is founded not only on enlightened self-interest but also on a deeply ingrained sense of shared heritage and national destiny. The Japanese, Swedes, Austrians, Swiss, and Germans, for example, view themselves as cultures whose strength and survival depend, to some extent, on sacrifices by the more fortunate among them. It is a matter of national duty and pride. Partly as a result, the distribution of income within these nations has been among the most equal of any countries (although the global division of labor is beginning to drive a wedge between their rich and poor and testing their commitment to economic equality). These nations, incidentally, experienced during the decades of the 1960s and 1970s some of the most spectacular records of growth of all industrialized nations.[1]

Could such sentiments be nurtured elsewhere? Should they be?

3

NATIONALISM can be a hazardous sentiment. The same "we're all in it together" attitude that elicits mutual sacrifice within a nation can easily degenerate into jingoistic contempt for all things foreign. Indeed, the two emotions tend to reinforce one another. It is a commonplace notion in Britain that the nation's citizens have never since displayed such virtue and solidarity as when they

---

[1]Much has been written about the "developmental state" of modern Japan. South Korea and Hong Kong, once touted by orthodox free marketeers as models of laissez-faire economic individualism, on closer inspection look remarkably like their more advanced neighbor to the north. See, for example, Alice Amsden, *Asia's Next Giant* (New York: Oxford University Press, 1989), and M. Castells and L. Tyson, "High Technology and the Changing International Division of Production," in R. Purcell (ed.), *The Newly Industrializing Countries in the World Economy* (Boulder, Colo.: Lynne Rienner, 1989). Austria, Switzerland, and Sweden represent a different path, of course, but these nations also are characterized by systems of internal bargaining which soften adjustment for their least fortunate citizens and elicit sacrifices from their most fortunate. See, for example, Peter Katzenstein, *Corporatism and Change: Austria, Switzerland, and the Politics of Industry* (Ithaca, N.Y.: Cornell University Press, 1989).

fought Hitler. America's Cold War with the Soviet Union inspired, and provided justification for, billions of dollars of public expenditure on highways, education, and research. The willingness of talented Japanese citizens to work long hours and receive relatively low incomes for the honor of doing their part for their country is fueled by the same set of emotions that makes it difficult for the Japanese to open their borders to foreign products and immigrants.

History offers ample warning of how "zero-sum" nationalism —the assumption that either we win or they win—can corrode public values to the point where citizens support policies that marginally improve their own welfare while harming everyone else on the planet, thus forcing other nations to do the same in defense. Armaments escalate; trade barriers rise; cold wars turn hot. The same social discipline and fierce loyalty that have elicited sacrifices among Germans and Japanese have also, in this century, generated mind-numbing atrocities.

Unbridled nationalism can also cause civic values to degenerate at home. Nations grow paranoid about foreign agents in their midst; civil liberties are restricted on grounds of national security. Neighbors begin to distrust one another. Tribal allegiances can even tear nation-states apart. The violence that periodically erupts between Greek and Turkish Cypriots, Armenians and Azerbaijanis, Albanians and Serbs, Flemings and Walloons, Vietnamese and Cambodians, Israelis and Palestinians, Sikhs and other Indians, Tamils and Sinhalese, and Lebanon's Christian and Moslem sects is grim evidence of the costs of tribal loyalty.

The argument against zero-sum nationalism, and in favor of a larger and more cosmopolitan perspective, seems especially strong in light of the growing inequalities in the world. The gap between the top fifth and bottom four-fifths of incomes within the United States or Britain is negligible in comparison with the gap between the top fifth and bottom four-fifths of the world's population. North America, Western Europe, and East Asia— together comprising the top fifth—account for three-quarters of the gross world product and 80 percent of the value of world trade. As these wealthy regions have become uncoupled from the rest of the world, much of what remains behind is sinking precipitously into hopeless poverty.

Between 1970 and 1980, the number of undernourished people in developing nations (excluding China) increased from 650 million to 730 million. Since 1980, economic growth rates in most of these nations have slowed and real wages have dropped further. In Africa and Latin America, per capita incomes were substantially lower in 1990 than in 1980. Commodity prices have plummeted; indebtedness to global banks has crippled many underdeveloped economies, as more than $50 billion is transferred each year to advanced nations. The ravages of deforestation, erosion, and large-scale farming have taken their toll on much of the Third World. Meanwhile, the world's poor populations are giving birth at a much higher rate than are the world's rich. Sixty percent of the 12,000 children born into the world each hour join families whose annual per-person incomes are lower than $350. In 1990, just over 5 billion human beings lived on the planet; their number is expected to reach 8 billion by 2025, and 16 billion by the end of the twenty-first century. The number of impoverished people has grown dramatically in Brazil, Chile, Ghana, Jamaica, Peru, and the Philippines. Life expectancy has declined in nine sub-Saharan African countries; deaths from malnutrition among infants and children have increased.[2]

A focus on national well-being is also dangerously narrow in relation to other problems on which global cooperation is essential: acid rain, the depletion of the ozone, the pollution of oceans, the use of fossil fuels and global warming, the destruction of species-rich tropical rain forests, the proliferation of nuclear weapons, the drug trade, the spread of AIDS, international terrorism. Narrowly nationalistic attitudes render solutions to these and other transnational crises all the more difficult to achieve.

4

ZERO-SUM nationalism also endangers global economic prosperity. The neomercantilist premise that either they win or we win is simply incorrect. As one nation's workers become more insightful and educated, they are able to add more wealth to the world.

[2]See *Global Outlook 2000* (New York: United Nations 1990), pp. 202–21, 285–97.

Everyone on the planet benefits from smaller and more powerful semiconductor chips regardless of who makes them.

It is true, of course, that the nation whose workers first gain the insights are likely to benefit disproportionately. This advantage may cause other nations' citizens to feel *relatively* poorer, notwithstanding their absolute gain. Sociologists have long noted the phenomenon of "relative deprivation," whereby people evaluate their well-being in light of others' wealth. The average citizen of Great Britain is in absolute terms far better off than twenty years ago but feels poorer now that the average Italian has pulled ahead. When I ask my students whether they would prefer living in a world in which every American is 25 percent wealthier than now and every Japanese is much wealthier than the average American, or in one in which Americans are only 10 percent wealthier than now but ahead of the average Japanese, a large number usually vote for the second option. People may be willing to forgo absolute gains to prevent their perceived rivals from enjoying even greater gains. While understandable, such zero-sum impulses are hardly to be commended as a principle of international economic behavior. Since economic advances rarely benefit the citizens of all nations in equal proportion, such an approach, if widely adopted, would block most efforts to increase global wealth.

Economic interdependence runs so deep, in fact, that any zero-sum strategy is likely to boomerang, as the members of the Organization of Petroleum Exporting Countries discovered in the 1970s when their sky-high oil prices plunged the world into recession and reduced the demand for oil. Today, no nation's central banker can control its money supply or the value of its currency without the help of other nations' central bankers, nor can a nation unilaterally raise its interest rates or run large budget surpluses or deficits without others' cooperation or acquiescence. These days, every advanced nation depends on others as a market for, and source of, its goods. The Japanese need a strong and prosperous America as a market for their goods and a place to invest their money. If any step they might take were to precipitate a steep economic decline in the United States, the results would be disastrous for the Japanese as well.

But what if foreigners dominate a major technology, as it seems likely the Japanese soon will with advanced semiconductors, high-definition television, and dozens of other gadgets? Again, we should beware of zero-sum assumptions. The Japanese mastery of particular technologies will not foreclose technological progress in the United States or elsewhere. Technologies are not commodities for which world demand is finite, nor do they come in fixed quantities that either they get or we get. Technologies are domains of knowledge. They are like the outer branches of a giant bush on which countless other branches are growing all the time. While a nation's citizens need direct experience in researching, designing, and fabricating technologies on outer branches if they are to share in future growth, these need not be exactly the same branches that are occupied by another nation's work force.

5

THE COSMOPOLITAN man or woman with a sense of global citizenship is thus able to maintain appropriate perspective on the world's problems and possibilities. Devoid of strong patriotic impulse, the global symbolic analyst is likely to resist zero-sum solutions and thus behave more responsibly (in this sense) than citizens whose frame of reference is narrower.

But will the cosmopolitan with a global perspective choose to act fairly and compassionately? Will our current and future symbolic analysts—lacking any special sense of responsibility toward a particular nation and its citizens—share their wealth with the less fortunate of the world and devote their resources and energies to improving the chances that others may contribute to the world's wealth? Here we find the darker side of cosmopolitanism. For without strong attachments and loyalties extending beyond family and friends, symbolic analysts may never develop the habits and attitudes of social responsibility. They will be world citizens, but without accepting or even acknowledging any of the obligations that citizenship in a polity normally implies. They will resist zero-sum solutions, but they may also resist all other solutions that require sacrifice and commitment. Without a real political community in which to learn, refine, and practice the ideals of justice and fairness, they may find these ideals to be meaningless abstractions.

Senses of justice and generosity are learned. The learning has many roots, but significant among them is membership in a political community. We learn to feel responsible for others because we share with them a common history, we participate with them in a common culture, we face with them a common fate. As the social philosopher Michael Ignatieff has written, "We think of ourselves not as human beings first, but as sons, and daughters . . . tribesmen, and neighbors. It is this dense web of relations and the meanings which they give to life which satisfies the needs which really matter to us."[3]

That we share with others nothing more than our humanity may be insufficient to elicit much sacrifice. The management consultant living in Chappaqua and commuting to a steel-and-glass tower on Park Avenue, and dealing with clients all over the world, may feel slightly more responsibility toward a poor family living 3,000 miles away in East Los Angeles than to a poor family of Mexicans living 3,200 miles away in Tijuana, but the extra measure of affinity may not be enough to command his or her energies or resources. A citizen of the world, the management consultant may feel no particular bond with any society.

Cosmopolitanism can also engender resignation. Even if the symbolic analyst is sensitive to the problems that plague the world, these dilemmas may seem so intractable and overpowering in their global dimension that any attempt to remedy them appears futile. The greatest enemy of progress is a sense of hopelessness; from a vantage point that takes in the full enormity of the world's ills, real progress may seem beyond reach. Within smaller political units like towns, cities, states, and even nations, problems may seem soluble; even a tiny improvement can seem large on this smaller scale. As a result, where the nationalist or localist is apt to feel that a sacrifice is both valorous and potentially effective, the cosmopolitan may be overcome by its apparent uselessness.[4]

The reader has only to reflect upon personal experience. Nothing more surely stills reformist zeal than a faithful reading of *The New York Times* or other great newspaper of the world, in which the global dimensions of hunger, disease, racism, environmental depredation, and political injustice are detailed daily. It should

---

[3] Michael Ignatieff, *The Needs of Strangers* (New York: Viking Penguin, 1985), p. 29.

[4] Jonathan Glover, "It Makes No Difference Whether or Not I Do It," *Supplemental Proceedings of the Aristotelian Society*, New York, 1975.

not come as a surprise, then, that all great social movements have begun locally. Those who aim to reform the world in one great swoop often have difficulty signing up credulous recruits.

In short, while a cosmopolitan view provides a useful and appropriate perspective on many of the world's problems and avoids the pitfalls of zero-sum thinking, it may discourage the very steps necessary to remedy the problems it illuminates. It is not clear that mankind is significantly better off with an abundance of wise cosmopolitans feeling indifferent or ineffective in the face of the world's ills than it is with a bunch of foolish nationalists intent on making their particular society Number One.

6

BUT MUST we choose between zero-sum nationalism and impassive cosmopolitanism? Do these two positions describe the only alternative modes of future citizenship? Unfortunately, much of the debate we hear about America's national interest in the global economy is framed in just these dichotomous terms. On one side are zero-sum nationalists, typically representing the views of routine producers and in-person servers, urging that government advance the nation's economic interests—even at the expense of others around the globe. In their view, unless we become more assertive, foreigners will continue to increase their market shares at our expense in industry after industry—exploiting our openness, gaining competitive advantage over us, ultimately robbing us of control over our destinies. On the other side are laissez-faire cosmopolitans, usually representing the views of symbolic analysts, arguing that government should simply stay out. In their view, profit-seeking individuals and firms are far better able to decide what gets produced where; governments only mess things up. Free movement of all factors of production across national boundaries ultimately will improve everyone's lot.

What is being lost in this debate is a third, superior position: a positive economic nationalism, in which each nation's citizens take primary responsibility for enhancing the capacities of their countrymen for full and productive lives, but who also work with other nations to ensure that these improvements do not come at others' expense. This position is not that of the laissez-faire cosmopolitan, because it rests on a sense of national purpose—of principled historic and cultural connection to a common political endeavor. It seeks to encourage new learning within the nation, to smooth the transition of the labor force from older industries, to educate and train the nation's workers, to improve the nation's infrastructure, and to create international rules of fair play for accomplishing all these things. The objectives of such investments are unambiguously public.

Neither is this the position of a zero-sum nationalist: Here the overarching goal is to enhance global welfare rather than to advance one nation's well-being by reducing another's. There is not a fixed amount of world profit to be divided or a limited market to be shared. It is not "their" corporations against "ours" in a fight for dominance in world commerce. We meet instead on an infinitely expanding terrain of human skills and knowledge. Human capital, unlike physical or financial capital, has no inherent bounds.

Indeed, *these* nationalist sentiments are likely to result in greater global wealth than will cosmopolitan sentiments founded upon loyalty to no nation. For like villagers whose diligence in tending to their own gardens results in a bounteous harvest for all, citizens who feel a special obligation to cultivate the talents and abilities of their compatriots end up contributing to the well-being of compatriots and noncompatriots alike. One nation's well-being is enhanced whenever other nations improve the capacities of their own citizens. To extend the metaphor, while each garden tender may feel competitive with every other, each also understands that the success of the total harvest requires cooperation. While each has a primary responsibility to tend his own garden, each has a secondary responsibility to ensure—and a genuine interest in seeing—that all gardens flourish.

Thus positive economic nationalism would eschew trade barriers against the products of any work force as well as obstacles to the movement of money and ideas across borders. Even were such obstacles enforceable, they would only serve to reduce the capacity of each nation's work force to enjoy the fruits of investments made in them, and in others. But not all government intervention would be avoided. Instead, this approach would encourage public spending within each nation in any manner that enhanced the capacities of its citizens to lead full and productive lives—including pre- and postnatal care, childcare and preschool preparation, excellent primary and secondary education, access to college regardless of financial condition, training and retraining, and good infrastructure. Such investments would form the core of national economic policy.

Positive nationalism also would tolerate—even invite—public subsidies to firms that undertook within the nation's borders high-value-added production (complex design, engineering, fabrication, systems integration, and so forth), so that the subsidy-granting nation's work force could gain sophisticated on-the-job skills. But it would draw no distinctions based on the nationalities of the firm's shareholders or top executives. To ensure against zero-sum ploys in which nations bid against one another to attract the same set of global firms and related technologies, nations would negotiate over the appropriate levels and targets of such subsidies. The result would be a kind of "GATT for direct investment"—a logical extension of the General Agreement on Tariffs and Trade that the United States sponsored after World War II—setting out the rules by which nations could bid for high-value-added investments by global corporations. Barred would be threats to close the domestic market unless certain investments were undertaken within it, for such threats would likely unravel into zero-sum contests. Instead, the rules would seek to define fair tactics, depending upon the characteristics of the national economy and the type of investment being sought. For example, the amount of permissible subsidy might be directly proportional to the size of the nation's work force but inversely proportional to its average skills. Nations with large and relatively unskilled work forces would be allowed greater leeway in bidding for global investment than nations with smaller and more highly skilled work forces.

Other kinds of subsidies would be pooled and parceled out to where they could do the most good, as the European Community has begun to do regionally. For example, nations would jointly fund basic research whose fruits are likely to travel almost immediately across international borders—projects such as the high-energy particle accelerator, the human genome, and the exploration of space. (Single governments are unlikely to support many such projects on their own, given that the entire world so easily benefits from them.) How such funds were apportioned, and toward what ends, would, of course, be subject to negotiation.

Positive economic nationalism also would ease the transition of a work force out of older industries and technologies in which there was worldwide overcapacity. This might take the form of severance payments, relocation assistance, extra training grants, extra unemployment insurance, regional economic aid, and funds for retooling or upgrading machinery toward higher-value-added production. Since every nation benefits when overcapacity anywhere is reduced, these subsidies might come from a common fund established jointly by all nations. Payments into the fund could be apportioned according to how much of that particular industry's capacity lay within each nation's borders at the start.

Finally, positive economic nationalism would seek to develop the capacities of the work forces of the Third World—not as a means of forestalling world communism or stabilizing Third World regimes so that global companies can safely extract raw materials and sell products within them—but as a means of promoting indigenous development and thereby enhancing global wealth. To this end, the shift of high-volume, standardized production to Third World nations would be welcomed, and markets in advanced economies would be open to them. Advanced nations would reduce the Third World's debt burden, make new lending available, and monitor the loans more carefully than in the past.

7

THE PRESSURES of global change have fragmented the electorate. Routine producers and in-person servers—tending toward zero-sum nationalism—fear that foreigners, the Japanese in particular, are taking over the nation's assets and secretly influencing national politics. They resent low-wage workers in South-east Asia and Latin America who are inheriting many of the nation's routine production jobs and seem in addition to be swarming into the nation's cities. Many symbolic analysts—tending toward laissez-faire cosmopolitanism—feel no particular urgency about the economic plight of other citizens, on the one hand, and, on the other, feel ineffectual and overwhelmed with regard to many of the larger problems facing the rest of the world.

Neither constituency, in other words, is naturally disposed to positive nationalism. Those who are threatened by global competition feel that they have much to lose and little to gain from an approach that seeks to enhance world wealth, while those who are benefiting the most from the blurring of national borders sense that they have much to lose and little to gain from government intervention intended to spread such benefits.

The direction we are heading is reasonably clear. If the future could be predicted on the basis of trends already underway, laissez-faire cosmopolitanism would become the dominant economic and social philosophy of advanced nations. Left to unfold on its own, the worldwide division of labor not only will create vast disparities of wealth within nations but may also reduce the willingness of global winners to do anything to reverse this trend toward inequality—either within the nation or without. Symbolic analysts, who hold most of the cards in this game, could be confident of "victory." But what of the losers?

We are presented with a rare historical moment in which the threat of worldwide conflict seems remote and the transformations of economies and technology are blurring the lines between nations. The modern nation-state, some two hundred years old, is no longer what it once was: Vanishing is a nationalism founded upon the practical necessities of economic interdependence within borders and security against foreigners outside. There is thus an opportunity for us, as for every society, to redefine who we are, why we have joined together, and what we owe each other and the other inhabitants of the world. The choice is ours to make. We are no more slaves to present trends than to vestiges of the past. We can, if we choose, assert that our mutual obligations as citizens extend beyond our economic usefulness to one another, and act accordingly.

A Note on Additional Sources

Like any work of synthesis and interpretation, the foregoing has depended upon a wide range of studies, surveys, and analyses drawn from many different fields. I have also relied extensively on interviews undertaken over a period of several years. Striking the proper balance between analysis and synthesis—or what Isaiah Berlin might have called the expert hedgehog and the interdisciplinary fox—is, of course, a perilous exercise, and the reader is owed an accounting of major sources in addition to those specifically cited in the text.

For understanding the development of the idea of economic nationalism, and the centrality of the national corporation in that evolution, I have found particularly useful Fernand Braudel's monumental three-volume study, *Civilization and Capitalism, 15th–18th Centuries* (American ed.; New York: Harper & Row, 1984), which helps place economic nationalism in the broader context of the emergence of the nation-state and the era of mercantilism. Eric Hobsbawm's *The Age of Empire, 1875–1914* (New York: Pantheon, 1987) provides a useful summary of forces ushering in the modern era of national economic competition. A particularly comprehensive history of European industrialization, and its political context, is found in Sidney Pollard's *Peaceful Conquest: The Industrialization of Europe: 1760–1970* (Oxford: Oxford University Press, 1981). On the evolution of nationalism in general, a useful survey is Carlton J. H. Hayes's *The Historical Evolution of Modern Nationalism* (New York: Macmillan, 1948). Boyd C. Shafer's *Nationalism: Myth and Reality* (New York: Harcourt, Brace & World, 1955) places the development of nationalism in a broader social and economic framework.

For a history of the development of the core corporation in the United States, Alfred Chandler's *The Visible Hand: The Managerial Revolution in American Business* (Cambridge: Harvard University Press, 1977) is unsurpassed. On the relation between this development and American politics, Thomas McCraw's essay "Rethinking the Trust Question," in his edited volume *Regulation in Perspective* (Cambridge: Harvard Business School, 1981), is especially helpful, as is his biographical study *Prophets of Regulation* (Cambridge: Harvard University Press, 1984). Morton Horwitz's *The Transformation of*

American Law: 1780–1860 (Cambridge: Harvard University Press, 1977) offers a thoughtful analysis of the role of the common law in the development of American industry. Louis Galambos and Joseph Pratt provide a useful overview of the rise of the unique relationship between American business and government in the United States in *The Rise of the Corporate Commonwealth* (New York: Basic Books, 1988). The intimacy of the relationship is delineated by Grant McConnell in *Private Power and American Democracy* (New York: Knopf, 1966) and by Jonathan R. T. Hughes, *The Governmental Habit: Economic Controls from Colonial Times to the Present* (New York: Basic Books, 1977). The relationship can be understood as one element of the eighteenth-century European liberal tradition, as interpreted by Louis Hartz in his now classic *The Liberal Tradition in America* (New York: Harcourt, Brace & World, 1955) and by James Weinstein in *The Corporate Ideal in the Liberal State, 1900–1918* (Boston: Beacon Press, 1968).

Useful in placing the development of the American corporation during the twentieth century into political perspective are Ellis Hawley's *The New Deal and the Problem of Monopoly* (Princeton: Princeton University Press, 1966), Richard Hofstadter's *The Age of Reform* (New York: Knopf, 1955), and James Willard Hurst's *Law and Markets in U.S. History* (Madison: University of Wisconsin Press, 1981). For understanding the relationship between the corporation and American nationalism during much of this century I also have relied extensively on contemporaneous accounts found in popular journals such as *Fortune* magazine and *The New Republic*.

On the emergence of localized areas of expertise, which I have termed "symbolic-analytic zones," a large and growing number of studies have been undertaken in recent years. Among the most important forerunners are Raymond Vernon's *Metropolis 1985* (Cambridge: Harvard University Press, 1960) and M. Hall's *Made in New York* (Cambridge: Harvard University Press, 1959), both of which suggest how locales attract and develop skilled pools of labor. Recent applications and refinements of these ideas, which I have found especially useful, include Annalee Saxenian, "The Urban Contradictions of Silicon Valley: Regional Growth and the Restructuring of the Semiconductor Industry," in L. Sawers and W. Tabb (eds.), *Sunbelt/Snowbelt* (New York: Oxford University Press, 1984); Bennett Harrison, "Regional Restructuring and Good Business Climates: The Economic Transformation of New England," in the same volume; R. Miller and M. Cote, "Growing the Next Silicon Valley," *Harvard Business Review*, July–August 1985, pp. 114–23; Ann Markusen, "Defense Spending and the Geography of High Technology Industries," in J. Rees (ed.), *Technology, Regions, and Policy* (Totowa, N.J.: Rowman & Littlefield, 1986); and Nancy Dorfman, "Route 128: The Development of a Regional High Technology Center," *Research Policy*, Vol. 12 (1983), pp. 299–316. Helpful syntheses of this emerging literature can be found in Peter Doeringer et al., *Invisible Factors in Local Economic Development* (New York: Oxford University Press, 1987), and in U.S. Congress, Office of Technology Assessment, *Technology, Innovation, and Regional*

Economic Development (Washington, D.C.: U.S. Government Printing Office, 1987).

Readers interested in how formal education can develop critical thinking confront a broad and expanding literature. I have found several works to be especially valuable. Donald A. Schon's *The Reflective Practitioner: How Professionals Think in Action* (New York: Basic Books, 1983) offers an insightful and provocative analysis of how people come to take responsibility for their continued learning, and on the relationship between abstract reasoning and practical action. In the vast literature on experimental learning, two works stand out: D. A. Kolb's "On Management and the Learning Process," in D. A. Kolb et al. (eds.), *Organizational Psychology: A Book of Readings* (2nd ed.; Englewood Cliffs, N.J.: Prentice Hall, 1974), and A. Whimbey and J. Lockhead, *Problem-solving and Comprehension* (Philadelphia: Franklin Institute Press, 1982). A particularly interesting assessment of how to teach "higher-order" thinking skills is found in Lauren Resnick, *Education and Learning to Think* (Washington, D.C.: National Academy Press, 1987).

Finally, for an understanding of recent economic and political changes, especially those occurring since the late 1970s, I have relied on interviews with private- and public-sector officials, all of whom have been extremely generous with their time. None of them or their organizations bear any responsibility for the data or conclusions contained in this book.

In the private sector, my sources have been employees of a sampling of companies including both large and small enterprises, manufacturers and service providers (as traditionally defined), privately held and publicly held, foreign-owned and American-owned. They include Aries Computer, Arthur Andersen & Company, AT&T, AT&T Bell Laboratories, Atex Corporation, Bell South, British Steel, Bull HN, Burlington Northern Corporation, Cargill, La Cie Minière Québec, Cincinnati Milacron Inc., Consolidated Edison, CSX Corporation, Erving Paper Mills, First Bank of Minneapolis, First Commercial Bank of Arkansas, Frito-Lay, Fujisankei Communications, Fujitsu Microelectronics Inc., General Foods Corp., GTE Inc., Honeywell Inc., IBM, IBM Canada, Imo Deleval Inc., John Hancock Mutual Life Insurance Co., Kendall Corp., Loram Companies, McKinsey & Company, NEC Corporation, Newmont Mining Corp., Newsday Corp., Onex Corp., Polysar Inc., Prescott Ball & Turben Inc., Prime Computer Inc., R. R. Donnelley Inc., Sara Lee Corp., Schott America Inc., Scotts Hospitalities (Canada), Shamrock Holdings Corp., Sony, Square D Corp., Steelcase Corp., Sun Chemical Corp., Touche Ross Inc., Towers Perrin Company, The Williams Companies, and Wyatt Company.

In the public and not-for-profit sectors, my sources have included employees of the federal, state, and local governments in the United States, as well as of several foreign governments and of labor organizations. They include the Association des Directeurs de Recherche Industrielle du Québec, Commonwealth of Kentucky Department of Economic Development, Commonwealth of Massachusetts Department of Economic Development,

Growth Opportunity Alliance of Lawrence, Massachusetts, Industrial Development Research Council of San Antonio, Texas, Industrial Union Department of the AFL-CIO, International Trade Commission of the United States, Ministry of Finance of Japan, Ministry of International Trade and Industry of Japan, New York State Office of Employee Relations, Port Authority of New York and New Jersey, the Province of Ontario, Science and Engineering Council of Great Britain, State of Michigan Department of Commerce, State of Minnesota Bureau of Mediation Services, La Secretaría de Programacida y Presupuesto de México, the U.S. Trade Representative, and the Western Pennsylvania Advanced Technology Center.

Index

A vivid and controversial analysis of what nations must
do if their citizens are to flourish in the world
economy of the future.

Robert B. Reich is a professor at Harvard's John F. Kennedy
School of Government, and one of America's foremost political
economists. He was an influential adviser in the 1992 election
campaign and is now President Clinton's new Labor Secretary.

"Will become essential reading for anyone wanting to understand
the social consequences of the emerging global economy."
David Sainsbury, Chairman, J Sainsbury plc

"Bob Reich lives at the frontier of our understanding of political
economy, and in this book he has pushed that frontier further
than anyone else. No one can read this book without being
moved. No one will be quite the same afterwards. Some will be
moved to action. A few will be moved to fury or despair, but
even they will be moved to discard the vestigial thinking which is
poisoning both the American and British political economies."
Sir Charles Villiers, former chairman, British Steel

"The world's economy is becoming global, with immeasurable
consequences for corporate management, governments, politics,
and people. There is no more provocative, brilliant or perceptive
guide to this economic transformation than Robert Reich's
The Work of Nations."
The Rt. Hon. Shirley Williams

ISBN 0-671-71275-6

9 780671 712754 >

£7.99 net